All the Land

THE GERMAN LIST

All the Land

JO LENDLE

Translated by Katy Derbyshire

LONDON NEW YORK CALCUTTA

This publication has been supported by a grant from
the Goethe-Institut India

Seagull Books, 2019

Originally published as *Alles Land*

© Deutsche Verlags-Anstalt, 2011

A division of Verlagsgruppe Random House GmbH, Munich, Germany

First published in English translation by Seagull Books, 2019

English translation © Katy Derbyshire, 2019

ISBN 978 0 8574 2 606 2

British Library Cataloguing-in-Publication Data

A catalogue record for this book is available from the British Library.

Typeset by Seagull Books, Calcutta, India
Printed and bound by Hyam Enterprises, Calcutta, India

Doubt not, go forward; if thou doubt, the beasts will tear thee piecemeal.

Alfred Tennyson

No horizon. The wind drives snow across the ground like a pack of small animals, one following on another's heels. In the end they dissolve into the dull, empty white of the sky.

The snow does not bother us; the ski poles protrude from the driving flakes. But it's torture for the dogs. Their fur has long since frozen white. Sometimes they snap at one another and at the sled lines in mid-run; then their muzzles are visible, and their eyes clotted with snow. A strong south-westerly, fortunately from behind, the wind driving us on ahead of it. The snowflakes whirl, encircling sleds and dogs only to unite again before us. We are no hindrance.

The falling snow is rushing as though it too had a destination. It will be there before us.

There is no firm ground to be made out beneath the drifting snow; perhaps there is none. It's no use thinking of the crevasses. We set out twenty-eight hours ago and it is light still. Since then we have been moving along the inland ice, the home of the evil spirits, as the Greenlanders call it.

What will we find? During our wait on the ship, Wegener talked about Scott, how he and his people were discovered a day's journey from the lifesaving depot. The men carried their mineral samples with them to the very end, the rocks bearing impressions of plants. They were found beneath them, protected by their bodies.

Anyone who does not cling with every fibre to returning in one piece might easily lose his mind here. We move on without pause; none of us feels inclined to sleep. The last rocks have vanished. Beneath us kilometre-thick ice, measured by Wegener himself.

This is truly the loneliest place in the world.

Then the dark shape in the distance. A shadow, as it emerges on our approach, cast on the drifting snow as if on firm ground. Our sleds are now in a close pack.

For a long time, we cannot make out what is casting the shadow. No one says a word. Only when we slow down does it reveal itself—two crossed skis stuck in the firn, between them a splintered ski pole. As soon as we come to a standstill, the dogs lunge at the leather of their harnesses and devour it.

The Alfonsine Tables

Alfred Wegener had more siblings than one would wish upon a person. They stood around him and stared at him, elbowing each other and pointing at him, some even grabbing over the woven edge of the willow cradle to pinch him, out of love.

It cost his mother some effort to hold the children back. The birth had taken twenty-four hours, a whole day. It was hard to unsettle a woman like Anna Wegener, but attempting to restrain this horde had her at her wits' end.

The midwife had left mother and child alone for a moment to take the tub down to the scullery, she too exhausted from the long labour. As she stood up she'd felt dizzy, and she was shivering with tiredness. It was too cold in the room, too cold for a birth. She had gathered up all the white linens, the sheets and towels, and then not locked the door again from outside.

The children had not hesitated for an instant. Barely had the midwife disappeared down the cellar steps before they slipped in, one after another. They brought with them what was outside and what had played no role inside the room over the past twenty-four hours, as little as the shifts of day and night.

It was the long break-time outside the door; it was a Monday, the first day of November 1880. Outside it was All Hallows' Day, a holy day not celebrated in Berlin, the capital of the Kingdom of Prussia. No reason to close the school. The children had gone to class like any other morning. Their mother had heard their calls and shouts, the morning after that endless long night, followed

3

by quiet for a long time during the first lessons, and now the bell had rung over there. The children spent their long break at home, with their new brother.

There were considerably too many of them. Along with her four own children there were the other siblings, two dozen at least, from the upper-sixth down to those who had only joined them recently. Tall, pale dreamers and chubby country children with eyes glinting with jollity.

All boys, all with their hair cropped close, a constant shambles. They were the sons of deceased civil servants, teachers and pastors from the Mark Brandenburg, who lived with them in the orphanage. Alfred Wegener was born into a wild, noisy pack of boys that never left anyone in peace.

As different as the boys were, each of them wore his school clothing, black trousers, white shirt with its embroidered coat of arms, a cardigan to ward off the cold—the uniform of the Gymnasium zum Grauen Kloster. Alfred's father was a Classics teacher there. He had his pupils read Plato and Ovid and the psalms, as best they could. He had them write down what they understood until the very last of them had grasped what he read.

At lunchtime, after school finished for the day, the siblings came over to the orphanage. Alfred's father accompanied them; he was the head of the institution. His family lived under one roof with their wards. On Sundays, they all marched to the nearby Klosterkirche, where their father held the sermons.

On the seventh morning of his life, Alfred attended his first of these services, the next the week after and so on and on, together with all the others, always together, and never did one of them remain alone.

Alfred Wegener's forefathers had been pastors in Silesia and the Mark for centuries, in villages whose names had long since died out. On Sundays they had read the gospels to the congregation in low voices, they had taught children to pray and read and sing and hope. They had each of their names and birthdates in their minds, keeping a space alongside for the date of death. They knew the lives of every single parishioner, they baptized, married and buried them. In return, the peasant farmers provided them with everything they needed, and often their houses were the best in the village, built by all the parishioners together.

These forefathers had been headstrong men, confident towards church leaders and unresponsive to their instructions. They preferred to study the Holy Scripture themselves and interpret it as seemed best for those in their charge. They invented their own rituals and new songs for many voices.

Only gradually did their interests expand beyond the pastoral.

Alfred's father was the first in the line of his ancestors to write. He had begun with theological essays, which grew more and more frank each time and moved ever further from God at each attempt. Richard Wegener wrote by night when everyone and everything was asleep, perhaps even God. He could not have explained what was wrong about it. He merely felt that his writing distanced him from the world from which he came, from its rules and laws.

By day he promised himself to give up writing, but by night the boundlessness of the empty page tempted him anew. The outcome was a small collection of poems, to which he gave the title Poetic Orchard. He did not even show it to his wife.

A publisher in Cöthen was willing to print the book and Richard Wegener soon received his personal copy, bound in red linen. He burnt it in the fireplace.

By the time the fire went out, the book had turned to ash but not lost its shape. The title was still clearly visible, as was the cover plate with its drawing of a peasant garden, in the middle a crowing cockerel. Above it his name. He took the poker and stabbed at the ash until nothing was left but pale flakes.

Richard Wegener never wrote another poem. As he fell asleep he prayed his children would never learn of their father's digressions. They were to keep to God's paths.

He had met his wife in Wittstock. He had been twenty-four at the time and still studying theology. He wanted to give something to the world. Anna Schwarz had lost her parents at a young age; Richard had always had a weakness for orphans. He saw her at a reception held by the dean, where she helped in the household. Anna walked among the rows of guests with a jug of iced water; it was a scorching hot afternoon. There was a small washhouse used for curing and brewing next to the parish hall. Later he claimed Anna had made eyes at him. She countered that she had merely wondered why he kept staring at her.

She had that face even then, with the big blue eyes. He shivered that afternoon in the dean's garden from all the ice water he had her bring him. Her surname appealed to him—he imagined everyone would come to the wedding in black. Not until he set out for home did it occur to him that he was in no position to maintain a family. From that day on he did everything to change that.

Just under a year later, he had his degree certificate in hand and found a position as a curate in the province of Posen. It brought him 300 thalers' annual salary and the collection from the Christmas services. On the feast of John the Baptist 1868, at the first cooing of the doves, he had led Anna to the altar. On their entrance to the church everyone rose from the pews, one long black rustle of frock coats and taffeta.

When Alfred's mother took care of the laundry in the morning she laid her youngest child on the floor of the parental bedroom on the first floor of the house on Friedrichsgracht. The boy was now nine months old. It was summer and everything was in motion, all except Alfred. He spent his mornings on a woollen blanket, not moving an inch. Sometimes his parents worried he might lie like that for ever, and they argued quietly over whether they ought to help him to move his limbs or whether motion would come of its own accord, from God.

Alfred lay on his front on his blanket, his head tipped back. A strip of light fell through a gap between the curtains, dancing dust motes. Above the dark bed hung the faces of his grandparents, looking down at him. In the open clock case, the pendulum kept time running. There was an excess of smells in the room. It smelt of lavender, of dust, of the woollen loops beneath his chin. It smelt of the taste in his mouth and the bodies of his parents when they pressed him to them. Between the bedposts stood their chamber pot, covered by a grey cloth.

All at once something moved, right before Alfred's face, a black flake. He screwed up his eyes.

It was an ant. Alfred let out a gurgling laugh, pleased. The ant too lifted its head and stretched out its front legs. At last he managed to raise his arms as well. He wanted to touch the creature, clenching his fist over and over but hitting only his own temples and mid-air. Only after a while did his fist finally meet the ant, and he squashed it with a squeal of joy.

Behind it came a second ant and behind that yet more. It was a small colony, a diligently crawling line of fidgety specks. It proceeded underneath the bed, around the chamber pot and along the skirting board to the door.

A thread of saliva dripped onto the back of Alfred's hand. He braced his arms against the blanket and pressed his body upwards. The small body swaddled in a nest of white nappy reared up and fell sideways. Alfred rolled off the blanket, the whole room wrapping itself around him until he bumped into the edge of the bed and came to a stop on his back. He heard himself breathing. From their wooden frames, his grandparents watched his strivings.

Alfred reached out a hand and grabbed for the foot of the bed. His fingers clutched around the dark-brown wood, then he tensed his arm and turned himself slowly back onto his belly. Now he recognized everything. Carefully, he pulled at the bed and instead slid forwards. How easy it was. He pushed himself along with his hands. He soon touched the frame with his forehead and bent his head until he disappeared underneath the bed. He dived into the tide of ants.

The underside of the mattress was ripped. The web of steel springs sagged in the middle, scratching his skin, catching in the fabric of his nappy and tearing it. He pushed himself on incessantly. It was gloomy down here and the chamber pot emitted a dark sound when Alfred bumped it with his forehead. He was patting at ants with his hands, ants long since crawling over his body and face, losing themselves in the folds of his nappy and nipping at his skin. Alfred cried but went on pulling himself along. The gap leading out into the room was lit up ahead of him.

Once he had pushed himself from under the bed back into the open air, Alfred laid his cheek on the floorboards for a moment to catch his breath. He stroked his fist over his face and raised his head.

The door ahead of him was ajar. His mother left it open to hear him if he cried. Alfred saw the column of ants marching on in the shadow of the doorframe and dissolving in the distance, a crawling line. From the corner of his eye he saw his grandparents' gaze following him. They wouldn't be able to stop him.

The way out to the corridor was as easy as pie. The bannisters were thin; Alfred crawled up to the top of the stairs.

He breasted the first steps headfirst, braking his fall by turns with his forehead, nose and chin. He turned a somersault, the nappy cushioning his landing. He stayed put like that for a moment. Then he let himself down step by step.

He didn't know what awaited him at the end of his journey. Never had he been nearly as alert as now. On the edges of the steps was a layer of dust, which disappeared when he stroked at it.

He found the ants again at the foot of the staircase. Their trail led across the stone floor and he had no trouble following them now. Not until the end of the hallway did Alfred come up against a door, which was white. He leant his weight against it but it refused to open. Only the ants squeezed through a crack beneath the skirting board.

Alfred watched them disappearing and all at once he was overwhelmed by a storm of unhappiness, cold and hunger. He pushed up against the crack as though he might warm himself by it.

It was Tony who found him, his older sister, when she came home from school before the others. No one could explain how he had managed to get there. From then on the door stayed closed when his mother put him down for a nap.

Alfred spent a whole summer afternoon sitting next to Käte in the garden, each with a shoe in their lap, while his sister showed him how to tie a bow. It was very quiet in the garden. They had laid newspaper under the soles to stop their clothes from getting dirty. Alfred looked down at his hands, the thin shoelaces entwined between them. His fingers picked up one end and shaped it into a loop, wrapped the other lace around it, but before they managed to make another loop, the first one slipped away from them. Alfred watched his stubby fingers. He knew exactly what they had to do but they simply wouldn't do it. Over and over he started again, his

9

lips pursed, until his fingers started trembling in the end. He felt almost like cutting them off.

His sister laughed when he threw his shoe on the grass. She gave him another patient display and Alfred made a new attempt. He didn't even notice Käte still laughing at him, at his tongue sticking out of his mouth with all the effort. It leapt to and fro at his fingers' every movement; he couldn't help it. 'You'll end up tying your tongue in a knot, not your lace,' said Käte. Early in the evening he managed his first bow, long after his sister had gone inside. Alfred repeated his new game until his mother came to fetch him for dinner.

Anna Wegener's main concern was for her three youngest children. Born with a year between them, they were less strong than the older ones and their mother feared for their health. Elderberries grew in the garden and she boiled up black syrup out of them, which was bitter but supposed to relieve the colds from which Käte, Kurt and Alfred suffered for six months of the year. She made sweet semolina dumplings and poured the syrup over them so that they'd eat it. She bought them train oil and told stories about the whale from which the oil came. When she came to the place where the catchers slung their harpoons at it, she inserted a full spoon into each of her children's mouths in turn. And she described how the whale tried to dive down one last time. The ship had almost gone under water. The children swallowed their medicine without resisting.

In the evenings, when Alfred and his brothers and sisters were asleep, Anna Wegener would lie on the settee and eat the quince loaf she baked in large quantities for herself. The other family members pulled a face when she put the dish on the table because it always turned out slightly bitter, though all it needed was a pinch of icing sugar. She would read the work of Pastor Sebastian Anton Kneipp. Despite being a Catholic, he had some views worth considering. She was impressed that a bath in the ice-cold Danube had cured his tuberculosis. She memorized one of his sentences: If you notice you have eaten, then you have eaten too much. At sunrise from then on, she and her three youngest went to the garden pond, took off their shoes and socks, and Käte, Kurt and Alfred jumped into the little pool with screams of excitement. They had to hold on to each other so as not to fall over in their enthusiasm. Sometimes the older children accompanied them but they weren't allowed in to tread water. They stood mute by the edge of the pond, annoyed to be in such good health.

Alfred's childhood stretched between the dining table, the school desk, the garden, the church and their large dormitory. The family children slept in there together with the orphans, their father's sense of justice not allowing it any other way.

Alfred's bed was by the window. On his bedside table was a snow globe, which he would pick up at bedtime to feel its smooth, cool shape. When the moon rose, its light refracted in the glass. Then he would shake the globe and see the snow descending inaudibly like sand in an hourglass. Inside was Cologne Cathedral, small and proud like Alfred himself. The toy had been a gift from his uncle on Alfred's birth, when the cathedral had just been finished. 'Six hundred years after the first turn of the sod,' the uncle had said to Anna. Good thing the boy had been finished quicker.

Speed was the word on everyone's lips. There were new plans everywhere. At breakfast, their father looked up from his newspaper and said they wanted to build a new railway in Berlin now, under the ground. He read aloud the planned journey times and Alfred learnt them by heart. From Warschauer Strasse to Stralauer Tor, the train would take only one minute. Alfred would not even have tied his shoelaces in that time.

There was a waffle iron for the kitchen stove. On the last Sunday before Advent, Anna lifted the round middle piece out of the stovetop with the tongs and then one ring after another, from the smaller ones at the centre to the outer rings, the flames flaring ever higher, and Alfred standing next to her was afraid they might reach him, but then came his mother and placed the waffle pan precisely over the hole. While the iron heated she prepared the batter, and then it was baking time. Anna pulled the hot waffles into segments with her bare hands, then shared them out. The children compared the size of their pieces and tested out how they fitted together. Willi, Alfred's oldest brother, would always complain he had got a bad deal, but no one took any notice. Every child was allowed to sprinkle icing sugar on their own waffles.

When their mother left the room once, Willi leant down to Alfred and asked whether he'd ever been to the perpetual ice. Cautiously, Alfred shook his head. 'In here,' said Willi, 'is the perpetual ice,' and he held out the icing-sugar tin. Curious, Alfred moved closer to the holes in the lid as Willi tapped the metal tin from below, and Alfred had a face dusted with white.

The other children's laughter, the wrestling for the icing-sugar tin and the clouds rising into the air and drifting across the room as he tried to wrest the sugar away from Willi. Alfred's worry over whether it was allowed, and his appalling rage overlaying everything. At last he got hold of the tin with both hands and tugged at it, but it was only the lid he was holding. Laughing, Willi took a step towards him and shook the entire contents out over him. By the time their mother came back the room was a white desert. In it, only the children petrified with shock and the black stove throbbing with heat.

For Christmas, each of the children got a set of wax crayons in all colours. They sat side by side at the long table, filling sheet after sheet. The skin-coloured crayons were the most popular, needing repeated sharpening. In the end, Alfred gave his to Kurt to make him happy. He never drew people anyway.

The year's end—everywhere drumming, bangs and shots, noise from all sides. Alfred had never been out on the street at night before, not without his parents. By the time they set out he had suddenly lost all desire to go along, but his brothers and sisters acted as though they experienced this kind of thing every night. And so he had left the house with the others, wrapped up in stiff coats, shawls and fur gloves, and Alfred had seen stars in the sky, suspended unmoving between the hurriedly drifting clouds. The water in the canal was frozen, the ice covered by snow. Their father said it would be a beautiful New Year, and Alfred was once again amazed at all his father knew. His father would hold the sermon in the school hall the next morning, on Matthew 7:7; his mother had whispered as much because it was Alfred's baptismal motto. Ask, and it shall be given you; seek, and ye shall find; knock, and it shall be opened unto you. All the children from the orphanage would be there listening, and at the end a few of them would stay in their seats as usual, not wanting to go back to their dormitory, away from the beautiful words.

Their mother had given them frying pans and lids, which they banged together to make the racket that belonged to the last day of the year.

Alfred tried to hold his ears closed but didn't manage. They had barely crossed the bridge before Willi placed a cast-iron casserole over his head, to which he was now administering rhythmic blows with a wooden spoon. Alfred attempted to smile from beneath it; it was the first time he'd been allowed along. It was his job to stay close to the clear sound, the empty soda bottles that Käte was clinking together, walking at the very front. Alfred was carrying the big tin milk can and whenever Willi took a break,

Alfred beat at the metal with a stirrer, a dull thud, and for a moment there was nothing else to be heard but his beats and their quiet echo back from the houses on the other side of the road.

In the darkness beneath his saucepan, Alfred tried to picture where they were walking. To begin with it was easy to follow their path, out of the house and along the bank, past the baker's shop that smelt of dough even during the night. Then he grew dizzy from all the noise and it was hard enough to pay attention to the direction of the soda bottles' chiming. Once he thought he recognized the sounds of the pub, but wouldn't they have to cross Gertraudtenstrasse after it? And they did; he could feel the kerbstone beneath his feet and there were the rails for the horse-drawn trams. There were no carriages on the road. Now they must be by the dairy shop where his mother sent him with the can in the mornings. Alfred imagined how dark the windows were now, always shining so milky white in the morning.

His fingers got cold and he took the can and the beater in one hand and put the other in his coat pocket. At his feet he could see the snow they were walking on. When they passed one of the gaslights it shone brighter and looked even colder. The snow crystals glinted like thousands of tiny stars. It seemed to Alfred as if Willi were drumming harder and harder, his head barely noticing the quiet between the beats. All at once, Alfred saw blotches before the black walls of the casserole, as though he were walking through a nocturnal snowstorm, all alone. He could hear nothing above all the noise, tears running down his cheeks but he couldn't wipe them away. In the end he simply sat down on the ground; the others pulled the pan off his head and rubbed his face with snow until everything was right again.

Outside the house was the Schleusengraben Canal, where they played whenever the weather allowed. At the banks, posts peeked out of the water like lost souls. The piles sported heads of grass hair that told them apart, the Dandy, the Mademoiselle, the Veteran, the Elf. At noon the anglers hung their nets over them to dry, then the Mademoiselle had a veil and the Elf looked like a caged animal.

They usually stayed at the canal's lower level outside the house, between the Jungfern Bridge and Grüne Strasse. Only when they didn't want to be seen did the children go upstream of the lock, or balanced across the iron cantilevers of the Gertraudten Bridge to the square at Spittelmarkt, where they played tag around the tall streetlamps and watched the horse-drawn trams. They ran across to the Cölln side of the canal and daydreamt outside the windows of the Technical Institute, admiring the rococo candles at Hildebrand Wax, the optical instruments of the lorgnette factory; they saw the giant letters of the Kompass works rising to the sky, and they strolled along Mühlendamm like ladies and gentlemen, always two by two, hand in hand so that no one was lost in the crowd. On the way back from their excursions they raced the last leg and sat down, sweat-soaked, on the Jungfern Bridge outside the house, where they threw stones in the water until dinnertime. They watched the low barges gliding slowly along the narrow channel beneath their feet.

Sometimes a lone white-veiled figure joined them on the bridge. An old wedding custom demanded that every bride crossed it on the way to the altar, her groom waiting for her on the other side. If all was quiet there was nothing in the way of the marriage. If the boards creaked, however, there was reason to doubt her virginity. The boards always creaked, though, the wedding party shrieked with laughter, the bride blushed beneath her veil, making her look all the more delightful, the groom put on a brave face and everyone proceeded to the church in good cheer.

The brothers and sisters stayed until the last lockage. Whenever a dinghy came along or a boat with a taller structure, they leapt to the bridge's huge crank wheels with chains running over them. On command, four of them began to turn the wheels like helmsmen in a storm, the others firing them on. The chains tautened with a rattle and the bridge's boards rose slowly as though the earth were opening up and divided into halves, which slid calmly upwards. Once the bridge was open the children made way for the boatmen and stood in a row along the low parapet like sailors along a ship's rail, their hands raised to their caps in salute. Only the brothers on the cranks kept their hands calmly on their steering wheels and looked out to the distance, as if on a great expedition.

The performance never failed. The last in line climbed swiftly over the rails to the boat and accepted the toll fee.

As the years passed, the children grew fewer. On the day after Alfred's sixth birthday they buried Käte, who had failed to recover from a bout of pneumonia. Willi died the following year when he broke the surface while skating on the canal and never came up again. He must have drifted off under the ice. The search long abandoned, Alfred was still sitting by the bank that evening and waiting for it all to have been a joke. He thought he could hear Willi's drumbeats from New Year's Eve again. That night, he couldn't rid himself of the sight of the black hole in the ice. His father sat by his bed and advised him to forget the image. Willi was in the Lord now. But Alfred knew full well he was in the canal.

He asked, 'Where does the canal go to?'

'To the River Spree.'

'And then?'

'To the Havel.'

'And the Havel?'

'Flows into the Elbe.'

'Where does the Elbe end?'

'In the North Sea,' said his father.

Alfred had never heard of a North Sea.

Before the open casket, his father read from Genesis. 'Is not the whole land before thee? Separate thyself, I pray thee, from me.' Alfred was glad he couldn't see over the edge into the empty coffin.

On the way to the burial he held his mother's hand. They stood in a large circle around the freshly dug grave, the whole family with all the orphanage children, and no one said a word. Early April, their good shoes splashed with mud. Then Alfred stepped forward, reached into his suit pocket, knelt by the opening and placed his snow globe on his brother's coffin.

Back with his mother, he buried his head in her lap. She stroked the crown of his head but he couldn't stop crying. She reminded him how cheerful Willi had been, only making him weep more loudly. In the end she said, 'Life is God's work of art. No one can predict whether it will turn out well or fail. We have no choice but to admire his works and be glad when they succeed.'

Alfred stopped crying. Right there, his face hidden in his mother's black dress, he came up with a plan to make his life a success. He did not want to deal God another disappointment.

For all the ceremony on Sundays, the orphanage had a strict routine on Saturdays. They weren't real days, Kurt once said, they were nothing but preparations for Sunday. Right after getting up, the children had to change their sheets. And though they knew how cool and firm their pillows would feel that evening, they grumbled in the mornings as they struggled to get the scratchy blankets into their linen covers. Then they would sweep and scrub the dormitory, Alfred sometimes feigning a cough and allowed to replace the burnt-down candles.

Before noon each of them washed their clothes and then themselves. They climbed into the hot tub in pairs and scrubbed each other's backs until their skin glowed red with cleanliness. Once they had all bathed the children lined up, wrapped in their towels, in a long row before their mother. The washroom was still swathed in steam, a damp cloud surrounding them, luscious and heavy, like the Holy Spirit. Anna Wegener lifted one child after another onto her lap to cut their nails. Her left hand enfolded fingers or toes, the right held her silver scissors. She took her time over the ritual.

As she cut, their mother told stories. They were usually tales from the testaments, which she altered for the children, embellished and reconnected. In her Gospel, the 5,000 were fed not only loaves and fishes but also chicken, potatoes and biscuits. The children wished for more and more dishes from Jesus, and their mother made sure every one of them ended up on the table. Her expulsion of the money changers from the temple led to fisticuffs and the parable of the mustard seed ended up with a sausage.

On one of those Saturdays, when it was Alfred's turn to have his nails cut, Anna Wegener told the story of the creation. Alfred clambered onto his mother's lap and leant against her bent arm. She took his left hand, inserted the tip of the closed scissors under the edge of his thumbnail and pulled it slowly across. The metal transformed the black and left nothing but a pale strip of fingernail. One finger after another had its turn, while his mother told the tale of light and darkness and how the Lord divided them from one another. How He divided the firmament from the earth and the dry land from the water. The creation seemed to be one long story of divisions. Now his mother stabbed the tip of the scissors into Alfred's nail bed, picking for the dark specks she had not yet caught. Alfred pursed his lips. Kurt, the next in line, asked, 'Where did God get all the ideas for His creation? He only had seven days' time. I'd have thought of the sun and the moon too, but then there are the grasses and herbs, the birds, all the wild animals and the whales.' And people, Alfred added silently.

His mother had moved on to his toes, where the nails were thicker. 'I'm going to tell you a secret,' she said. 'God had a plan. Everything was already written down, every detail. That's why He was so quick at his work.' She took Alfred's last toe and slowly cut a crescent-shaped strip of nail off it. When she'd finished she picked up the cutting and flicked it into the bowl at her feet.

'And where's the plan now?' Alfred asked quietly.

His mother thought for a moment. 'He tore it up when He didn't need it any more. On Sunday afternoon, after He was finished, He tore it up and threw it away.'

'And where are the pieces?' asked Kurt.

'We don't know,' their mother said. 'Scattered across the world.'

Someone ought to collect them up, Alfred thought. Someone ought to hold them up to one another and see whether they fitted together. And if they fitted we could tell whether the plan had been a success.

From further back in the line, one of the orphans asked whether it was a true story. Alfred's mother let her son down from her lap. 'No,' she answered, 'it's a legend.' Then she helped Kurt up onto her knees.

Twinned and Accompanied Halos

Alfred started school in the late summer of 1887. In his satchel he found a bible, a new exercise book, a pretzel, a bag of boiled sweets and a compass. His siblings accompanied him to his first lesson. They stood outside in the corridor and waved as he entered the classroom. Though Alfred had long been looking forward to being a schoolboy, a strange emptiness crept up on him.

His brothers and sisters had made dark insinuations, drowned out by widespread sniggering before they came to an end. Alfred didn't mind learning but he feared having to sit so tightly packed with the others.

The classroom was already fully occupied; there had been so much to talk about on the way there. A space was made for him on the edge of the front bench. When Alfred hung his satchel on the desk hook he bumped up against a map stand. He set the large map swaying but it didn't fall down. Alfred deciphered the heading: THE EARTH. He was in the right place.

Over the past months, he had asked each of his siblings to show him one letter; that added up to the alphabet. The room was large, but not large enough for all the children. The blackboard at the front, with hooks on the wall alongside it holding a set of compasses, a ruler and a violin. In front of them stood the teacher's desk, replete with a globe. The air in the classroom was stuffy even in the morning.

What Alfred was looking forward to unreservedly was the bread rolls named after the Kaiser, which every schoolchild was given on the Kaiser's birthday. For years, he had watched his brothers and sisters coming home with their crusty white rolls one day in March, each missing only the tiniest of nibbles around the edges. For the rest of the day they made such a drama that they might have been given nectar and ambrosia. As soon as Alfred got close to them they'd sniff at their rolls and sigh, only to bite tiny morsels off them. None of them had ever thought of sharing with him.

They now had the third kaiser in one year. Wilhelm Friedrich had died in early March, days before they would have celebrated his birthday. His son Friedrich Wilhelm was sickly at his coronation and died after ninety-nine days without ever having a royal birthday. On the day of his death, his oldest son Friedrich Wilhelm was appointed as his successor, a January child. And so Alfred didn't get a single kaiser roll in all of his first year at school, despite the three kaisers.

All in all, school proved a disappointment. He found it hard to bear the sound of pencils on slates. Next to him sat a small, squinting boy who occasionally brought toffees to school and smelt bad. His name was Gregor and he pinched Alfred's thigh under the desk. He would copy in arithmetic, making Alfred press himself up against the wall. Sometimes Gregor would cry if the teacher asked him something.

Break time was frightening for Alfred because he didn't know the other children. He could barely tell them apart. Not until they all filed back into the classroom did he run once across the empty schoolyard, wishing he had more time.

The teacher had only one eye, one leg and a stick. The other eye and leg had been lost in the war, and the teacher jammed the stick under his arm when he hobbled into the classroom on his crutches.

What they had to pay heed to was good posture. The pupils were to look straight ahead with backs straight and legs together. Secondly, no one was to speak unless spoken to. That was called obedience. Anyone spoken to answered in full sentences. That was commanded by humility. The most effort for Alfred arose from the fourth rule: neatness. After several months they switched to fountain pens, which was even harder for him than using the slate pencil. The exercise books had lines printed in them, between which their letters had to go.

The teacher said, 'He who crosses the lines crosses the law.'

He taught religion, German, arithmetic, drawing, singing and gymnastics, and also the sciences, Alfred's favourite subject. In these lessons, he was allowed to fill his exercise book with everything that interested him anyway—he stuck autumn leaves to the pages, copied down the astounding pattern of a bird's egg and kept a daily record of the weather development. The black ink he had used to draw the egg pressed through to the rear side of the paper. Turning the page, a shiver ran down Alfred's neck as he realized that the pattern looked like that from the inside; this was the first thing the bird saw in its life. Did a bird start blinking before it hatched? Alfred imagined it must be lonely inside an egg.

At the end of the year, new children joined the class and sat in the front row, where Alfred had just been. He was allowed to move back a bench while Gregor stayed put. Alfred got on better with his new neighbour; the two of them moved back again the next summer, and so it went slowly on, away from the teacher, bench by bench.

Although Alfred was not easy game for his siblings' pleasure-seeking, they soon learnt how to tempt him. As soon as they offered to play hide-and-seek he was in on it. In the summer holidays they invented their own version, which they called hunt-the-rabbit, and they started playing the minute they finished breakfast. There were too many of them for one to seek all the others, so one child would hide and the others would set out in search. The seekers would stand in a circle, close their eyes and count to a hundred, murmuring; it sounded like the Lord's Prayer. Then they'd rub their eyes and set forth after the rabbit.

They would prowl separately around the yard and through the rooms where they were allowed to play, the whole house with the exception of the library, the kitchen and their parents' bedroom.

At the beginning they'd call hints at each other when they met, sharing where they'd already looked and where they were going now. Soon, though, each of them would concentrate on their own search and avoid the others.

The rules of the game had it that the first person to find the rabbit would not shout out in joy, but quietly slip into the hiding place alongside the prey. And so the house and the yard gradually emptied out while the rabbit had less and less space. Child after child squeezed in under the bed, behind the door, into the wardrobe, where their fellows greeted them in whispers, holding their hands over their mouths as soon as they started to explain why they hadn't thought anyone would be here.

Alfred loved the insidious isolation as the game grew imperceptibly quieter and he came to be surrounded only by silence, the empty yard, abandoned rooms, sometimes an imagined giggle. He never knew when the moment had come when he was the last one seeking. As he ran through the rooms keeping a distracted eye open, being left behind felt like winning.

Sometimes he ran on even though he had long since guessed where the others were, enjoying an extra lap of the house. He felt like the only survivor of a battle. No one could know what he knew; he pretended not to see a brotherly foot poking out, not to hear a whisper, not to notice the protrusions in the curtains on the way to the veranda. All at once he saw things that had never caught his eye before. Evidently, one had to disregard the familiar to find something new. He was standing in the yard as he thought that, in the shade of the walls, but up on the crest of the barn's roof were the first rays of early sunshine. It was going to be a beautiful day. He walked on like that, his gaze fixed on the sky, on the cirrus clouds neatly combed by the north wind, looking in the morning light as though they had no weight at all.

It was a pot of red geraniums that tripped him up, recently put out by his mother after the greenfly got the upper hand. Alfred stumbled and landed with his face in the nettles at the foot of the garden wall. Although he had hurt himself, he lay there for a moment, his bleeding knee gripped in his hands, not feeling like crying. When he opened his eyes he saw a caterpillar in among the stinging nettles.

It was plump, bright red and prickly, and he squatted down in front of the leaf it was eating. It tickled when he took the caterpillar in his hand. After watching it for long enough, the tiny black feet, the pale veil along its belly, the constrictions after each segment, he closed his fingers around it, stood up and went to the hiding place. There had been growing unrest behind a pile of planks for some time. His brothers and sisters were grateful to be released, crawling out one after another and admiring his treasure with him. Heinrich, an older orphan, found a large matchbox; Alfred placed the caterpillar in there along with a few nettle leaves and put the box in his pocket.

The ant situation did not improve. That summer, they marched into the kitchen from all directions, even crawling up the heating pipe from the washroom. At breakfast, they invaded the bread-basket and the bowl of pickled onions. Alfred's sister Tony had started by enticing a couple of them onto her finger and taking them outside, but there were no fewer ants on her proud return.

Their father slapped at them, their mother swiped them away with a cloth, the children flicked them across the smooth table top at one another. Once, when Alfred was helping his mother clear the table, he secretly cut one of them in half at the thinnest point with the fruit knife. He had heard that some creatures grew new limbs and lived on but ants were presumably not among them.

Their mother stuffed cloth in the gaps through which they got in and soaked the cloth in petroleum. Nothing changed. Heinrich found a good stick in the yard and beat long and hard at the ant trail, eventually returning to the house sweat-soaked and scared because there only ever seemed to be more of them. Tony took the rolling pin and rolled it calmly and evenly along the trail from the kitchen cupboard to the back door, which was effective but looked horrific, prompting the others to wrest the sticky rolling pin away from her. Alfred made a silent pledge to go without rolled-out biscuits that Christmas. Their mother came out with a kettle of boiling water and poured it carefully over the stones in the yard, all the way over to the flowerbeds. Alfred leant over the cobbles and watched the ants' small bodies being rinsed along the gaps between the stones, no longer even twitching. It was doubtlessly an effective procedure but they couldn't walk around with boiling water all day long.

It was Alfred who came up with the trap idea. At first he had considered something flammable but that wasn't even necessary. He fetched the pan from the carriage shed, the one Willi had put over his head that New Year's Eve. He put it down in the yard, got his mother to pour half a bottle of beer into it, and shook icing sugar onto it until it formed a firm island. Then he called the others and together they stood around the arrangement, his very first experiment.

It wasn't long before an ant scaled the steep wall of the casserole. Having arrived at the top, it looked around and walked to and fro along the brim for a moment, as though it had just reached the boundary to the land of milk and honey. Then it paused and climbed back down the outer wall, criss-crossing the cobbles before it returned to the edge of the vessel, perhaps simply wanting to eke out the anticipation a little. The icing-sugar island had broken up in the meantime, its pieces floating at a leisurely pace on the beer.

When they collided with other pieces they united into larger formations, broke apart again elsewhere and so on and on, a slow dance. One of the islands drifted to the edge and stayed there; the ant landed on it as it plunged down to paradise. The inside of the pan was enamelled—there was no way back. Not for this ant and not for all the others that soon followed, some plunging straight into the floods, some managing to climb onto their fellows and form small rafts, which quickly sank. Others found temporary salvation on one of the icing sugar islands and floated around on them. There must have been hundreds of them by the end, the small islands black with ants. Agitated, they ran from one coast to the other but there was no rescue in sight.

On the last day of the summer holidays, they were playing horse-and-coach in the yard when Alfred threw aside the riding crop and ran into the house. On the stairs, he shouted in a cracked voice, 'Where are my trousers?' His mother stared in confusion from above and it took him terribly long to explain it all—the fall, his knee, the matchbox. His mother laughed; the trousers were still at the tailor. Alfred asked where the workshop was. 'In the Krosigk building,' she answered, 'the patch ought to be done by now.'

She gave him a coin and he ran out of the house, not seeing the newspaper boy standing on the corner, almost running into a horse and carriage, dashing down Friedrichsgracht and across the Grünstrasse Bridge; outside the distillery, a man shouted after him and raised his hand, but Alfred couldn't waste time deciding whether it was a greeting or a curse. Only when he leapt wheezing up the three steps to the tailor's workshop was he certain he had made up part of the lost time.

The tailor was an elderly man. He was smooth-shaven, though a beard would have mercifully concealed his pockmarked face. In response to Alfred's panted question, he ran a hand over his scabbed cheeks, then stabbed his needle in the black gabardine he was working on, rose to his feet with a groan and disappeared behind a curtain to the next room. Alfred leant against a roll of canvas and tried to catch his breath. The workshop was strewn with fabric cuttings, crumpled patterns, measuring tapes and yarns in all shades. All of a sudden Alfred started coughing, worse and worse, unable to stop. He raised his arms to get some air and it only improved when the tailor emerged from behind the cloth with the carefully folded pair of trousers, though his eyes were still watering. The old man wanted to show him the repair he'd made but Alfred held out the coin, got the trousers wrapped in paper and left the shop without a word of thanks.

On the way back he dawdled, walking slowly along Wallstrasse, watched a boy at the crossroads whipping a top along before him, and only stopped on the canal embankment. There, he lay his bundle on the ground, untied the knot and folded back the paper. He gingerly opened the button of the pocket and reached inside, and the matchbox really was still there. Alfred removed it and sat down by the water. What awaited him inside the box? And could anything be changed now, by a wish, a prayer? He asked himself whether it would help simply not to open the box, to delay the certainty of death. In the end, Alfred was not even sure the caterpillar had even existed before he landed next to it in the nettle patch.

Then he took a deep breath and pushed open the box. A whole nest of decayed leaves was inside it, crumbs, colourless dry clumps, between them strange threads but no caterpillar. Instead he found a sheath of parchment, torn open and empty; when he lifted it out he saw that it was transparent, a hollow cocoon. His fingers pushed the leaves aside and discovered something moving in the corner of the box.

It was a butterfly, or perhaps it was merely the ghost of a butterfly. Grey, stunted, its feelers bent over to one side, one wing broken. Alfred picked up the creature by one leg and lifted it onto the palm of his hand. The butterfly made a motion that might have become a flutter, had it possessed what was necessary for such a thing—healthy wings and strength. Or perhaps it wasn't the butterfly twitching but only a reflex of its small, broken body. Alfred felt more miserable than ever before. He picked a blade of grass and held it out to the creature but the butterfly made no reaction. When Alfred stood up and jammed the folded trousers beneath one arm, the butterfly tipped over and stayed on its side. Alfred covered it with the other hand. He left the empty matchbox behind on the cobbles.

He carried it before him like a ceremonial object. By the time he got home the creature had still not moved. Alfred no longer believed it was alive. He considered returning it to the nettles, in case it might recover. But then he'd have to pass it every day. So he went down the steps to the canal and set the butterfly down on the water. The creature turned on its side, one wing splayed out vertically, and a gust of wind caught it and blew it ahead, out onto the canal.

That same day, Alfred went over to the Lustgarten on the other side of the palace. He roamed along the paths of the outer ring, paced up and down beneath the trees, his eyes fixed to the ground. A lady pushing a perambulator passed him several times, at some point stopping and asking whether he was looking for conkers. If so, he was looking in the wrong place. He would have explained but the baby began to cry and she moved on. An elderly gentleman enquired after what he had lost and offered to help him look.

When he heard what Alfred wanted he laughed at him. 'You can't look for them, you just find them.'

He was right, as it turned out. Only over a week later did he make his find, on the way back from church. The caterpillar was perched on a dandelion in the gutter and was smaller than the first one. Green, with a dense coating of hairs; he picked it up on one finger and told Tony to close her eyes, then he stroked her face with it. His sister shrieked with pleasure, drawing the others. When they saw what Alfred had they all held out their cheeks, and he had to run from one to the next with the creature until every last one had been stroked by the caterpillar's hairs. Tony wished for a necklace of caterpillars and Kurt immediately came up with a plan—all they had to do was tie a thick stalk of the caterpillars' favourite grass around her neck and balance the creatures along it. Alfred imagined the furry green strip squirming around his sister's neck, crawling imperceptibly onward.

At home, he put the caterpillar in a pickling jar on his bedside table. Waking up in the morning, his first glance was at the jar, as was his last after evening prayers. The caterpillar quickly gained weight; sometimes Alfred found the jar full of new gifts: grasses, flowers, a gooseberry, even crumbs of bread and slices of sausage donated by one of his siblings.

When Alfred woke up on the seventh day, the caterpillar was gone. He had sealed off the jar with perforated parchment—when he checked, a small cocoon was suspended beneath it. It had pupated. At the top end, the furry remains of the caterpillar's tail peeked out, falling off by that very evening.

The other children now came every morning and wanted to touch the chrysalis. Alfred was kept fully occupied with protecting his foundling. In the meantime, he had taken to carrying the jar everywhere he went, and so it stood at his place at the breakfast table and accompanied him throughout the day. While the other children played in the afternoon, Alfred sat next to them, the jar on his lap, guarding it proudly.

After a week, Alfred noticed in the morning that the chrysalis looked different to before, more transparent; he almost thought he could see patterns behind the white skin. Alfred decided to stay in bed, pretending to have a stomach ache. His mother was surprised but when Alfred screwed up his face in pain she brought him the heavy hot water bottle, wrapped him in his blankets and closed the door quietly.

It took a terribly long time. Unchanged, the chrysalis hung from the lid looking tight enough to burst. Alfred tried to make the sheath break open through sheer willpower. He stared at the small pale sac, held his breath and pressed as though he might bring the butterfly into the world himself. A few times, he leant over and tapped the glass, in case the creature needed one last impetus to set it in motion. But nothing happened. He couldn't even tell what was top and what was bottom of the butterfly.

For a moment he considered simply freeing the creature from its husk himself, but Heinrich had warned him that a butterfly could not survive without the physical challenge of its birth. Alfred's tired eyes kept closing and he had to rub them. By now he really did have a stomach ache, out of hunger. Aside from which, he urgently needed the bathroom.

Only when the white shape made a sudden motion did Alfred emerge from his thoughts with a start. The chrysalis was still closed but it was now swaying to and fro. Alfred was just about to shout when the sheath broke open at the lower end.

A creature stretched its way out, a head with giant eyes, a proboscis that rolled up into a spiral, and then followed the cramped body, the butterfly pushing its way out in a single fluid motion and sliding out of its shell. The folds opened up and gave way to the joints of the tiny legs with which the butterfly held onto the chrysalis, now hanging pale and spent from the lid, and then it opened its wings, white like two small, fragile sails, spreading them very gradually and then dangling there motionless, as though what had to be done had been done, and only after a long while did Alfred dare to breathe again.

He kept the butterfly in its jar to begin with. He showed it to his brothers and sister when they came home, he showed it to his mother and father, and he looked at it himself over and over. He made dozens of sketches, including of the moment of its hatching, from memory, but none of them approached the beauty of the actual event. Alfred put flowers brushed with sugar water in the jar and the creature really did land on them and lick at the petals. On the third evening, his mother asked how much longer he wanted to keep the butterfly, and Heinrich also told him the time had come tó set it free. During the night, Alfred stared over at the white spot perched on the edge of the jar, looking like it wanted to get out. When Alfred closed his eyes he saw it fluttering inside the jar for the first time, then settling on the bottom and slowly opening and closing its wings over and over. Alfred saw all the images he wanted to retain, wanted to keep for himself like precious treasure, and when the dawn came he crept down to his mother's sewing box in the parlour and quietly climbed the stairs again, carefully opened the jar, reached inside and stabbed a pin gently through the butterfly's slim abdomen. He pinned it to the wall above his bed. After a while, the creature gave up its struggle.

Then he sat by the canal again, his legs dangling, the Kompass works' sign reflected in the water before the darkening sky. Alfred wanted to make his mark. Every evening, the day closed over him like water over a cast stone. And no matter how many stones he threw in the lock over the years, the water level never rose even a finger's width.

On the Origins of Lesser Whirlwinds

Alfred met a girl at church. She caught his eye because she held her hands to her lips as she prayed. As they left the building, they arranged to meet up next time. During that week, he looked forward to Sunday in a different way than usual. He had forgotten to ask her name and so when he thought of her, he called her Squirrel in his mind. She looked a little squirrel-like.

The week grew endless, with Saturday especially dragging itself out beyond measure. After lunch, Alfred vanished to the still-warm washroom all alone and drew in his exercise book, lying on the floor, with charcoal. To begin with he made patterns, then he simply drew a line as straight as possible across the page, from the left edge across the joint in the middle, where the line jolted slightly, and across to the right rim. He made a great effort not to draw over the side of the book, so as not to make marks on the floor, but he didn't always manage it. When he finished one page he turned it over and continued the line on the reverse, all the way through the book, imagining it as a long path, at the end of which he'd see Squirrel again.

That Sunday morning, the family of Wegener the preacher filed into the church two by two as usual, in the same formation as on school excursions. As the preliminary organ playing ended, the last of them had just entered the building. Alfred took a seat in the front row. That day, however, he didn't sit next to his mother, but pressed himself against the outer edge of the pew. He crept away at the beginning of the Lord's Prayer.

Squirrel was waiting behind the back pews. She looked even more rodent-like than the week before, her pointed nose, her wide-apart eyes, her small mouth. How pale she was. Her stubbly hair stood slightly on end, uncombed. Alfred had never seen a girl with short hair.

They squatted down on the stone flags and looked at each other, their hands in front of their mouths so they didn't laugh out loud, though Alfred's also because he quickly recited the end of the Lord's Prayer behind the protection of his fingers. Deliver us from evil. For the first time, he stumbled over the words. Squirrel asked him whether his father wore a cassock at home too, and Alfred told her about the Sunday when all the bands had been dirty.

'Bands?'

'The white collar above the cassock,' Alfred explained. 'My mother just took a napkin out of the drawer, folded it and tied it around his neck. Nobody noticed.'

Squirrel took his hands in hers to read his fortune. Her thumb stroked around his palm, all the way to between his fingers. It tickled and Alfred was uncertain whether what they were doing might not be superstition. He pulled his hand away and Squirrel said he was too young anyway; she couldn't make out the lines properly yet.

They had to whisper. His father's preaching voice came from above: For all the land which thou seest, to thee will I give it, and to thy seed for ever. Whenever Squirrel said something she leant forward and put her mouth up close to Alfred's ear. Then she sat there again and looked at him, her head bowed. The thing that most distinguished her from a squirrel was her skin, which was more beautiful than anything Alfred had seen in his life. His father was talking about Matthew verse 4 now. Just as he told how Jesus was showed all the kingdoms of the world at once from the high mountain, Squirrel reached out a hand for Alfred and grabbed at his face. Alfred flinched. She gave a silent laugh, put her finger on her lips and beckoned to him. He had something on his cheek, she whispered. Cautiously, she reached over and showed him what it was.

'An eyelash. You get to make a wish.' She paused. 'You can tell me your wish, of course.' She held up her finger with the black eyelash to his face and blew it away herself. Then she looked up at him from below.

Alfred said nothing. He knew you died if you lost all your eyelashes. His mother had told him so when one of hers had fallen out, and she'd laughed as she said it. Alfred considered telling Squirrel, but he didn't know whether they knew each other well enough yet. So he smiled as best he could. Sometimes silence was the better option.

They were back in their seats for Communion.

In bed that evening, he was annoyed that he'd already given his snow globe away. He thought about what he might give Squirrel instead, but nothing seemed valuable enough.

The next Sunday, Squirrel wasn't at church. Alfred worked himself up to asking her mother and found out that her good daughter was sick, but not what the sickness was. He said the collect inattentively and without enthusiasm and only gathered his mind for the silent intercession. All the way home, Kurt detailed a proof of God's existence he had come up with during the sermon. He talked himself deeper and deeper with increasing fervour—out of faith had come knowledge, the argumentation not merely logical but infallible, any error out of the question. Alfred did not follow his brother's arguments with his full attention.

At night he lay awake among his breathing siblings, beneath the dark dome of their sleep, reciting the illnesses he knew. Coughs, scabs, tuberculosis, warts. After some thought he added catarrh, diarrhoea, toothache. What else could it be? Hysteria? He was too concerned to come up with more than a dozen illnesses. And she'd been so pale. As soon as he closed his eyes he saw her white face close up. Might she be a snow squirrel? When the Klosterkirche bell struck midnight he cast off his blankets and crept barefoot down to the parlour. In the bureau behind the napkin rings were the two volumes of Good Health for Everyman. Sometimes, when their parents weren't looking, the older brothers took them out and studied the illustrations with horror and consternation. The subtitle promised a great deal: Medical advice for every age and every condition of human life, in cases of sickness of all kinds, including epidemics and endemics. That was exactly what he needed. The volumes were called Abdomen–Kyphosis and Labour–Zygomatic. Alfred hesitated briefly and then decided on both.

He found a box of matches, removed one of the long splints and made sure to hold it by the very end. Carefully, he lit a candle, wrapped himself up in the tablecloth and took a seat in the armchair. Then he opened up the first volume.

It was overwhelming. Alfred had never realized how many ways there were for the human body to perish. How vulnerable and weak a person was. In every drawing of a carbuncle, he thought he recognized Squirrel's beautiful skin, now disfigured by the hideous growth. The coloured plates showing longitudinal sections of scarred tissue reminded him of the pattern on her dress, even on the digestive diagrams he thought it must be her lung that was afflicted, her pancreas, her spleen. To begin with, he had licked his forefinger before turning each page, but disgust soon put a stop to that.

He learnt all manner of new names, sometimes uncertain whether they referred to parts of the human body or its afflictions. Yet he linked every one of them mentally with his new friend, who grew increasingly entangled in lymph nodes and intestinal loops, who suffered from gall bladders, follicles and prostates. With every new page, the prospect of ever seeing Squirrel alive again drifted further away. And if he ever did, he hardly dared to hope he would still recognize her.

By the time he closed the books late into the night, his head was spinning. On the stairs up to the dormitory, one hand on the bannisters so as not to fall over out of sheer exhaustion, he only knew one thing for sure—things did not look good for her.

In the morning he stayed in bed, unable to say precisely what he was suffering from. There were too many possibilities. It did him good to be alone in the darkened room, even though sinister images detached themselves from the bottom of his consciousness as he dozed, floating up to the surface. He sought refuge in sleep. For hours, he tossed to and fro on his pillow, watched anxiously from time to time by his mother, who interrupted his fever dreams with light meals and lukewarm tea. In the evening she sponged him down because his temperature refused to fall. Alfred woke in the middle of the night, disturbed by his own sighs. Halfway back to sleep he saw himself lying there, his body feeling alien, as if moving of its own accord and beginning to wander imperceptibly. Alfred felt as though wings were growing out of his back, curving to form a roof above his head. He lay beneath it, trembling with heat. A great roof, beneath which it was absolutely dark. He floated up, the wings bearing him, and the higher he got the brighter it grew around him, in the end so white that he woke with a start. In the semi-darkness of the dormitory, he made out the bedside table and reached for his cup of now cold chamomile tea, then he simply sat there, his chin resting on his knees, and looked out into the darkness so as not to close his eyes, where the images were waiting for him. His temperature fell the next morning and he felt strong enough to go to the bathroom alone. In the cold corridor, he heard his parents' voices from the kitchen, his father whispering and his mother saying, 'He could have died,' and he realized it was him they were talking about.

On Sundays after church, Squirrel was sometimes allowed to come home with him; one mouth more or less to feed made no difference. She had started school now too.

They all walked home together in their Sunday best, a long black-clad crocodile. The two of them dawdled behind the other children. It was a bright sunny day, the heat already pooling between the houses before noon, and Alfred had to take off his suit jacket. He threw it over his shoulder with the same swing as Heinrich, who was walking a little way ahead of them. When they got to Mühlendamm, Squirrel held him back by the jacket. He turned around to her but she merely pointed along the tram tracks.

Alfred saw the steeple of the Petrikirche, he saw the awnings outside Fettenborn's Conditorei with the coffeehouse guests sitting in their shade, he saw the sky-blue sky above them. Then he saw what Squirrel meant. At the end of the road, the cobbles shimmered like water. A tram was approaching from Molkenmarkt, the horses seemingly trotting through a shallow puddle.

'Do you know what kind of water that is?'

Alfred shrugged—what kind of water could something be that wasn't water?

Squirrel went on. 'If you fall in, you go under and die. We can only see the water from the distance. When it's our turn to die, we see it from close up.'

Alfred imagined what it must be like to float in a lake that was perfectly shallow. In a lake that didn't exist. He saw himself, suddenly minuscule in a huge, glittering surface that stretched to the horizon, beating his arms. He tried to rid himself of the image but found that he couldn't. He vowed to find out why it was impossible to drown in a lake like that.

When Alfred looked up he saw his parents and siblings stepping into the shimmer, their feet sinking into it, looking like they were walking through water, but it didn't trouble them; they simply walked on, deeper and deeper into it.

The city air made Alfred pale and tired. Or that was how it seemed to Anna Wegener, who watched her youngest child with growing distress. Everything gave her reason for concern, his cough, the way he rubbed his temples, his stubbornly pouted lips, his gentle features. Even his grey eyes had lost their piercing quality and looked dull and doubting. And so his father went and bought the old director's house of the closed-down glassworks near Rheinsberg. It was the house where his wife was born but she had grown up with relatives after her parents' early death. The long low building was on the banks of Lake Schlaborn; he found it abandoned and empty. He spent two days criss-crossing the villages, buying up Anna's parents' mahogany furniture, their mirrors and pictures, which had been dispersed around the area. And then it was a home again.

They now went there for all holidays, for harvest festival, Saint Nicolas' Day, after Christmas. When the horse-drawn omnibus took them to the Stettin Station on Invalidenstrasse, the wheels sang to the children. We're off to our Hütte, we're off to our Hütte! In the rattling train carriage, they told tales of all there was to do out there, by the lake, in the light, in the woods. At last the train gave one last whistle and they climbed down onto the wet, sandy ground next to the tracks. While their parents took a cart with the luggage, the children walked through the underbrush.

How wonderfully quiet it was in the forest. In a long row, all the siblings walked side by side, the snow still on the ground out here crunching beneath their boots. The pine trunks stood bare, between them oaks and beeches, some of them tipped over. Finding beechnuts under the snow, they tossed away their gloves and collected until their fingers almost froze. Afterwards they stood together in the twilight, their breath steaming, and peeled the nuts with fingernails and teeth like rodents. They ate until none of them had a single beechnut left and then they ran on, even closer together than before.

By the time they reached the lake they were sweaty and tired. The water glinted in the last of the daylight. Their mother stood in the open door and helped the smaller boys out of their coats.

There was soup made of bread and fish, and they only ever went to sleep after looking at the stars from the gable windows. There were so many that their eyes watered.

In the morning they ran out onto the lake before breakfast, one of them always slipping on the smooth ice, the others helping him up, and together they slid all the way to the middle, their arms outstretched as though they were flying. They held long, merciless snowball fights between continuously changing camps, simply because it was so tempting to throw snow at those on their own side.

By the time they returned home half-frozen, their father had lit the fire. They sat close by the hearth with chattering teeth until they gradually warmed up. Their parents had to promise them they'd always come out here from now on.

And that was what they did. As soon as they arrived they would run out onto the ice with the big drill and bore a hole through which to fetch water, or they let down crusts of bread on a line until a stickleback took the bait, shocking them so much they let it go again. They told their parents it had been a catfish. They fetched cartloads of wood from the forest and sawed and hacked the trunks behind the house. With the soot from the fireplace, they drew black lines beneath their eyes to look like savages; they were members of a remote tribe with their own cruel rituals and gods just as unrelenting. They found out they could use the soot to melt holes in the ice, and they kept fetching new ash with the dustpan until the lake was dotted with black stains like a sieve. They climbed into the snowy crowns of the oaks in front of the house and tried to hit the guttering from above with snowballs. Alfred dug up frogs and slowworms hibernating in the earth and defrosted them by the fire to see what happened to them.

They skated along the canal to the glassy smooth Zootzensee Lake and on to Flecken Zechlin. On every new lake they came to lay an untouched layer of frost, in which they scratched their patterns with wide swings like symbols on a blank sheet of paper, as though writing gigantic letters no one could read, unless there were someone looking down on them from far above. Alfred tried not to think of Willi. They were the first people in the world, all alone in the silence of the day, not shattered by a single bird's call. Only from the banks, from the edges, sounded the unending working of the ice, cracking and dull.

The children slept in the attic, a low room that ran along the length of the house. The cold scored frost ferns into the panes of their windows.

Alfred squatted on the floor and drew them. Page after page, he filled his exercise book with the patterns and gave them names, which he consolidated into classes. There were round and angular patterns, wreaths and rays, there were crowns, rods and fans, there were patterns that opened up like ferns, and there were irregular scratches that Alfred found ugly but also documented in his collection, for the sake of completeness. Thus, he learnt the peace and calm of science.

Out here in Zechlinerhütte, Alfred decided to become a natural scientist. He was old enough now. His uncle had given him a book, which he read every evening. It was about time and how it had passed. Alfred wrote down what he didn't understand and asked Heinrich about it before breakfast. He copied the names of the periods into his book and recited them until he knew them by heart: Carboniferous, Permian, Triassic, Jurassic, Cretaceous, Palaeogene, Neogene, Quarternary. He read that there had once been tropical hippopotami on the Rhine, which took some effort to imagine.

At night he sometimes remembered Squirrel, her skin. When the images became too much he wrote her a letter in his mind, explaining that he had no time for her for the foreseeable future. His research would sadly not permit a meeting.

He wondered where she had gone.

For Christmas, he got an electrostatic machine. Kurt found a chemistry book under the tree. The brothers decided both presents were to belong to them together. They forged plans at bedtime, coming up with lists of all they wanted to learn, categorized by subject area. It would not be long before no one could fool them any more.

Heinrich had been given a jigsaw puzzle showing the whole world, dismantled into a thousand pieces. For days on end, the boys sat on the floorboards in front of the fireplace and tried to put it together, but the sameness of the oceans foiled their hopes. The continents were soon assembled but there was no way to determine how they fitted together, and so the children lost interest one after another.

After the holidays, Alfred and Kurt begged for a room for their experiments and their mother let them have an unused corner next to the scullery. She didn't tell their father. Every penny of pocket money was spent at the pharmacy. They set off for school listlessly in the morning. At midday, though, they could hardly wait—buying carbide on the way, tossing their coats on the hook at home, running over to their laboratory, depositing a few spoons of the powder in a tin, dripping a little water on it and swiftly closing the lid tight, stabbing a hole in it with a pin. When they held a lit match before the opening a flame shot out. Using their mother's nail scissors, Alfred corrected his brother's singed forelock.

They found an old bicycle lamp at a junkshop, which cost them almost their entire savings. With the five remaining pfennigs, they bought a pocket-sized wire brush for carbide burners. Now they had light whenever they needed it. They experimented with the ratio of fuel to water, the diameter of the opening, the amount of carbide they used. Alfred noted: 'Depending on long or short period of light required, use more or less of the material.' They began tests on the maximum burning length. After a brief interruption, Alfred noted: 'The lamp must not be fully filled under any circumstances, as carbide expands on reaction (explosive effect).'

Without the lamp, they had to come up with new experiments. Kurt had the idea of putting some of the carbide in the gaps between the backyard cobbles, along which ants were still marching incessantly. Some of them quickly approached the grains, climbed onto them and tried to move them away. After a very brief period, none of the ants moved a muscle, and nor was any motion to be seen in the more distant gaps. Alfred noted: 'The ground moisture is sufficient to form acetylene, which has a specific weight apparently greater than air, as it penetrates to the creatures' underground tunnels. The gas has proven to be more toxic than suspected. Experiments therefore suspended.'

At dancing school he met Squirrel again, matured into a young woman. He would not have recognized her in the line of girls as they stood facing one another, but when her eyes fell on him she rearranged her face into that smile from behind the last pew.

The dancing mistress, an elderly woman with deep shadows beneath her eyes, clapped once, stepped between the two rows and began the first lesson. She looked around and said in a dark voice that she needed a man. Then she pointed a long slim finger at Alfred.

The surprised happiness of a moment ago gave way to sheer panic. The other boys smirked as Alfred stepped into the middle of the room. The dancing mistress took his hands and laid them on her back and her hip. Her hair smelt of tobacco.

She called out: 'This young gentleman will now gallantly follow my every step!' Then she signalled to the little man slumped at the piano and the notes of a waltz issued slowly forth. The woman moved one foot back and then slid the other to the side, Alfred following her with his feet as best he could. Sometimes Tony had played at dancing a waltz with him to the music coming out of the pub by the canal. It was the same now, except it was not for fun.

When the piece came to an end the mistress asked in a loud voice whether he now trusted he could teach it to a young lady. A few of the boys whistled through their teeth, and squeals sounded from the girls' side.

Alfred nodded mutely.

'Which one do you like?'

Alfred showed her. The floor creaked as Squirrel walked towards him.

She was still fragile but had grown tall in the meantime. Her hair was down in the style of Eleonora Duse. As she came closer he thought she would tower over him. Fortunately, though, he had grown as well. She too lowered her eyes. Not until the last moment before they touched did they both look up again. He put his hands on her sides as he had just learnt. It felt different than with the teacher. To his amazement he did not have to show her where her hands went.

The little man began to play again. They listened for two or three bars, Alfred feeling Squirrel swaying, then he moved one foot forward and she followed. To the side and back again and the slight turn as they went. Over her shoulder, he looked out of the window to where smoke rose from chimneys, vanishing in the clear sky. The little man played a trill. Alfred cast a brief glance at her face; her eyes were closed.

During the break she explained why she had stopped coming, back then. 'My mother died and I was sent to Bad Muskau to my grandparents. But now Father has married again and I was able to come back.'

She laughed when he admitted his secret name for her. Alfred decided to stick to Squirrel.

At the end of the afternoon, outside on the street, he held out his hand to her and she reached for it and did not let go. They both looked down at their hands, where Squirrel's fingers stroked across his knuckles, over the wart on his thumb, over his short scratchy fingernails. Since he'd taken to chewing them, there was no need for his mother to cut his nails any more.

From the corner of his eye he saw her lower her gaze. He looked at her face, the wild loose hair that would not stay tucked behind her ears. The skin on her cheeks. Her nose was no longer as pointed as back then at the Lord's Prayer but her eyes were still far apart. He looked down at her neck and further. He wished to write an essay for her. Or about her. About her body in particular.

When he looked down at their hands he noticed she had stopped stroking him. His fingers now gripped her hand tightly. Shocked, he let go and leapt back. His face bright red, he nodded at her several times. She raised her shoulders and looked for a moment like a small scared animal once again.

Then he turned around and walked away without looking back at her. On the way home he asked himself what he had intended with his nods.

In any case, he would not see her again. What was dancing good for? He was long since promised to another—to science.

The Countenance of the Moon

Das Neue Jahrhundert came by post. 'Like a cat scratching at the door to a gentleman's study, the German woman asks: May I cycle? May I write novels? May I study medicine? May I read Zola?' The journal's title had seduced him into ordering a sample copy—The New Century. His landlord Messerschmidt had burst in on his breakfast to bring him the post. Alfred Wegener topped up his coffee and went on reading. There was a report on the construction of rolling walkways for the World Exhibition in Paris, an observation on the fragile British fortunes in the Boer War. Stormberg, Magersfontein, Colenso, all these lost battles, but it was all too weak of mind for him, too libertarian, ultimately too Catholic.

The coffee was not strong enough either. Wegener put the cup back on the table. He flicked hastily through the rest of the newspaper, but he was not interested in the Civil Code having come into effect as of the first of January, no matter how excitedly his Heidelberger Tageblatt commented on the matter. He was not interested in the centennial celebrations held by Wilhelm II in far-off Berlin, and nor was he interested that the Kaiser then set off for Stettin to launch the Deutschland, even if it was the largest and fastest ship in the Reich ten times over.

For him, the new century had begun with cirri. Typical weather ahead of a warm front, falling pressure, high-étage clouds—it wouldn't stay nice for long. He felt tense and nervous himself, and his head was buzzing in addition.

Beneath the newspaper he found an envelope and opened it: 'The accused Alfred Wegener, student, is charged with having committed gross nuisance and disturbance of the peace at three o'clock in the night of the 2nd of the mth., by means of roaming the main road to the marketplace covered in a white sheet and thereby indecently causing disturbance of the peace through excessively loud shouting. Constable Eiermann.'

Eiermann. That cretin. Wegener took another sip and returned the letter to its envelope. Everyone here knew the police constable; they had spotted him a mile off. Nobody else wore his cap even remotely as skewed on top of his bald skull. The others had got away unscathed because they hadn't been singing. The song of the Eskiman and his Eskiwife; Wegener had thought up one verse after another, to his own amazement. And he'd refused to stop just because a moustachioed egghead came strolling around the corner.

He'd have to go to the police station later; Eiermann had charged him a penalty. Five marks—that was two weeks' rent. Wegener was lodging with a childless couple. At the end of the penalty notice was a passage stating that non-supplication would result in two days' immediate imprisonment. For a moment, Wegener considered whether that might not be a better option. But the prospect of sitting in a crowded cell amid all kinds of delinquents was not attractive.

He planned to buy a bicycle at last that afternoon, for his way to the college. He would have to do without the Wanderer model, then. The catalogue page was on the table: 'Those undeterred by a slightly higher price should choose the trusted brand'—that was out of the question now.

Stukenbrok, then. Wegener had to look for the page in the pile: 'First-class specialities in bicycles, sewing machines and weapons. Even my cheapest models are reliable.' He'd take his word for it.

In the end the penalty came to seven marks, Wegener having made somewhat of a scene at the police station. In the courtyard of the velocipede shop, he went from vehicle to vehicle with the master on his heels, a man as thin as a rake and barely older than himself, who gesticulated with oil-smeared hands during his explanations. Dark stripes crossed his temples as he was constantly attempting to push a curl back from his forehead, a lock of hair that did not exist. He had a slight squint and he blinked a great deal. There was conjecture among doctors that the use of a bicycle entailed sexual excitement, impotence and character damage. This man did nothing to invalidate that thesis, at least. And yet, Wegener appreciated the enthusiasm with which he presented his recommendations. The way he was in his element. Why not do the same and open a business? But what would he sell, what was his element?

Wegener elucidated his financial possibilities. The salesman fell silent for a moment and then advised a Deutschland Cycle. He led him to the model in question. The front mudguard flaunted a small plaque with the inscription: 'My field is the world.' Wegener walked once around it and then nodded. He liked it. In the end there was even enough money for a small tropical helmet. He had seen people wearing such things recently, as protection from the sun. He tried it on and asked how he looked.

The salesman laughed. 'It suits anyone. In Paris even the ladies wear them while cycling. With a veil to keep off the flies.'

The question remained in his mind—where was he to shine? He could have shone anywhere. Instead, he was hiding his light. He had left school as Primus omnium, but for what? Every morning he went to a different institute and grabbed a handful of basic works in the library, retiring with them to a corner. Vertebrate Palaeontology, Introduction to Maritime Law, Practical Course on Conception—it was all fine for him. After twenty pages at most he returned the volumes to the shelves. Why did he have to understand it? It was all written down already. Should he ever be in a calamity, he would find whatever could be said about any conceivable subject right here. Everyone was talking about the rise of mathematics and expecting God knows what insights from the field. Wegener did not appreciate arithmetic. He had no wish to spend his life on pieces of paper.

Physics had come to an end, that was the general conviction. All that could be described had been described. And so? There was always the indescribable. Had scientists not simply restricted themselves to explaining tangible matters? All that held still enough to be weighed had been weighed. All that fitted onto a slide had been microscoped. Who was studying the unpredictability of a whirlwind? Wegener felt a craving to get behind things, to devote himself to the inconceivable, the fleeting. To get as close to the calculation of the incalculable as humanly possible.

He attended Valentiner's general astronomy course. Quincke lectured in murmurs on experimental physics. Wegener was not the only one woken only by the trampling of students leaving the room. Who cared about the spectral distribution of a distant sun, when it existed without the slightest doubt? What was the constant path of a moon around Jupiter compared to the flickering heat of the road that Squirrel had showed him, and the way it had vanished on coming closer?

After a few weeks he stayed away from lectures. Instead, he joined a fraternity and was soon more often in the fencing hall than in college. He drank beer. A fellow student wrote home that Wegener was thoroughly letting off steam. Only one single lecture did he attend to the full that first year—Mysteries of Celestial Mechanics, a private course, but gratis.

In the spring he moved to Innsbruck to focus on other ideas. Instead of studying, he spent his no-longer-abundant bills of exchange on mountain boots, crampons, picks and rope. Thus equipped, he devoted days on end to exploring the geology and botany of the Stubai, Ötztal, Tyrolean and Zillertal Alps.

He passed the forest line, the tree line and the snow line, crossing boundaries as though travelling to a colder country. And all that was so clearly distinguished from a distance merged together here in a disturbing manner, up close. Isolated dwarf pines, fields of mountain pine, pastures, then patches of firn. He saw marmots popping up out of nowhere, just as shocked as himself for a long moment, before vanishing again with a sharp whistle. He saw the light and the way it was lost between the peaks. As soon as he reached the first field of solid snow he fell backward into the white and lay there, swaddled by the material in a calming manner. Whenever his doubts returned he stomped up to the nearest ridge and gazed down into the valleys. Descending, his knees ached.

For a few weeks he stopped shaving. In the evenings he watched the Alpenglow through his window and thought about religion. Was that what he was looking for? God had always been one of them, part of the family. Then they had lost sight of one another. Was God trying to show himself out here, in the beauty of His creation?

Wegener returned to Berlin that summer. He moved back in with his parents, who found their son altered. They did not probe. He helped in the garden. How young the orphans were. In the evening, once his new siblings were asleep, he sat around the long table with his parents and talked about science. His father was silent; his mother served home-baked treats. For the first time, Wegener enjoyed her quince loaf. Only at the end of the evening when his mother had gone to bed did his father begin to speak.

Quietly, he asked his son about his faith. Alfred gulped, playing out possible responses that were easier to say than the truth. Then he admitted he had not been to church for months.

'Why not?'

'They deny doubt.' Alfred fixed his eyes on his father over a corner of his quince loaf slice. 'And you? Are you without doubt?'

For a moment his father remained mute, and that silence betrayed him even as he began to speak, after all, in his preacher's voice. 'He who gives in to doubt loses the ground beneath his feet. He who once begins to doubt is lost, there is no going back.'

Alfred interrupted him. 'I don't believe you. I don't believe your psalms. I don't believe anything is revealed in them.'

'Where then?'

'In nature.' Alfred took a deep breath. 'We must read nature's book.'

'Even there it is not written where the next lightning bolt will strike. It is in God's hand alone.'

'Which God are you talking about—Zeus?'

'Guard your tongue. You'll never know where a snowflake will fall, despite your weather studies. You won't manage to catch a shooting star.'

'I will try. And if I don't achieve it, there will be others after me.' Wegener breathed deeply. 'Man's thirst for knowledge is unstoppable.'

'I demand humility.'

'Before God?'

'Before me.' Now it was his father taking a deep breath. 'The science of nature is nothing but man's work. What you read in nature is your own poetry.'

'You do nothing else with your bible.' Alfred cast a quick glance before adding, 'You're much more of a poet than I.'

His father's eyes narrowed. 'Watch what you say.' He had risen to his feet.

Alfred stood likewise. He moved behind his chair and gripped the back of it. 'I'm more likely to find the truth in the natural sciences than you in God's word.'

'Is that supposed to be a bet?'

'Call it what you like.'

'What shall we bet for?'

'The kingdom of heaven?'

'Don't make jokes.'

His father left him standing in the room.

He wanted everything, whatever that might be. Wegner cycled to the university on his Deutschland Cycle. He took Planck's course on heat theory, which left quite an impression. He felt a need to know everything, especially now. What had Wilhelm said in his Hun speech? No pardon shall be given. No prisoners shall be taken. Wegener had no desire to take prisoners either. No pardon, least of all for himself.

He attended Theory of Solar Eclipses, Tidal Theory, Theory of Special Disturbances, as well as Selected Chapters from Error Theory. He took every course as it came, feeling it would all be useful to him at some point. He studied the calculation of cloud height. Under Wolf, he learnt meteorology and noted the causes of the climate in an exercise book: '(1) Location, (2) Height, (3) Airstreams. The latter in particular. Very complicated.' He underlined the last part. Cycling home from the institute in the dark, along the canal, he felt he was vibrating.

At the age of twenty-four he gained his doctorate. His dissertation was less than forty pages long; he nevertheless managed to slip in a quote by Alfonso the Wise: 'Had God consulted me before embarking on Creation, I would have advised greater simplicity.'

As Wegener stepped forward to accept the honour he received a standing ovation. At the foot of the certificate was the line: Sagacitatis et industriae specimen laudabile. At home he looked up what it meant.

At night, Wegener went walking along the River Spree, observing the pockmarked face of the moon. There was still no tenable theory that might explain what had made such a mess of the satellite. A majority of the scientific world assumed it was extinguished volcanoes, but what kind of volcanoes would leave such gigantic craters? There again, what other cause came into question?

It was the same as ever. In the beginning was presumably a catastrophe. How few changes in the universe were not triggered by catastrophe. To be precise, he could not think of a single one. What triggered these catastrophes, though?

Had they asked him, thought Wegener as he crossed Jungfern Bridge, he would have assumed an external cause. Most causes came from outside. He might be a little inebriated. A brief moment of support against the bridge's parapet was necessary. The moon floated in the canal's water, looking no more unreal down there than in the sky. Wegener found a pebble and slung it over the parapet. The stone hit the moon between the eyes, contorting its face. A circular wave rose aloft, moved inwards, flung a few drops of water up from its middle and then flowed away at the edges.

Wegener screwed up his eyes. For an instant, he had seen the image of a crater. Perhaps it was nothing but reflected light, like so much. He had better stay put for a while and take the air.

Walking on again, he felt better. He felt his way through the black carriage entrance. All the windows to the courtyard were dark. In one corner lay the pile of rough marlstone delivered that morning. In the silvery lunar light, it looked like moonstone. The pebbles crunched beneath his shoes as Wegener climbed up the pile. At the top, he bent down for a particularly large clump and threw it hard at the others.

Nothing happened, aside from a single pebble bouncing off his boot. No trace of a crater; the stones were far too heavy and rough, but weren't the stones on the moon equally so?

In the kitchen he made tea, first burning his tongue and then leaving it on the table until the drink was cold.

He looked out of the window, behind which was nothing but darkness and the moon. It was all much smaller down here.

From the pantry, he fetched several bags of icing sugar and tipped it all onto the kitchen table. He took a handful of cherries from the bowl by the window and ate a couple before he dared to sling the last one with all his might into the icing sugar landscape.

Once the dust had settled the cherry lay on the ground of a crater. A small circular rampart had formed around it, with steeply sloped edges. In the middle of the crater rose a tiny pillar, the cherry next to it. It had burst, its juice colouring the ground of the crater red. The stone had been half expelled. Using his fingers, Wegener detached the flesh and put it in his mouth. It tasted sweet from the sugar adhering to it. He swept the experiment into the dustpan and went up to sleep.

In bed, he noted: 'Reduction in dimensions must entail a reduction of the mineral hardness. I should like to pursue this idea further.' He slept badly that night. Later, he made light again and added: 'Determined search for meteorite craters would presumably also yield findings on Earth.'

His brother Kurt persuaded him to sign up with him for the Jean Pleinars Cup, a gas ballooning competition. Kurt was now working as an assistant at the Aeronautical Observatory in Lindenberg and an experienced pilot. Only on their way did the two of them admit they were interested more in ballooning together than in winning. What use was it to stay in the air for as long as possible?

They found a guesthouse and shared a bed beneath a heavy down quilt. Kurt sweated strongly and nor did Alfred get much sleep. When the landlady came to wake them with a pot of rosehip tea before sunrise, the two of them were long since booted and spurred on the edge of the bed. The tea was sweet; they drank as though they had just escaped a blazing storm.

As the day dawned they arrived in the field at the edge of the town. They were the only participants who had never competed before, the youngest by some distance, and the only ones who did not own their flying equipment. They had been lent it by the airship battalion for a night flight. That was where their gas came from too, for thirty-four pfennigs per cubic metre.

The first balloons began to right themselves like sleepy giants, their baskets alongside them decked with bunting and flags. Photographers strode from one to the next, magnesium flashing at every turn.

The pilots had pride written on their faces as though they were hunters and had just bagged the giant creatures next to them. At the edge of the field a long table was erected, behind which sat the commission in black coats and hats. The brothers registered there, allocated the last starting number.

Lift-offs came at minutes' intervals. One balloon after another clipped the lines and rose into the young day. While Kurt was still occupied with the ropes, Alfred was already in the basket, watching the huge brightly coloured balls set loose from the ground one at a time, to float slowly and unerringly up into the sky. Had the other objects simply not yet noticed that this was now the direction in which gravity pulled? As if someone had turned over the snow globe in which they all lived, and the fat bright drops simply came away first before everything else was to follow slightly later, the carriages parked at the edge of the field along with their grazing horses, the table with the competition organizers, the spectators' picnic baskets and possibly the spectators themselves. All the cones in the surrounding woods would no longer fall to the ground but rise to the sky, just like the stones, the leaves in autumn, all the animals of the wood and all the land and all the people, each for himself, up and up to never-ending heights.

A referee startled Wegener out of such thoughts. He stepped up with a clipboard, from which he read the starting times. He informed the brothers they were to make themselves ready now. Kurt clambered into the basket, the referee released the rope and the two of them lifted off. They had thirty-eight sacks of ballast on board.

The balloon quickly gained altitude. Below, the houses remained in place, the fields and the land. The crawling on the ground. Never before had Wegener felt so light and at the same time so fearful, a stimulating fear. Above him only the balloon, the huge nothingness to which they clung like to a belief. With every metre's altitude, breathing grew easier. Away at last from the ground and its uncertainties, its creeping creatures. Away from the ants.

Climbing steadily, the balloon crossed Kremmen and Lake Ruppin to the northwest. The other airships were recognizable as distant dots in the sky, above and below them, but one after another was blown out of their vision. Wegener made a mental note to think on a more appropriate occasion about whether the flow behaviour of individual air layers might justify its own study.

Late that morning they flew over Wittstock, where their parents had first met. Delighted, both brothers spotted the dean's courtyard, but when they pointed they realized they meant different buildings. Before they managed to agree on one house the wind drove them onwards.

At noon they reached the Baltic at Wismar. The sea dark green, few billows to be seen due to the offshore wind. They had with them four pork cutlets, two bottles of mineral water, two oranges and two pounds of chocolate, of which each of the two crew members now received one bar.

At medium altitude, they passed the west coast of Fehmarn. They were convinced the temperature fell above the open sea but they agreed there was no plausible reason for it to do so. On the horizon, they made out the southern tip of Langeland. They ate one cutlet each.

Evening came as they were flying over Horsens on the coast of Jutland. The wind abated. Unfortunately, they established they had forgotten their coats in the excitement of starting. Kurt was of the opinion Alfred had put them over the back of a chair when he showed their identification papers. A barely excusable mistake. Alfred, however, was certain he had seen Kurt putting them down on the grass before they lifted off, to have his hands free for checking the ropes.

They had agreed on air temperature measurements at fifteen-minute intervals, so as to obtain some scientific benefit from the flight. In their light summer jackets, however, they were so directly exposed to the temperature that they were soon capable of estimating the values, and refrained from further readings from the thermometer they had brought along. The swift consumption of a large amount of chocolate kept them warm until Alfred insisted on rationing.

Concerned they might drift out to sea during the night, they decided to take turns keeping guard. Their fear of being overcome by sleep proved unfounded, however, inasmuch as their trembling effectively prevented any thought of sleep.

At some point the breeze turned to the east and they drifted gently out over the Kattegat in the early hours of the morning. They were astounded by how long it took before the sun's first rays began to warm them. For breakfast, they each ate their second cutlet, then took turns to doze for a while. The wind took them along the Danish coast back in a southerly direction, past Samsø and Fünen. The islands looked enticing. They climbed to 2,500 metres to evade the temptations of human civilization. In the afternoon the wind picked up; they ate their oranges.

On crossing the coastline, their course took a dangerous westerly turn, prompting the brothers to consider breaking off the flight. Concern that they might be sent out over the North Sea during the evening offered a good reason to end their undertaking. Just as they were preparing the basket for a landing, the wind turned anew and they flew south again. They had long since stopped looking out for their competitors.

When the sun touched the horizon for the second time they unwrapped the last two bars of chocolate from their paper. Chewing, Alfred said he could not remember ever eating anything as delicious. Kurt sucked wordlessly at his piece, his face contorted with pleasure. Later, he began pacing the cramped basket. One step forwards, one step back, expending the majority of his energy on turning. As he watched his brother, Alfred noticed himself clenching his eyes shut repeatedly, although the sun had set some time ago.

They knew they could have landed at any time. Yet now that they were up here, they saw no need to return to the ground before their strength was exhausted. Except—how could one be certain that one's own strength was exhausted?

The second night was absolutely clear, the sky strewn with stars. During his watch, Alfred occupied himself with inventing constellations by joining the dots in new ways. Despite knowing the balloon obscured the upper section of the sky, in the end he thought even the cope of heaven were full of stars. Nor was his blinking getting any better. The mineral water had long since dwindled. But the balloon's outer surface was wet with dew and the ropes too gathered moisture. From time to time Alfred found the energy to lick at them.

Then he stood there, his chest leaning against the edge of the basket, and looked down. The ground was in absolute darkness. There could be no thought of landing now. When they reached Hannover, Alfred noticed how low the wet balloon was meanwhile flying. He saw the glow of gas lanterns directly below him, almost thinking they might collide with the city's smokestacks. Through the chimneys, the embers in the fireplaces shone up to them.

Now he realized what the woven basket reminded him of— his childhood cradle, waiting in his parents' attic for some new purpose.

It grew light over Göttingen. Over Hannoversch Münden the sun went up. Everything would be fine now. They decided to attempt an ascent, letting the morning sun lift them to 3,700 metres. To climb more quickly, they wanted to jettison ballast. It emerged, however, that the two of them were no longer capable of lifting the sack over the edge of the basket. At sixteen degrees below freezing their trembling increased, worsened by muscular cramps and repeated faints.

Alfred was lying in one corner of the basket, his head bedded on one of the raffia containers, when from the corner of his eye he saw Kurt raising a finger in the opposite corner. He feared his brother wanted to rise even further. Only after a while did he realize Kurt merely wished to attract his attention. He raised his head. Kurt now pointed his finger downwards and raised his eyebrows. Alfred nodded again.

They prepared everything for landing and Kurt let down the drop line. The wind had grown stronger. Soon the basket was tilting, the rope on the ground, and Alfred leant his full weight against the edge of the basket. Then there was a jerk and Alfred held the torn end of the rope in his hand. His brother immediately pulled the rip line to empty the balloon. Just before the basket hit the ground they leapt up into the poles. Alfred was dragged along the ground, a grassy field, clumps of earth, roots, a molehill, then a field border, gripping at the undergrowth with his feet. Thus he came to a stop, his cheek bedded on a dandelion pillow, his stiff collar dug into the earth like a ploughshare.

When he sat upright he saw that his boots had been torn from his feet but he located them both again, likewise his house-keys and hat. After a while his brother turned up as well, accompanied by two fieldworkers.

They had touched down near Laubach in Spessart, fifty-two hours after starting. The news of their record-breaking flight spread like wildfire. A reporter came riding over from Aschaffenburg, on a nervous white horse. Wegener was sitting on the grass, leant against the basket, when the rider arrived. The man leapt down and set about arranging a tripod. His horse approached and sniffed at Wegener like a dog. He plucked a tuft of grass and held it out but the horse merely snorted and turned away. Meanwhile, the reporter shot a few pictures that were published in the region's newssheets the next morning. Over the following days the national and international newspapers reported on the event, all of them referring to the Comte de la Vaulx and his long-standing record for the world's longest balloon flight.

And these two greenhorns were supposed not only to have outdone France's most respected airman, but humiliated him? Surpassed his record by half, claiming to have been in the air a whole seventeen hours longer than the legend? Barely anyone accorded them credibility.

Wegener wrote in his notebook that evening: 'The world from above. There will soon be as many people alive on Earth as ever died. I ought to pursue this thought.'

The Ground of the Atlantic Ocean

Early in 1906, he read in the newspaper about a plan for a Danish expedition to north-eastern Greenland, which was to spend two summers charting the coastline. Under the writer Mylius-Erichsen's command, they would attempt to cross the ice of the Greenland Sea to reach the spot where the Germania expedition had been forced to turn back in 1870, and set up a base. From there, they hoped to explore the unknown section to Cape Bridgman.

A base station in the ice. All that could be studied there! Wegener closed his eyes. It required some effort to gather his wishes. He commanded himself to breathe more calmly and divided up the plans shooting through his mind. There would be the meteorological surveys, the hydrological, the terrestrial magnetic aspects, the atmospheric electric and the atmospheric studies, for which he felt particularly responsible. There were—seeing as one were there in the first place—the botanical, zoological and paleontological surveys, of course a number of geological questions occurred to him, then the glaciological problem, and there might even be ethnographical tasks. There was no need for him to explore everything himself.

The next thing he gathered was his clothing. He would not need much; he did not anticipate staying longer than two days. He set out with a small case that afternoon, purchased a ticket at the station and boarded the night train to Copenhagen. Mylius-Erichsen had to see him.

Standing by the open window of the compartment, he leant out with his face screwed up. The evening wind brought tears to his eyes. Why did travelling north feel like ascending into the air? When it grew dark outside he closed the window. He saw himself in the glass, his hair ruffled out of shape. How old was he? A quarter of a century. It was high time for a great deed.

In Warnemünde they shunted onto the new train ferry. They would cross on the Prinsessin Alexandrine, a single-track paddle ferry; Wegener had seen the white ship in the water from the wharf. Sadly, leaving the car was not permitted. The rocking of the waves lulled him into sleep.

When he awoke they were approaching Copenhagen. The main station a building site, though the Danish flag already flew from the scaffolding for the rectangular towers. He disembarked, complete with his hat and small case; it was early morning.

How many ships sailed between the buildings! It was barely recognizable whether the city was built on land or on water. Wegener handed the coachman one of the notes he had exchanged and received a handful of strange coins in return. Then he rang at the door.

It was a troll that opened up. A stooped figure with a furry body, pointed beard and piercing eyes peered cautiously out of the dark corridor, hair concealed beneath a dwarf's cap. For a moment Wegener considered running away, but he had no chance of escaping this creature with his suitcase. So he took a deep breath and said his name.

'I am seeking Mr Ludvig Mylius-Erichsen. With regards to his expedition, in which I propose to participate as a scientist from Germany.'

The creature laughed and asked him in. It spoke German with an accent as though it had come straight from the depths of the earth. The door opened entirely, then the figure pushed back its hood, held out its hand and introduced itself. It was none other than the man of the house. He apologized for his habit, Wegener having surprised him as he tried on a few souvenirs from his last trip that he intended to use on the forthcoming expedition. Would he care to feel it? Seal fur, a jacket to be pulled over the head. Wegener ran his hand along Mylius-Erichsen's upper arm; it felt soft.

The hallway and every room they passed through as they talked was full of bookshelves. Even in the kitchen, where they took seats at a table, volumes were piled on the windowsill. Mylius-Erichsen lived alone. He was only slightly older than Wegener, looking rather more human here in the light from the window. The beard would take some getting used to, however. In conversation, it emerged that his particular passion was for the world of Nordic sagas. Despite his youth, he had already led an expedition to Greenland. He had spent two years exploring and recording the myths of the polar Eskimos. He fetched the pictures painted during their trip. The round faces with tired eyes, as though they had seen quite other things than a shivering painter. Mylius-Erichsen didn't stop telling one saga after another. Wegener was amazed at what outlandish things one could study.

At last they returned to the planned trip. Mylius-Erichsen wanted to gather a handful of scientists from various fields and allow each one his freedom to research. Already standing by the door, he came to the subject of pecuniary matters—each man would receive the same small pay, from the expedition leader to the stoker. 'For,' he said, pushing the hood back over his head with a smile, 'we cannot do without any one man. And all will be putting their lives at risk. There is no more a man can give.'

Overjoyed, Wegener returned to Berlin the next day and announced to his parents that he was invited, along with five further researchers, two first lieutenants, several cartographers and two painters, to embark upon the journey that summer.

His father was appalled. He had always given Alfred a free hand for his occasionally bizarre ideas, he said, but now he had to speak out. 'I wish for my son to take on a pensionable position, not challenge God's mercy at the North Pole.'

Alfred said nothing. His mother brought drinks. They argued all afternoon. More quince loaf appeared from time to time. Sometimes his mother went out to tell the new siblings to quieten down.

By the time darkness fell Alfred's father had realized his son would not be persuaded against his plan. In the hallway, he wished him a murmured God's blessing.

The next morning, Wegener began writing letters. He planned to use kites and balloons to study the atmosphere in Greenland, so he needed apparatus and instruments. He appealed to the appropriate institutions to provide him with the necessary equipment.

'In the hope that you might forgive this inconvenience due to my great wish to carry the expedition's aerological programme to a satisfactory end, I remain respectfully your humble servant.' He filled the margins of several newspaper pages with his name until the signature appeared sufficiently worldly. To the minister of war, he sent a request for the loan of 200 steel flasks from the inventory of the Royal Airship Battalion for transporting hydrogen. He asked the German South Polar Expedition of 1901 to 1903 to send the ice drills they had purchased. He addressed envelopes, filled and sealed them, took them to the post office. His fingers smelt of ink.

A few days later he received the first response, postmarked Großborstel. The letter came from a Professor Köppen, the head of the local kite station. He invited dear Doctor Wegener to present the aims of his undertaking in a conversation.

A first warm day of spring, and Wegener took a hackney cab from Hamburg. He had recently begun cultivating a small moustache, which he occasionally stroked. The cloudless sky in the rear window was so empty that even an expert could draw no conclusions.

Anemograph wheels and flags whirled in the professor's garden, recording the winds. They spoke about meteorology. From time to time Köppen ran a hand through his white beard and his brows were equally white, dangling in front of his eyes. He was particularly interested in Wegener's studies on whirlwinds. He had to admit he had avoided such things all his life.

'Which things?' asked Wegener.

'All too intangible things. Meteorology already deals with rather ephemeral matters. Nothing ever stands still. But you, sir, seem to be rather obsessed with them.'

'What gives you that impression, Professor?'

Wegener had told him about his interest in the nature of funnel clouds—tornadoes that came out of nowhere and then raged for seconds or minutes, only to vanish as though merely imaginary. They were almost un-researched, simply because they were never there when they were needed. He had let himself get carried away and spoken of his thoughts on the crater-forming influence of meteorites on the surface of the moon, which seemed very real to him but might appear rather other-worldly to the uninitiated.

A young woman brought drinks. She wore a bright red scarf, though she had no need to distract from her face.

Professor Köppen noticed his guest's interest and introduced her as his daughter, Else. She too an absolute tornado—he sometimes didn't know which way was which with her.

Wegener commented that was what the certainty of science was for.

Else curtsied, her cheeks taking on the colour of her scarf for several moments.

'Very much so,' said Köppen once his daughter has returned to the house. Although he was not always even certain, in science, of how certain one could be of it.

Wegener looked at the professor in amazement. 'But is that not what keeps us upright?'

'My good man,' Köppen replied, wiping his lips. 'You display, as I said, a remarkable propensity for haziness. Are you aware of that? We are all meteorologists, but most of us came to the field out of a perfectly down-to-earth interest in the coming day's weather. Whether it will stay dry. Where the wind will come from. How cold it will be. If you like, we formalize country lore. You, sir, however, have chosen, of all things in this truly insufficiently secured field, the height of clouds, the shape of snow crystals and the secrets of turbulences and air vortexes. And you bring along an additional passion for the phenomenon of fata morgana. To say nothing of fantasies such as the fall of shooting stars. How could one refrain from wondering at such interests?'

Wegener turned up his collar. The day was growing a little cool after all. Shooting stars. He could have made a number of objections. Instead he said, 'But that is nothing but coincidence, Professor. These subjects simply occur to me and I pursue them. What scientist would eschew a phenomenon when there is something to explore?'

The professor smiled. He took out his tobacco and offered it to his guest. Wegener had no experience and turned it down, commenting that he had left his smoking equipment at home. Köppen had a second set at hand. For a while the two men filled their pipes in silence. Then it was Köppen who said, 'Please don't misunderstand me, sir. I have no objections to these thoughts; quite the opposite. You will laugh when I tell you it is an old dream of mine to bring order to phenomena for which we do not even have words. The impressions in the moment of falling asleep, the gradations of pain, ideas on the individual's sense of loneliness amid people.' He gathered up a few excess strands of tobacco and sprinkled them back into the bag.

Wegener did not look at the professor as he replied, 'I know what you are talking about.' He took a deep breath. 'Those are certainly challenges to which we have no answers. But will we ever find them? Will a child be able to explain to his mother, a hundred years from now, what he experiences in a fever dream? And are we the right men to study these internal lands?'

Köppen lit his pipe. It was the last match in the box, so he leant forward and gave a light to his guest. Wegener had filled his pipe so firmly that the tobacco refused to burn. How terribly unpleasant. He inhaled and blew by turn. By the time the tobacco was finally alight the flame had reached the professor's fingers.

Köppen made no comment. He waved the match out, blew briefly on his fingertips and leant back in his chair. Then they simply sat and smoked. Wegener felt as though he had never done anything else.

Else brought a plate of pastries, which they left untouched. She soon returned with a deck chair, took a scrutinizing glance at the sky and settled down nearby, as though by chance. Draped across her seat, she held a book that she read without turning the pages. A flock of pigeons fluttered over the garden and vanished into the horizon.

Wegener grew a little dizzy from the tobacco smoke. He would have liked to go on talking about these things, yet he did not want to show exaggerated interest in them. Only very gradually did his shock abate over Köppen having convicted him of a tendency for nebulosity. It gave way to surprise that the old man indulged in such questions himself.

Silently, Wegener formulated a thought for his notebook— 'The mainlands of knowledge are discovered.' It was time to venture out, onto the water, onto the floes, no matter how they might sway.

After a while Else stood up and came to clear the coffee table. She conjured up an apron and tied it around her waist. The two men watched her walking to the house with the tray. Once she had disappeared to the kitchen, Köppen said, 'What a feminine outline.'

Wegener attempted to laugh. He would have liked to answer, so that it was not so quiet in the garden. It was just that nothing occurred to him, with the best will in the world. So he simply said the first thing that went through his mind. 'Do you think so? I was just thinking, what a childlike outline.' He nearly added—almost orphan-like.

The conversation had shown him once again that he needed something to hold onto. He was in search of solidity, something natural. He could not think what it might be.

Mrs Köppen called them to the table for veal and dumplings. Over dinner, her husband spoke about kite strings and how to transport them, while his wife remained silent. Else too held her gaze downwards, which gave Wegener an opportunity to look at her.

He spent the night in the attic room. In the morning the men breakfasted without many words, made self-conscious by the previous day's admissions. On the occasional table next to Wegener, a goldfish swam in a bowl and stared at him mutely.

Else poured coffee and then stayed standing at the table. Her plaits were intertwined in a complicated manner behind her head. She apparently planned to join the conversation before Wegener left, and she bombarded him with questions about his plans at the 'North Pole', as she called it.

After breakfast the professor showed Wegener around his kite station and they discussed how Köppen might support the planned expedition, then he took his guest to the train in his automobile. The trundling journey along the cobbles of Eppendorfer Chaussee made Wegener sleepy. He felt good, leaning his head against the glass and looking out of the window. Dark red brick houses, between them the static ribbon of the Alster, above it all a few ragged cirrus clouds. Far too late, Wegener noticed they had arrived at the station some time ago.

'Please excuse me, Professor, I must have trailed off for a moment.' Wegener reached for the case between his feet.

'Trailing seems to be your main occupation today. You would have made a good comet.' Köppen laughed and slapped him on the shoulder. 'Do you know where the name of our science stems from, my good meteorologist?'

Wegener stared ahead. Beyond the front window, a group of black-clothed women stomped up the steps to the station. Then he whispered, 'Meteor . . . '

Why had he not noticed it before?

'My good man,' Köppen fixed the handbrake, 'it is the very same word. Meteoros means "floating high in the sky". Aristotle uses the term to refer to every celestial phenomenon for which there is no explanation. Whereas the distant stars were immutable, subject to the rules of astronomy, everything closer remained unpredictable. The moon formed the boundary between these two worlds. Astronomy described the cosmos beyond the moon's orbit, while all that was sub-lunar was meteorology.'

'That means we are studying floating?'

'Let's say floating phenomena. We ought to be, at least, according to the name.'

They had got out of the car. Köppen accompanied him into the station and they shook hands on the platform. Köppen's grip was so firm that tears came to Wegener's eyes. He wondered whether it was mere cordiality or a test.

He had taken a few steps when he turned around and asked Köppen to give his regards to his daughter, the forewind.

'I beg your pardon?' the professor replied.

'I meant to say . . .'

'You mean whirlwind, am I right? I called her that yesterday.' Köppen smiled.

'Exactly. Both. Neither. Please just give Else my best regards.' Wegener turned around and hastened away.

Back in Berlin, the first thing he did was to buy a curved pipe. It would keep him occupied on the trip. He tried out a number of kinds of tobacco and eventually settled on Danmark brand. He could purchase a large stock of it in Copenhagen before leaving.

Crates containing shipments from the various institutes gradually piled up in the orphanage's backyard. Wegener checked, added missing items, improved, repacked. He drafted page-long plans for the balloon and kite ascents in the ice. The Feast of Saint John 1906 was set as the date of departure.

On the last morning, a letter arrived from Großborstel. Köppen wished Wegener success. In the postscript he mentioned that Else had not stopped enthusing about their guest—how relaxed the doctor had appeared despite all his imminent adventures! Wegener made a mental note to reply from Copenhagen.

His mother and Kurt accompanied him there and Heinrich also came over, having found a position in Schleswig. The Danmark was anchored at New Harbour, a plain three-masted ship with an impressive stern. Wegener boarded via a plank and had to lower his head before entering the mess, where everyone was already gathered.

Wegener felt strangely solemn, greeting these men with whom he was to spend so much time. First Lieutenant Koch, a haggard cartographer, dashed towards him and introduced himself as his cabin-mate. He was some ten years older than Wegener and spoke passable German, fortunately. Koch led him to the captain, Alf Trolle. Wegener had to ask several times before he was certain he had understood the name correctly. No great surprise that the expedition leader had placed them in the hands of such a mariner. The ornithologist Arner Manniche appeared a little frightened, despite his moustache as long as a bird's wings. Then there was Hakon Jarner, a geologist and engineer from the Polytechnical College, a botanist by the name of Lundager, and a number of others whose hands Wegener merely shook, his head buzzing from all the people in such confined quarters.

Wegener had asked Mylius-Erichsen by letter to be released for a while for his own research on Greenland, hoping to explore the conditions on the edge of the inland ice during the polar night, preferably for several months and preferably alone. When Mylius-Erichsen approached him now he held out his hand to him, looked him in the eyes and then slowly shook his head, as though perplexed or at least uncomprehending. In the end he said he was happy to allow all of them the greatest freedom for their research, even though he could not understand each individual study. Depending on the conditions, he was willing to see what might become of Wegener's planned polar exile.

Then he rang the ship's bell at the entrance to the mess. All heads turned to him and the expedition leader said he had pre-pared a short speech, which he now proposed to hold. The men took seats and Mylius-Erichsen spoke of what they would need up there—a pair of willing hands, two open eyes and all the strength and stamina inherent to healthy young men. Nothing more was necessary, he said. That surprised Wegener. Had they not each been selected due to a particular skill? Mylius-Erichsen's address ended with a prospect of the future. The fortunate man who helped lift even a corner of the curtain before uncharted lands and seas, even a single time, would continue to feel the call of the unknown. He would not shake it off and would continue venturing out, again and again, as long as he possibly could. It was no doubt meant as a promise, though the way he said it made it sound more like a threat.

During these few days, Wegener enjoyed walking the promenade alone, impatient to put out to sea. The time of the mainland was over. Sometimes, when he was drawn to the lighthouse, everything seemed to him like a dream, uncertain of whether it would end well. When he returned to the harbour, the Danmark lay at anchor, large and mute. A sleeping watchdog that would make sure no harm came to them.

They put out to unending cheers from quayside spectators. Wegener saw his mother and his two brothers growing smaller. Would people cheer like that when they returned?

The Climates of Geological Prehistory

Alfred Wegener was glad not to be a whaler. He huddled on a pile of ropes, his eyes fixed on the barely recognizable horizon. It was the only thing on this blessed boat that stayed remotely still. It did him good to hold firm to it with his gaze.

From here, at the centre of the seesawing, there was no way to determine what was swaying more, his own guts or the belly of the ship. Immediately after their departure, looking out from the deck over at the whalers' sloops, Koch had attempted to explain to him how a ship behaves in waves. 'What is known as swell is composed of two independent motions.' Using his hands, he had drawn the stamping and rolling so vividly on the cold sea air that Wegener was overcome for the first time by something akin to seasickness. There had been none of this strange trundling from deep below on the Spree barges. It felt as though the whole world were restless.

In the meantime, he had come to relate personally to every detail Koch had tried to demonstrate. Only his limitation to stamping and rolling seemed wrong to Wegener. He could easily have added some dozen further motions to the slim nautical dictionary—first, the drunken lurching between two waves, then the jerky shaking on the crest of a wave, like a wet dog coming back to dry land; furthermore, the entire ship's delayed nodding, which could be exacerbated to a gigantic, perfectly executed bow. There was the slight deflection of the stern, coupled with a gentle leaning of the upper deck, and he also held a sinister memory of the gradual rising of the ship's entire rump, ended only by the sudden plunge into the bottomlessness of a wave trough. And of course he knew each motion's corresponding reaction inside his stomach. Fortunately, the only capsizes to date had taken place there.

Four hours' watch were followed by four hours' off-watch. Wegener soon learnt that the best option was to lie down to sleep without delay. He also gained control of his nausea and slept as deeply as a sunken ship in the depths of the sea. He barely encountered his cabin-mate, one waking the other for the next shift. They looked each other in the eye for mere moments, each from his own side of fatigue, one exhausted from the watch and the other wrecked by too little sleep.

The shifts were regularly reassigned to allow the expedition members to get to know one another. A few days after they had entered the polar circle without further ceremony, Wegener was put on the dog watch with Mylius-Erichsen. He jerked out of his daze when Koch shook him and stumbled onto deck shortly before midnight.

The older man was sitting at the prow, his first inspection round done. The air was noticeably cooler here. They were now making slower progress, passing their first icebergs from time to time. Though Wegener knew that Mylius-Erichsen disapproved of smoking, he was glad to have his pipe to hold on to. He showed him the tobacco packet and even the expedition leader had to laugh when he saw the word Danmark. 'So you're smoking our ship!'

They were silent for a while. Wegener turned to the ship's rail, rested his elbows on it and closed his eyes. He knew very well that was forbidden on the watch. Yet in fact he saw everything unchanged—the black water ahead of them and above it the black-veiled sky. It was only the wind he felt more strongly with his eyes closed, cold and wet from the spray. Though his stomach was coping better now, he was grateful not to have to endure out here with the whaling fleets, on a sea that made no bones about its dislike for people. Hunting down a beast that never showed itself. Did the whalers never lose faith in the existence of their quarry? And was train oil popular on board?

Wegener rubbed his eyelids so as to stay awake. Why did Mylius-Erichsen not simply speak to him? Wegener asked him about his time with the Eskimos. The man patted the edge of the lifeboat next to him. As he sat there, his thick coat bulged from all the layers of clothing beneath it, as though the lean man had a belly. Wegener joined him and Mylius-Erichsen's high voice began speaking the strange German that Wegener had found curiously appropriate to the man on their first meeting.

'They have lived well there for a long time. They were there when the Vikings came, bringing nothing but husbandry and inbreeding. The Vikings called them dwarves and mocked them, but in the end the dwarves beat them.'

As he spoke, Mylius-Erichsen watched him out of the corner of his eye. He looked like a descendant of those Vikings, in the darkness.

Continuing, he twisted his mouth. 'They are friendly people. Usually. One must not make the mistake of interpreting the inclination of their eyes as a smile.'

Though Mylius-Erichsen paused for a moment, his lips remained open. A cloud of breath hovered before his mouth as though he were still speaking, merely inaudibly.

'They know astoundingly little fear. Otherwise they would not have dealt with the Vikings. The only thing they actually fear is leaving the coastal regions and moving up to the inland ice. They call it sermerssuaq, the great ice cover. Their settlements lie immediately below it; they have it in view at all times. They believe the spirits live there. No one may enter their home.'

Wegener blew his nose and then asked to hear one of their sagas.

'There is the story,' Mylius-Erichsen began, 'of the death ship. One of the few tales they tell along the entire coast, because it was originally not their own; the Vikings brought it. People sit together and stare straight ahead, an old mother sitting alongside, patching boots. One gets the impression boot-patching were the only thing that counted in her life. And really, none of these mothers will let a guest into her home without checking his footwear, coupled with the advice to keep it in good condition at all times.'

Mylius-Erichsen raised his head, and Wegener did not know whether he was looking at him or his boots. He would have liked to check their state but he did not dare look down.

'Only after a while,' continued Mylius-Erichsen, 'does one of the others begin to tell a story. The death ship is called Naglfar. The giant Hrymr will captain it when the time comes. At the end of days he stands on deck, no different to us here, and steers the frost giants to the final battle against the gods. The entire ship is made of the fingernails of the dead. It is the largest ship and the most beautiful. It is not yet finished, but once it is completed Ragnarök will begin, the end of the world. That's why they cut the fingernails of everyone who dies. As short as possible so that the ship grows less quickly. When they finish their story they grin at you, either uncertain or friendly, it's never easy to tell. Since then, I've kept my fingernails short.'

Alfred Wegener looked at his hands but they were inside his mittens. He drew his thumbs out of their pockets and ran them over the tips of his fingers. In his excitement before their departure, he had bitten them so short that the death ship would have no use for them.

Mylius-Erichsen went on talking about the truth inherent to each folk tale. Wegener made no comment. He distrusted such things. Once, he had asked his mother at bedtime what would happen to Sleeping Beauty if she really woke up after a hundred years. In reality, not a single one of her friends would be alive.

In the morning they discovered ice blooms in the sea. Thousands of calyxes on the perfectly smooth surface, scattered as though on a spring meadow. Captain Trolle had heard of the phenomenon but never seen it—the brine of the surface water crystallized into delicate forms, a few centimetres in size. They throttled the engines and glided slowly through the spectacle. For days they had heard the constant noise of the pumping machines and now they were silent at once. As far as the eye could see, they were surrounded by an ocean of radiant white flowers.

Friis and Bertelsen, the two painters, immediately positioned themselves at the ship's rail and captured the sight. Wegener would have liked to join them, but a glance at their easels convinced him the task was better entrusted to them.

A long search for the three-colour camera, finally found beneath a pile of sacks. It was still too dark for photography, however. Koch fetched up a few samples of the blooms with a net, walked along the crew lined up backboard and handed one to each of them. The painters interrupted their panoramas to sketch the fine details. Lundager seemed to be counting something, probably mentally comparing the arrangement of the sparkling petals with every flower he knew. Wegener licked at his; it was as salty as the deep-blue sea. God must have been righteously in love when he created this piece of flora. Mylius-Erichsen put his flower on his bare hand and watched it slowly melt.

Wegener was assigned an assistant, Peter Freuchen, a medical student as blond as a character from a Nordic saga. Even as Wegener was explaining the instruments to him for the first time, the thermograph measurements proved disagreeable. The equipment plotted the ship's every vibration, of which there was no lack. They would have to store it in suspension. They also needed to remove the dried fish from the top of the thermometer case so that it was better ventilated. 'We don't want,' Freuchen commented to show his comprehension, 'to measure the temperature of the fish.' Wegener gave a cautious smile.

The two of them walked from one instrument to the next, Wegener instructing his assistant on the art of reading them out. Calmly, pipe in hand, he went through the values, explained measurement procedures, checked plausibility, made estimates.

'One needs a feeling for whether a value is likely. Most people believe the instruments more than themselves. One can't blame them; they haven't learnt any different. In reality, though, reading instruments is nothing but interpretation. A battle between the machine and the mind.'

Wegener looked up and asked, 'Do you have a girl?'

Freuchen said no.

Wegener continued. 'It's like with women. They insist on their view of the world, but the man will make sure to guide them in secret.'

Freuchen gave a mute nod. Wegener nodded likewise.

He drew on his pipe. Both men stared into space, apparently unmoving, and yet everything in the small cabin—the two scientists, their measurement devices, the entire equipment—was subject to the constant motion of the swell.

'That's what we learnt,' said Wegener and took another drag. 'And yet,' he continued after a while, 'we have to acknowledge that in the end it might be them who prove right, in an unforeseen way. We must not lose our willingness to let them surprise us.'

Freuchen did not look as if he knew whether Wegener was speaking of his instruments or of women.

A seaman walked past the open door, stopped and put his head in. He asked what they were doing and proved particularly fascinated by the hygrometer. They were soon joined by Boatswain's Mate Thostrup, who sat down and followed their activities. It was not long before the machinist and the second mate crept in and stood silently against the wall. When Captain Trolle himself joined the group, Wegener asked rather harshly how he might assist the gentlemen.

It emerged that there was a column for humidity in the ship's log, which had never been filled out. From then on, the instruments in Wegener's cabin were consulted several times a day by all members of the crew.

Though they all had plenty to do, they took every opportunity to stand at the ship's rail and look out. The shapes of the drifting ice, as varied as clouds. And of such rich colours that Wegener was veritably consternated. The extent of this beauty surprised him. By night, a thin mist lay above the water, sallow in the light of the midnight sun. In the mornings it all began to shine again, down to the pale-green fast ice beneath the water line. Impossible to tell from where the light came. The giant chunks floating on the water as though they had always been there. Their ice contained all hues. Wegener stood there and had to grip the rail, so enchantingly violet was the floe they were passing.

Had someone asked him his wish, he would have wished to go on land on each of these islands. To stay there. It was only the wind bringing tears to his eyes, yet still he wiped them away before anyone saw.

They installed the camera; the views were simply too wondrous. Their sole concern was whether the prints would show what they saw. The camera took three pictures at intervals. After every exposure they had to move the sliding frame holding the plates. The first exposure behind red, the second behind blue, the last behind green glass. The result was three different views, no different to the way their minds worked. They made their own images, none of them knowing how they related to one another— Freuchen's impression, his own and that of the camera. What colour did Wegener's filter show?

Professor Miethe had registered the procedure for a patent only a few years previously. A list delivered with the device told Wegener the length of the exposure. For 'good light in winter', the blue and green plates required ten seconds each, while red called for twenty-five seconds. At full speed, they would have to ensure they did not lose their photo subjects from the viewfinder during the process.

They photographed like men possessed for a good hour. In the end, Freuchen said he wondered whether they might spot Santa Claus on the prints. He did spend his summers in this part of the world, after all.

That same afternoon, there was an alarm. Before Wegener could gather his wits, everyone dashed with their belongings to the boats, which they loaded in haste. Wegener joined them, wishing he could call a halt to the frantic activity, or at least call for insight. Jensen ran out of the galley to the rail, his torso bare, one arm gripping his impressive belly in the vain attempt to warm it against the icy wind. In the other hand he clutched a small frying pan. Friis pushed past him, an empty easel under one arm. The second cartographer Hagerup squatted on deck, disoriented and trembling. Johannsen and Manniche wound the wheels like dervishes, attempting to let one of the lifeboats down into the water. It was suspended upside down in mid-air.

Before Wegener could call to them that they were winding in different directions, the boat had already slipped out of its harnesses and plummeted onto the water like a sea swallow on the attack. The ship's bell was still ringing but its noise was almost drowned out by the dogs' barking. Wegener saw his comrades now letting down the other lifeboats, their faces contorted as though the cold water had already reached them and frozen them in one blow. He himself, to his own amazement, was entirely free from fear. He slipped his pipe into his inside pocket and was the last to leave the ship, along with the captain.

They rowed to an ice floe, climbed onto it and drew the lifeboats out of the water. Then they stood at the edge and looked over at their ship, which miraculously failed to sink. Abandoned, it rested in the water, strangely proud as though it had no need of its masters. After a while Mylius-Erichsen reported that it had been a practice alarm and they could go back on board.

No one said a word. How little tension remained once the fear had evaporated. Before they re-embarked, however, Mylius-Erichsen continued, he would look through the rescued equipment; their departure had not been marked by great prudence. He inspected the load, shooing away anyone who tried to assist him.

They were lacking all that was necessary. The only provisions were three crates of mixed pickles on board one boat. Mylius-Erichsen held a stern lecture as they stood useless and lost on the ice floe, like a far-travelled colony of penguins. He accused his men of having lost their heads. He wished for their sake and his own that something like this never happened on the ice. He reminded them they were not here for their own amusement. They would all have to answer to the history of science.

'Books will be written about us one day. Consider that in all that you do,' he told them, looking so sombre that Wegener hoped the books would not be illustrated.

They rowed back to the ship in silence but their mood did not improve on arrival. The dogs had broken into the kitchen and the pantry, the salon and even the engine room, and made a terrible mess. The off-watch was cancelled, a full clean begun.

At night Wegener lay in his bunk and saw his comrades in his mind's eye, leaping about as though facing Ragnarök. One could only hope they would deal with the end of the world in a calmer fashion. Why had the danger left him so unmoved? Was there such a thing as a desire for an end? If anything, the lack of order had disturbed him. Headlessness gave him a headache, that much he knew.

They named the place where they landed Danmarkshavn. It lay in the protected Dove Bay, crowded lastly by such dense ice floes that they feared they might be enclosed by ice over winter.

They spent the next few weeks unloading, building a wooden house that they called the Villa and putting the instruments into operation.

They explored the surrounding area. The bay was on the outer coast directly by Cape Bismarck, where the German expedition under Koldewey had had to give up. They were separated from the open sea by a peninsula and surrounded by hills. The ground was bedrock. They made excursions, on foot or with the sleds, finding fossilized wood, ammonites in sandstone and occasional polar bears, some of which they photographed, others they hunted down. They gave names to everything they saw—Storm Bay, Walrus Peninsula, Signal Mountain. They established the cardinal directions.

Wegener collected a series of minor but valuable experiences: how to repair a broken sled (through deft, reckless improvisation), how to quickly disentangle the dogs' tug line, how to prevent the beasts from running around after stopping (one had to stand on the leads so that the dogs had little room for manoeuvre).

He scolded himself for not bringing a better timepiece; his own watch could not weather the hardships of outside readings, first telling the wrong time and then breaking down entirely. Koch offered to lend him his pocket chronometer as necessary, and Wegener accepted although it hurt his pride. Without time measurements, however, many of his observations would be pointless.

He gradually came to know his comrades' peculiarities, some of them more so than he would have liked. Freuchen's compliant nature, Thostrup's tendency for permanent haste, particularly evident on sled trips—he did not manage the dogs' strength economically, didn't have a canine mind.

Koch, however, he envied for his efficacy. Everything he did was well thought out. When it came to his work he could be reckless, but Wegener admired that too. He hoped to learn self-reliance from him.

He was aware that the others likely now thought him a paragon of activity, but he himself saw only how he remained below his abilities and failed to reach his goals at every turn.

Freuchen helped him to unpack the balloons, which were stuck together terribly from the journey. As soon as they spread them out, the dogs ran over them and everything was covered in dirt again. They raised kites, 1,500 metres, 2,400 metres; they could study whatever came to mind—everything was new.

At night they kept watch by the sleds to stop the dogs from biting off their leads. Mylius-Erichsen hoped this would reduce the day's work to twenty-four hours. At this point, the daily repairs went on further and further into the morning.

The end of October brought a sharp deterioration. Moods! During a magnetic observation, Wegener dropped Koch's chronometer. The moment when the box slipped out of his hand and he saw it in mid-air, the sensation of an unnatural simultaneity—it was all there at that instant, shock, shame, desperate certainty that it was impossible to repair the damage out here. He saw it all coming, unable to influence the development: his hand now empty, beyond it the chronometer, falling so slowly to the ground as if it had dropped not only from his hand but also out of time, which—no longer measured—refused to pass. Only then did the instrument reach the ground. Wegener's breath froze for a moment and then he picked up the box, squatted down and opened it from the back. The balance wheel was broken.

Wegener was terribly embarrassed, to face Koch but no less with regard to his duty to science. He was in a vile mood for days and made unbearable company.

Wolves howled in the evenings but no one ever caught sight of them. It was gradually growing colder.

Wegener assailed the task of the base station on the edge of the inland ice, planning to set it up inside the Mörke Fjord. He would go there alone and stay there alone, and he was looking forward to it.

They sat so close to one another in the Villa that one man could not move without embarrassing the next. The idea of spending time apart was compelling. Wegener longed for new company—and his own seemed particularly exclusive.

Along with Freuchen, he set out in search of a location and found one that appeared to combine the place's meteorological characteristics in an outstanding manner.

In two fairly long sled journeys, they transported sufficient material to build a small hut, and a further trip brought fuel and provisions for the winter. Wegener named the station Pustervig. Mylius-Erichsen had approved the plan in theory, so he would most likely be agreed with its actual implementation on his return. Together with Hagen and the Greenlander Brønlund, he had set out on a sledge journey to the north to map the last unknown stretches of the coast. They ought to have been back some time ago.

Frost Supersaturation and Cirri

With a dog and a sled full of instruments, Wegener set out. He called the dog Feldmann; he was the kind of comrade who did him good. Half a day's travel took them to the Laxau River, on which he and Freuchen had built a raft out of barrels. Wegener had not considered how much effort it would be to get the load onto the raft without a second man. And the moment it was all loaded the dog ran off, Wegener unable to chase it without risking the boxes going overboard.

They had learnt from the Greenlanders not only to chastise the dogs, but also to direct them with strict commands. Here on the Laxau, Wegener yelled for all he was worth but the dog stayed calmly on land, a few paces away. When all the screaming proved no use, Wegener switched to asking; no one could hear him. He tried to convince the dog with good arguments, in the end almost begging. Eventually, the dog was persuaded and joined him on the swaying vessel, possibly out of boredom.

On the other side, they had to cross a range of fells. During their long descent to the Mörke Fjord a runner broke, but Wegener did not let that upset him. Using his pistol, he shot two holes into it and bound the pieces together with leather and wedges. As darkness fell, he reached his exile.

That evening a walk in the moonlight, which provided extraordinarily powerful impressions. A feeling of abandonment, excluding any possibility of consolation so entirely that nothing remained other than a clear, radiant sobriety, with Wegener unsure of whether he could bear it.

Back in the hut he breathed a sigh of relief, as though making an arrival for the first time in his life. A first night with not the slightest sound; at one point he woke and believed he was falling, with no consciousness of danger, simply because he would never hit the ground.

In the morning the same intoxicating certainty of being in the right place. How pitying the others had been when seeing him off, their concerned waves when he turned and looked back. In any case, what was loneliness—he had himself. He dressed, then stood in the doorway and looked out into nothingness. This was the right place for him.

It took him a long time to get the small stove burning and melt some snow. Taking his hot tea, he sat down at the wooden plank that was to serve as a table. He placed a pencil within arm's reach. Then he stood up, fetched the hunting knife Freuchen had given him on parting and chipped away at the pencil until its tip was soothingly perfect.

What was he to do here in his Pustervig station; what was he to do with his life in general? Why did man feel the need to achieve outstanding feats? It was not about himself.

What he knew was this—he had the power to doubt, possibly the strongest gift his creator had bestowed upon him, if there was a creator. His doubt had rent the ties to his father, to his origins, but it had not set him down anywhere. Was it God he did not trust? Why then did he not vent his doubt on God, but on nature's phenomena?

What he was looking for was a fixed point. He remembered how diligently Kurt had once sought proof of God's existence. Evening after evening, his brother had enumerated for him that there had to be something out there that was different to themselves. Better. And every time, Alfred had found an error somewhere, yet still did not believe the matter was therefore settled.

He decided not to set such traps for himself on the first day and got up to dig a latrine some distance behind the hut.

Setting up, putting the instruments into operation, allocating a sleeping spot to the dog, a wind-protected nook by the freshly carpentered thermometer hut. Realizing that the dog was a bitch. Feldmann was a woman. Did that alter their relationship in some way? Wegener kept the name nonetheless.

He caught himself whistling as he worked. He lacked for nothing. Sometimes the wind whistled back, then they blew a duet for a while until one of them ran out of breath. In the evening Feldmann sat outside the hut and howled, wolves howling back from the distance. Wegener hoped they would not come too close.

That night he stepped outside and could not believe his eyes. It was just as the old storytellers wrote—the sky was set alight. Northern Lights as they had not yet seen in all their time here, crossing the firmament from horizon to horizon, glimmering from within as though creating themselves anew at every moment.

Wegener ran to fetch the camera but just as he began the exposure, the apparition darted to another corner of the heavens before it had left an impression on the photographic plate. It was a hopeless undertaking, the phenomenon eluding his instruments at every turn. How was he to capture anything of this? As inconstant as the formation was, it clearly wanted to make a fool of him. Feldmann paid no attention to the spectacle.

Before sleeping, Wegener noted by the light of the carbide lamp, 'A glorious symphony of light played in deepest, most solemn silence above our heads, as though to ridicule our science—come here and study me! Tell me what I am!'

He did not know whom he meant by 'we'.

At night he recalled when he had seen his first photographic apparatus, on a Sunday walk with the family. At Jungfern Bridge they had come across a particularly magnificent wedding party, which crossed with them to the palace grounds. An ocean of salmon-pink, flamingo-pink, rhubarb-pink tulle, interrupted only by the vertical black of the frock coats and top hats.

The two groups had intermingled in an instant, the children far too excited by the dresses' radiant magnificence, the crowd of wedding-goers far too charmed by the boisterous siblings, particularly the numerous aunts. Kurt had made the bridesmaids blush to their flowered crowns with one of his stories, the bride had given the youngest of the children an apple. Alfred bit into it.

At that instant, the light went on. A flash of lightning in broad daylight, out of nowhere. Alfred turned around and looked into two mouths, opened as wide as a pair of huge eyes. They belonged to the groom and the bride's mother. They laughed resoundingly, clearly liking one another. But what where they laughing about, and why had it been so bright?

Alfred looked around some more and finally discovered the apparatus behind him, a black cloth, a rod with a birdie and a container for the just ignited magnesium, now disappearing in a rather large cloud.

Once the smoke had cleared, a bald-headed man appeared from beneath the cloth. Alfred had learnt at school what was concealed inside the black box—the picture he had just seen, the sight of a couple copied from nature, a man in dark clothes and his brand new mother-in-law, their gaping mouths. He knew it but he could not believe it was possible to preserve all that. Alfred would have given a great deal to see the photograph. Could the jollity in the woman's eyes really be captured?

He overcame his timidity and took the few steps towards the bald man. Might he have a look?

What did he want to look at?

'The picture.'

The photographer laughed. 'There is no picture.'

'But you just made it, sir. When those two were laughing. It's in there.'

The man shook his head. With a swift gesture, he opened the door to his apparatus. An empty chamber.

'Where has it gone?'

'Do you mean this?' The photographer raised his hand, holding a wooden frame.

'Let me see.' Alfred reached for it but the man pulled the frame away.

'That isn't a picture,' he said. 'It's the opposite.'

'What's the opposite of a picture?'

'It mustn't be exposed to light, or else it'll disappear.'

'Is the picture in the frame?'

'No more than honey in the comb. You have to fetch it out. Would you put a beehive on the breakfast table?' Alfred shook his head.

The man held out the frame. 'It looks no different to the frame the beekeeper takes out of the hive. He extracts the honey, I extract the picture.'

Alfred didn't understand what the man meant but he took the frame in his hand. There was no picture to be seen. As Alfred examined it from all directions, the photographer explained he would later go to a room as dark as the inside of his camera.

'And that's where you take it all out again? The people laughing?'

The man smiled. 'That's right. Or whatever happened in front of the camera. I capture everything with it.'

'Everything? Even the wind? And fear?'

'Only if they show themselves. You can see the wind in the flying leaves. How can you spot fear?'

'It makes you freeze stiff.'

'Then everyone in my pictures would be afraid. Photography freezes everyone.'

That had made sense to Alfred. It was certainly possible. Perhaps people were afraid they might never escape from the photograph.

The fewer impressions the days provided, the more time Wegener spent remembering. He thought of his siblings, of the winters in Zechlinerhütte (why was it always winter there in his memory?), of his mother, who had grown ever quieter over the years. He thought of Else and her father. Would Köppen be proud to see him here? His forename was Vladimir; with the best will in the world, Wegener could not imagine ever calling him that. But who knew what awaited him upon his return?

On the hill behind the hut, he discovered fresh tracks of musk oxen and set out on a hunt with Feldmann. After some time he came across a small herd. The animals were not bothered by the shooting, standing calmly still, looking around and only lowing when they took a bullet. As soon as he stood up and approached they bolted, shoulder to shoulder.

Wegener shot two young oxen and their mother, as well as a few hares on the way back. He spent the next few days skinning and dismembering the animals. He dug meat stores in the snow.

For reasons of weight he had brought only one book, a volume of Seligenrath's excellent encyclopaedia, originally intended for consultation purposes in the expedition library. When the time had come to seek a companion for the winter, his choice had been for the reference book; he anticipated the greatest stimulation from it. The challenge had been to select a single volume and eventually he opted for Volume III, F–J, to have all combinations of firn, frost and ice at hand.

By now he had finished the volume and felt the lack of any further reading matter, particularly the kind that might keep his mind occupied; he would have liked to exchange views on his reading with himself. The main works he thought of were Haeckel, Darwin, Chamberlain, Bölsche, Meyer's Popular Astronomy, Diesterweg and a number of Förster's books. Novels did not seem suitable, however. What satisfaction would he gain out here from reading a novel? On their first meeting, Köppen had accused him of a tendency to nebulosity. Did that accusation not apply to a far greater extent to lovers of literature? Novels appeared to him, to quote Köppen, insufficiently secured. In comparison to many a phenomenon he had experienced in books, a whirlwind was markedly tangible.

Wegener did find entertainment with the dog, however. It was particularly amusing when he threw Feldmann a piece of the freshly hunted meat, and the dog launched herself at it as though aiming to destroy a foe. How fat she had grown. How she bolted down her food. As though a whole pack of other dogs were waiting behind her, when in reality the two of them were the only living creatures far and wide.

At noon Wegener went down to the water with Feldmann and they walked along the shore. It occurred to him that some dogs liked fetching sticks, but was Feldmann such a dog? And where was he to get a stick? From an overhang, Wegener broke off an icicle, held it in front of his companion's nose and then hurled it away. Feldmann did not move a muscle.

The water of the Mörke Fjord was calm, with small icebergs drifting past at regular intervals. Wegener wondered what glacier was calving so bountifully. It must be somewhere beyond the hills between which the fjord disappeared. Wegener drew the blue-shimmering islands in charcoal to retain their diverse shapes, though the most beautiful thing to them was their motion, which his picture lacked. The icebergs were young and boisterous and could turn somersaults without warning, like immature sparrows splashing in an August puddle. How far away the summer was. As if every possibility of warmth were extinguished by this merciless frost.

The cold. Its objective was the fossilization of nature in its entirety. He last saw a ray of sunlight on Reformation Day. Even then the sun no longer managed to detach itself from the hills to the south, creeping along the horizon for hours on end. The next morning, Wegener awoke in the awareness of spending the day in twilight. He put water on the stove to thaw an apple.

It was his twenty-sixth birthday.

He longed for Else, who formed a counter-image in his imagination to his existence out here, her neat character, the tendency for precision learnt from her father. For her, science was a matter of course; she had grown up within it. He, by contrast, had had to fight for it, against the world of his forefathers, and it was no use convincing himself that struggle tied him all the more firmly to the sphere. It seemed to him he would remain an outsider. He was a guest to science. Else, however, had been born into it, without the slightest doubt.

At these moments, when he had been tossing and turning in his bed for hours with no idea of what the time might be, it seemed to him that she were the more capable of them.

Having initially harboured various suspicions as to why his companion's restricted diet enlarged her belly to such an extent, Wegener's finding was soon impossible to overlook. Feldmann was pregnant.

Wegener padded her bed with a blanket; that much comfort would have to suffice. Feldmann satisfied her increased hunger with frozen excrement from the latrine, where she obtained the best examples for herself. There was plenty to be going on with.

When Feldmann dropped, Wegener tried to move her and her offspring into a crate so as to bring the whole brood indoors. He did not succeed. He hoped the young would perish of their own accord so he would not have to wring their necks.

Slowly but unceasingly, the ice crystals grew. Even the air now grew more sluggish. Only the ice sighed, announcing the approaching high tide. It was an open battle, Wegener thinking during the day that the heat of his will might thaw it all, the firn landscapes, the white-shimmering edges of the fells, the icebergs themselves. In the evenings, though, he felt the cold drawing in around his hut, inching closer like a pack of wolves, patient. And in the mornings, when it would have been time for a new day, he lay in his tight sleeping bag and waited to gather enough energy to ring in the day, which no one else could call into life but him, no sound, no human actions, not a single ray of light. There were times when he lay there for hours, fighting his doubts as to whether all this actually existed. What would happen if he simply stayed put and did not let the day happen? Would he have conquered the day or would the day have won over him?

At the end of November the precipitation increased, the barometer falling. The air now so filled with snow that his view out of the small window extended not even a metre. Which was an estimate—there was nothing to serve as orientation. In any case, Wegener had to concede that the restriction barely altered the view.

On the way to an evening reading, he stepped out of the hut and saw nothing, literally nothing. The air was entirely full of new

94

snow, a wind of about fifteen metres and night as black as a raven. On his return from the instruments the hut was gone; he stumbled about, forwards and back again or in the direction he thought was back, walked up an unfamiliar rampart of snow and admitted he was getting lost in this fashion, was in fact lost already. Uncertain what to do, he stood still and observed his surroundings for some time. Then he saw a shimmer of light immediately in front of him. He was standing directly in front of the snowed-in window of his hut.

Before he went out for his readings the next morning he tipped coffee grounds against the snow-covered wall to help him find his way back.

What an effort it cost to deal with the petty tasks, to keep things in order, repairing his clothing, bodily hygiene, talking to himself as he had begun to do, leaving the hut. Even getting up in the morning called for a quantity of practical energy that was beyond him at times. To say nothing of the moral energy it demanded.

He had to repeat measurements more and more often because his mind was elsewhere. There was plenty of time to think of this and that. Usually, his mind turned to some memory of Europe, which he then plied for some time, thoughts of Else, career questions and other matters that were difficult to shake off again.

To be on the safe side, he had equipped the thermometer hut with the three clocks his comrades had lent him for the winter, to guarantee exact allocation of the measurements. A spring-driven chronograph, a pocket watch and a small pendulum timepiece. To begin with he was relieved at how evenly the clocks ran, having feared greater deviations. When only minimal adjustments were necessary even after weeks of falling temperatures, however, he grew suspicious. What if the cold had the same effect on all three? One morning when he stomped tired and cold through the snow, the clocks tried to convince him it was already forenoon. He clenched his teeth so as not to curse, removed his gloves and turned them all back with his bare hands.

As he fell asleep, he now often thought he heard a sound, a buzzing or a pumping noise, which was not possible of course. Was it the others coming to fetch him? Was it animals—but what animals could it be? Sometimes he went to the window and stood by the glass, seeing nothing. In the end he told himself repeatedly it was the wind or a kind of whistling in his ears, until he found sleep. Later he would jerk upright in his bed, woken by some kind of booming sound. Shivers ran down his back, he held his breath to listen to what it was, and in the end it proved to be nothing but the hammering of his own heart.

In the mornings it occurred now and then that he would walk out to the thermometer hut to read the temperature and, once returned, discover from the list that the values had already been entered. Had he really already been outside? It took some time until he was certain he had not confused the date. Certainties could slide in so many directions. And once they were in motion there was no way to establish what was still standing and what was floating. Wegener had the impression he was part of a greater movement yet unable to tell which way it was heading.

He saw his weakness before him like an enemy to be vanquished. He imagined them wrestling, the lassitude and he, and he worked himself up into this combat until he noticed in the end that he was the only one fighting. His opponent merely watched him constantly, unmoved. As though it could simply wait until exhaustion overpowered him.

At the end of each consideration he came to the one point upon which everything now turned: life was devoid of impressions. What liberation he felt when once the top of the opposite hill showed itself in the midday twilight, what lust for undertakings he took from it. Then night again. He was now constantly smoking. The solace of the tiny flame when he had to relight his pipe. The solace of the warm smoke with which he padded his freezing body. And so he sat and ruminated and stared as he did so at the small piece of ember in his hand.

He was shocked by the degree of his desire for external events. He took great pleasure from looking at the few photographs he had taken at the beginning of his stay. There was nothing to see in them other than what was before his eyes every day: the snow, his room, the blurred flag of the thermometer hut. Then, though, there was a picture to which he most looked forward when he flicked through the small pile of photographs, his hands gloved. He had constructed a remote release so as to have a picture of a person. The shot showed him, outside the door, grey for lack of light, his face half hidden beneath his hood. Looking at the picture, he smiled at himself and the photograph smiled cautiously back. He looked a little tense in the picture, which might have been due to his attention being focused on the remote release. The last picture in the pile was a shot of Feldmann, running towards him with her tail raised, pale eyes on the camera. Where was she, in fact? Wegener wondered when he had last seen his companion, when they had last ventured out together, when he had last put food out for the dog. He tried to recall their shared rituals but the images blurred. Slowly, he put on his fur shoes and set out to look for her. He found her outside in a nook of the thermometer hut, in the darkness, cold and stiff. No trace of her young. Her open eyes stared at nothing. For how long now?

Wegener had to admit he had underestimated the difficulties of wintering. How strange that the other expeditions had not mentioned this negative state of mind. His tobacco was soon running out, wasted on the winter's night. He spent half days studying the Northern Lights, stimulated by their brightness, their forms, their presence. He spotted shapes coming and going within them, reacting to one another, he let them tell him stories about them, light images in which he had great faith, more than his doubts.

On one occasion he thought it was his father's birthday, but he was no longer certain. Were they sitting together now with all the siblings, singing? He hummed the beginnings of a few of the songs they might choose, shocked by his own voice. Were they thinking of him, did they have any idea of how he was living here? There were a few candles in his reserves. To save petroleum, he affixed one to the desktop with wax and read for hours by its trembling flame.

On New Year's Eve he had to imagine the punch, lacking real alcohol. Instead, he treated himself to red wine chocolates until he managed to imagine feeling tipsy. He granted himself a solitary game of lead-pouring, dripping molten solder into water to predict the future. It was afternoon when he began, having covertly brought forward the evening reading. He melted some snow in a pan. Unable to locate the pliers immediately, he bent the rods of solder until they broke, put a few lumps on a spoon and held it over his candle. After half an hour, everything was covered in black soot but the pieces still hadn't melted, so he lit the soldering iron and held the spoon into its flame. How seductively the metal began to melt, how it glinted, how warm it looked. Wegener wished he could bathe in it, that silvery glow. Carefully, he poured the liquid into the pan and it froze in the water with a sharp hiss and sank to the bottom, motionless as a fly in amber. Wegener fished the shape out and examined it. A snake with a flat, slightly fattened head. And what was that to mean? That he was being seduced?

He repeated the experiment and placed the results alongside one another. Examined them in detail and held long, inconclusive debates with himself about the interpretation of their shapes. In front of him on the desk lay, in this order: a snake, an earthworm, a mouse with a long tail, an unrolled ball of wool, several tears, a handful of tadpoles. He could have come up with all kinds of prophecies. If he was honest, though, they all made him think of one thing—they looked like a collection of spermatozoa.

Wegener was glad his comrades were not with him. They might be playing the same game on the coast, sitting together around a table filling up round after round with these small silvery objects. They would vie loudly to decode one meaning after another, so as not to admit they were swimming in a sea of sperm.

At eleven thirty he decided to declare the New Year according to local time, and went to sleep.

The sex drive was a problem for which no one had prepared him. In the first weeks of his Pustervig isolation, he could not get enough of himself. As soon as he closed his eyes he was encircled by women. He filled his hut with them; they were available whenever he felt the desire. They were blonde, red-haired or brunette, voluptuous or gaunt, but they all had their eyes closed. Barely one of them was familiar to him. Sometimes he thought he recognized Else, in a corner, likewise naked as all the others, but her eyes open. She looked at him; that was how it was every time she appeared. She watched him.

When that happened he made an effort to dispel the other women quickly, and they really did simply dissolve one after another until he was alone with her. They were silent for a while. It was usually Else who started speaking at some point.

What are you doing here?

I'm researching.

I can see that. Are you making progress?

I was just about to make a discovery.

Until I came. What was your objective?

That was approximately how their conversations went, soon revolving in ever decreasing circles.

What did he want from Else, what did he fear? Would he really marry her? Did he want to say she was his wife? Did he want that of anyone?

And lastly—did he want children with her? When he stepped out into the semi-darkness outside the hut after his activities and rubbed himself clean with snow, he was overwhelmed by the number of conceptions he was wasting out in his wilderness.

For the first time, the thermometer fell below fifty degrees. Wegener had to bend far over to read it, frost blocking his view. What a short distance it was from his eyeball to the tiny column of mercury, and yet there was a heat differential between them of ninety degrees. It was a miracle that he was still managing to keep the cold out of his body. On his way back to the hut he saw himself from a great height, slowly trudging through the snow. The only movement in the rigidity all around, the sole warm point in the midst of an endless field of cold. It was a strange sight from up there; he enjoyed it until he noticed it was the perspective of a circling vulture—an observation that refused to be repressed by the knowledge that there were no vultures here.

He broke a molar on a hard ship's biscuit.

He had the idea of using an empty bread tin as a hot water bottle, and clung to it with legs drawn up as he fell asleep. To his misfortune, the tin was still in his sleeping bag when he established in the middle of the night that the lid was not watertight. He had woken in a warm puddle like in long-forgotten childhood days. Whence the fear that came over him at the thought? Then it occurred to him where he was, instead—in a tiny hut on the eastern coast of Greenland, alone, surrounded by perpetual ice. Had he decided to come here of his own accord? He could not immediately remember what he was doing here. It took days to dry the sleeping bag.

The broken tooth soon became infected; there was no doctor nearby. And so he began to rework a pair of flat-pointed pliers in the twilight of his room, to extract the root. He heated the metal to a glow in the soldering flame, then beat and filed it into shape. He could not grip the root, though, despite two hours of rummaging in his gum. Pre-boring with a screwdriver was no use either.

One morning outside the hut, he caught himself drawing a clumsy figure in the firn with a ski pole, so as to have a comrade by his side. He heard himself speaking to the figure and wanted to shake his head at such nonsense, yet he did not move. He drew Feldmann too, sitting on her haunches, head raised to her master made of snow. Wegener reproached himself for not having buried the dog; the wolves had taken her. He cried a little, the tears freezing on his eyelashes.

Freezing was now his main activity.

Sitting at his desk, he sometimes let his jaw dangle so that his mouth hung open, out of laziness and because no one could see it in any case.

At night he dreamt he was a gigantic dog. He had pulled himself free from his sled and run out into the nothingness, absolute white. When he woke with a start in his bed, it was dark. How pleasantly heavy his limbs were. It took a moment before he noticed to his amazement that he was apparently still a dog, the exhaustion affecting not just two legs but all four. He stayed in that position and remembered the pleasure of running on four paws. Until daybreak, he lay there and wallowed in that canine feeling, stroking his legs together and grooming himself.

Sometimes he rolled in the snow; no one was watching him. Sometimes he barked.

When the dream returned, Wegener tried to stay awake to evade the great power of its impressions. He convinced himself his watch was protecting the hut from attack by wild animals. In fact, for some time now the sight of a wild beast would have brought him more pleasure than fear. To his dreams, too, he submitted without resistance in the end.

Only in his sleep did he achieve more than at home, for that reason. He had seen the Northern Lights often enough now to have a vivid mental image of them, so he usually returned to bed immediately after the end of the short midday brightness. Eventually he fell entirely into a kind of hibernation, only rising to eat.

A man had to eat as much as he could stomach—he recited that to himself like a law when he indiscriminately opened one can after another in his waking moments. One night, he opened all the remaining meat stores in the vicinity of the hut, imagining he was a wolf, for scientific reasons. He was concerned with exploring their way of life, from the inside, a mimetic approach of which he retained only vague memories upon waking the next morning. On an inspection launched immediately after that, he found the stores ravaged, ripped chunks of meat in the snow with scraps bitten out of them, between them drops of red liquid, spat-out flesh. Wegener returned the larger pieces to the stores and covered the rest with snow. On that day he did three readings aside from the schedule, with unchanged values.

The tooth was now festering so much that it could eventually be removed with barely any resistance.

At last the days grew brighter. At the beginning of February, Wegener cast a shadow again for the first time, a shockingly slim, unfocused shape that he would have embraced in his enthusiasm, had it not bolted at his approach. The return of daylight gave him back something of his mental stability. He would undertake long treks across the firn at midday, towards the sun. When the territory allowed he would walk with his eyes closed, enjoying the light on his eyelids. He wished he never had to turn back. In these moments, he had no fear of getting lost in the ice. He followed the sun heading slowly west in a broad curve, trying to mentally calculate the algebraic curve of his traces in the snow. At some point, however, he would always call himself to order. And his return walk would treat him to the reflection of the light from all sides, another thing he could not get enough of, magnificent but absolutely dead nature.

What sounds were now to be heard in the general thaw! Although there was scant reason to expect visitors, he sometimes ran outside, sure of having heard the crunching of footsteps in the firn. But there was no one. Or only the wind and possibly a whistling in his ears.

He had little concentration for longer tasks. Often, he would stand at the telescope for hours, checking whether someone appeared on the horizon to see to him. The knowledge that he could now return at any time gave him strength.

He now only expected in the most general way that something might happen. There were too many possibilities for a specific hope. Or too few.

Despite all his longing, he retained a certain respect for his return home. How would he manage to re-accustom to the old world? For a brief time, he played with the idea of becoming a bon vivant on his return to Europe. He was gathering a great thirst for life, after all. He longed for Else and was glad every day anew of how clearly he could envisage her features. Yet there was also the fear that he was more concerned with the passion of this desire than with the passion of its fulfilment. As though the clarity of Else's image might begin to pale at the very moment when he stood facing her.

It was now light almost all the time.

Then he returned to his comrades, pulling the sled himself. Freuchen was the first to spot him and came striding towards him. They embraced, then faced one another. Mylius-Erichsen had been lost in the ice. Wegener was incapable of bearing the news. Freuchen pulled him to the hut by his arm. All the men welcomed him with joy but nothing followed. He had grown quieter, he noticed. Asked how he had fared, he gave evasive answers. What was he to say?

In the final nights when he lay down to sleep, he had felt something were slipping out of his hands. At first he thought he was sliding to and fro on his thin mattress. He had fastened himself to the bed with the belt from his trunk so as not to lose hold. That did not improve matters. He thought he felt the entire bed in motion, which could not be the case; it stood firm. Was it dreams? But he lay awake. How was he to retain the difference between day and night when it never grew dark? How was one to resist the idea, in this landscape of ice, that everything was sliding? In the end he thought the whole hut was gradually sliding down the firn to the water. He began to long for real dreams, not these imaginings, as he called them by then—the images before falling asleep or on waking or during breaks in his daily work. Instead, he began to avoid taking breaks, working like a wild thing. He had mapped the fjord, created geological profiles of the stream, he had come up with explanations of the world and cast each one aside again. He had worked until he had no time for digressions before falling asleep, so tired did he retire to his bed.

In the last nights, ships made of fingernails had set sail in his Pustervig dreams, ships steered by giants, a peaceful sight. Only when the dream returned had he realized that they were not sailing on the sea, but on burning land.

His search for a firm standpoint had not been a success. What if the feeling of floating possessed a firm basis, like the rest of the world did? A scientific basis like everything in which he believed? He would have to seek it, and as on every search for which the goal is not known, he would have to look in all possible and impossible places. In a strangely certain way, he—who was always questioning everything—had no doubt he would find it in the end.

The Formation of the Continents and Oceans

'Right worshipful Vice Chancellor, right honourable deans, honoured professors. Hereinafter an attempt shall be undertaken to interpret the form of the Earth, namely the continental shelves and the oceanic basins, on the basis of a single all-encompassing principle.'

A subdued murmur spread across the auditorium. Wegener wanted to continue but he had to swallow and clear his throat behind a raised hand. The noise swelled. It came from every direction, out of the wooden panelling on the walls, out of the heavy curtains at the edge of the stage, feeding on the slight creaks of the wooden seats here in the large lecture theatre of the Senckenberg Natural Science Society, on the myriad movements with which pince-nez were now adjusted, frock coats smoothed, eyes shaded. They wanted to unsettle him, register their doubts and reservations.

They knew what he wanted to tell them, having read the title of his lecture in the invitation: General Assembly of the Geological Association, with a guest contribution on 'New Ideas on the Formation of the Major Elements of the Earth's Crust'. They sensed what he was planning—to pull the firm ground out from beneath their feet.

They had not come to applaud. They wanted to see him founder.

It was three and a half years since the Danmark had reached Danish motherland. All the pennants, photographers, medals. Having meanwhile become an assistant at the Aeronautical Observatory in Lindenberg, Wegener had had to place an application to receive the honours. Accepting gifts required ministerial permission.

In his Pustervig isolation, he had sworn to avoid crowds of people and to steer clear of all human excitement. He did initiate one event immediately after his return, however—a slide presentation on his Greenlandic balloon ascents at the conference of the German Meteorological Society in Hamburg. It gave him an opportunity to see Professor Köppen and discuss with him not only the findings from the trip, but also the new thoughts now tirelessly haunting his mind.

Köppen had accepted Wegener's self-invitation with some cordiality. 'You're always welcome here. We need minds like yours in meteorology.' What had he meant by that? Merely because he had dared to brave the weather? Köppen had attended the lecture with his wife and daughter, sitting in the front row.

Else had become a young lady during his absence, and it suited her. She was enthusiastic, her father revealed before the lecture, about all unusual phenomena. He had the impression that Wegener also fell into that category, he remarked. Else had asked the director of her teaching college for a day's leave from school to see all that she now was presented with—the seductive slide projections and the scientist speaking so engagingly, still quite burnt by the Arctic sun.

She sat by his side at the formal dinner of beef medallions with gravy. Wegener made an effort to tease her and Else strained to parry with her own badinage. He sensed her shyness and brought out the photographs he now always carried, to relax the atmosphere. They were the same ones he had viewed so often in the polar night; he showed them to the guests sitting around him at the table. Each of them had questions—to be precise, there was little to see in them but white and black marks. Wegener noticed that explaining the pictures made his voice crack. Else leapt in with delightful extemporizations on whom or what the shots likely showed: tracks in the snow, an Arctic vixen with her young, melted shapes in a frozen waterway. What a marvellous companion she was. Out of the corner of his eye, Wegener noted she was watching him. He noticed she had the same look in her eye as an arctic fox. That suited her too.

Wegener moved to Marburg an der Lahn. He could have gone anywhere but of all the university towns, the small city on the river came closest to his Greenlandic isolation. He could gather the findings of his trip in peace there.

It was a Protestant university. The observatory's letter of recommendation had praised him as an outstanding man in every respect, as the prototype of a scholar gifted with rich thoughts, as an above-average person. Wegener wished he had not submitted the letter, so little did he recognize himself in its description.

A few days after he started work at Marburg the first female students were enrolled, a disturbing idea for Wegener. He gained his teaching qualification as an associate professor of astronomy and meteorology; no women attended his lectures. There was a small observatory where he spent many a night. He corresponded frequently with Köppen and less frequently with Köppen's daughter. To be precise, he merely sent her greetings, taking longer to formulate them than the entire preceding letter.

Wegener single-handedly founded an association for airship travel, which soon obtained its own balloon. He was now measuring incessantly, on the ground and in the air. On one ascent, he discovered boundaries between layers of warm and cooler air, which returned so regularly that he grew quite hot and cold himself. If he were to rise even higher? He discovered inversions and spheres and intermediate spheres; there was no end to it. He could have gone on writing essays evermore.

On viewing his Greenland notes, he was shocked by the vehemence of his thoughts. Here in his Marburg study, he dismissed them as one of the numerous side effects of that miserable winter. In the first weeks after his return he had attempted to forget his time at the Pustervig base, to grant no significance to the images still at the forefront of his mind. It was only when the memories grew more composed that he made cautious attempts to approach them, as though sipping at an overly hot drink, and he soon began to long once again for the endless days and nights in a hut at the end of the world.

Then he would remember the fate of Mylius-Erichsen, who had remained in the ice. The search party had found his companion Brønlund on Lambertsland. His body was discovered in a cavern in the earth close to the depot, draped with a reindeer skin for lack of a sleeping bag, his frozen feet wrapped in rags. His diary revealed that the three men had been forced to spend the summer on the far side of the fjord as the open water cut off their return journey. At last they had found an access route to the inland ice so as to embark on their return. Hagen was the first to be lost, then Mylius-Erichsen. He had not taken the Eskimo mother's advice to heart and had set out without a needle and thread. His boots were soon worn through and his feet eventually froze. Brønlund himself had arrived at the depot at the end of November, certain death in sight. He too had been unable to continue due to frostbite, least of all in darkness. He had placed his diary so that it was easy to find.

And yet there were moments when it actually seemed a more attractive proposal to Wegener to be far away and unreachable. When the students tortured him with their stupidity, when his applications for better remuneration gave rise to nothing but more and more correspondence, when his landlady woke him at the crack of dawn with the request not to leave his dirty walking boots on the stairs.

Or when no post came from Hamburg. Then it felt to Wegener as though he might as well be thousands of miles away. At such moments, the time of his expedition rose luminous in his mind, the undisturbed contemplation, the reduction of colours, the simplicity, the merciless regime of darkness and light.

During the subsequent summer, he used the weeks without teaching obligations to travel up to Hamburg. He left the train in Altona. The ladies on the platform wore their skirts above their ankles, unheard of in Marburg. At the top of the stairs stood Köppen with his hand raised, and Else appeared behind him, waving a handkerchief. Wegener couldn't tell whether she lowered her eyes as they greeted each other because he did so himself.

Köppen's beard had grown even longer. He now had white hairs growing out of his ears. He had brought along a boy, who took Wegener's luggage. They began discussing the state of their research projects even during the ride. The two men had recently agreed to send each other their work prior to publication.

Mrs Köppen had cooked again, welcoming him at the door in her apron. Wegener could not help feeling she was sizing him up. Standing before her and kneading his hands as though holding himself up by his own fingers, he would hardly have thought himself a pleasant conversation partner.

It was a familiar fear and he sometimes thought it applied less to the respective individual than to the entire species. Man was the only natural enemy left to man. Not that Marie Köppen could do anything about that. And her Brussels sprouts were delicious.

After the meal the Köppen Seniors announced they were taking a nap; he was welcome to do the same. The daughter of the house casually mentioned her plan to take a walk across the fields, on which he could of course accompany her if he felt an inclination for a little exercise.

They had barely left the last houses behind them before their conversation dried up. The land absolutely flat, nothing but fields, moor, isolated birds. The sea wind drove ragged clouds ahead of it, a broad street of cumuli; from below, there was no making out who was promenading along it.

After a quarter of an hour they reached a dyke, which Wegener climbed with a few fast strides, excited by the prospect of the sea behind it. When he reached the crown, however, all that opened up was more land, looking no different to the fields at his back.

Else too came up the steep slope, Wegener extending his hand for the last few steps. For a while they stood side by side. Else explained what lay before them: drainage ditches, newly gained land, in the distance the mud flats of the Wadden Sea and some islands concealed by the haze. He asked her the name of an island floating out there in the mist, but Else couldn't make it out.

'I suffer from glaucoma,' she said. 'It's nothing serious, but my lenses are slightly clouded.'

'I'm sorry.' Wegener now thought he could see a milky shimmer on her pupils, a paleness. 'I hope it doesn't cloud your mood.'

Else smiled. 'Not in the slightest.'

Wegener described the island to her, as best he could see in the mist, but Else couldn't think of the name.

They sat down on the edge of the embankment. At the foot of the dyke, a group of sheep pressed so close together to shelter from the wind that they looked like a single fluffy animal. Wegener reached for his tobacco pouch. Else lay back on the grass and closed her eyes. Getting his pipe started, Wegener watched her. Could she tell from behind her eyelids?

It was inexplicable to him why such beauty existed. Her ankles in sandals, the summery patterned skirt. Her belly was absolutely motionless, perfectly flat other than the few waves of her blouse above it. No sign of breathing. Ought he to check she was still alive?

He too felt the urge to gain new land. Previously, he had only heard of these brassieres that were now replacing the corset. She was clearly wearing such a model. Her neck appealed to him. How soft and white the skin was there. Her eyelashes trembled in the breeze as if it were an effort to keep her eyes closed.

Hoping to combat the dizziness suddenly seizing him, Wegener tried to calculate how many hairs a person possessed by estimating the number contained in individual tufts of her locks, at least approximately. In his attempt to determine how many such tufts were found on her head, though, he was forced to roam his eyes across those locks, which took him along in all directions, making him lose concentration every time.

So he simply fell back and lay there next to her, his eyes open, above him nothing but the empty sky. He swallowed and hoped Else wouldn't hear. After a while he too closed his eyes, yet the feeling refused to go away. That slight dizziness as though he were moving very gradually, not of his own accord. Very slowly, almost unnoticeably, as he lay there next to her on the grass, which was cold. He felt the ground's moisture seeping through his shirt. Someone tugged at his hair but it could only be the wind. Wegener thought he noticed a movement of the Earth as though it were migrating beneath him, impossible to halt. Was he drifting away from Else? At last he summoned up the courage to reach over to her with his eyes closed, to hold onto her so that the awful feeling would finally disappear. Later, he wondered how she had noticed he was not merely attempting an approach. Has he gripped her wrist too tightly? He simply lay there and held onto her, and she rose onto one elbow and asked what the matter was. He merely shook his head mutely.

112

The sheep had scattered across the marshland in the meantime, each now standing isolated. On the way back it was Else who reached for his hand, this time undoubtedly an attempted approach. For a moment they walked in silence, and then he began to tell her about his measurements and findings, about his work on the travel notes; he had re-read his comments on the mysterious buzzing he had heard in Pustervig and already formulated a number of thoughts on the subject, which he hoped to publish in Mitteilungen über Grönland under the title 'The Sound of Dove Bay'. Else listened to him. She did not let go of his hand.

Else sent a postcard to Marburg. It was the first time she had written herself. The card was a sketch of a summer retreat, the transition of a beach to the water, cumuli piled high above it. For the first time, he possessed a sample of Else's handwriting. During his forays into the library in his first semester at Heidelberg he had read an introduction to graphology, which he attempted to recall as he studied the characteristics of her script. The girlish loops of the initial letters, the slight swing of the downward strokes, the marked descenders that stood for depth, among other things, but also, if he remembered correctly, for hidden propensities.

In her note, Else reported she had made the same excursion the next day, with the sad sensation of being alone this time. Perhaps her blurred vision would improve, she wrote. She had thought again about their conversation on the way home, during which she had not managed to ask him the question on the tip of her tongue—what was he actually looking for?

Wegener decided to wait a few days before responding. He was concerned to avoid any impression of urgent insistence, yet at the same he wanted to put some effort into his choice of words. It would not be a letter of the usual kind, at least. What if he were to answer simply, 'A companion like you'?

In the end he abandoned all his drafts and wrote instead to
- Köppen, asking a straightforward question on the custom in
Hamburg with regard to dowries.

Köppen's response was effusive. He had measured the idea in his
heart and felt much joy at it. Wegener answered by return of post
with a long letter that barely made it clear whether he planned to
marry the daughter or her father. 'It is impossible for me to say
precisely how much I look forward to our work together. I always
fear pathos.' He agreed with Köppen that Else should stay at her
parents' home until he found a lifetime post.

On the staircase, he ran into his landlady and took the opportunity to inform her of his new status. She was happy for him
and likewise for herself, as she would keep her tenant for a
while longer. He knew what people said about the locals—the
Marburgers lived off a student in the attic and two goats in the
cellar.

From the post office he went straight to the institute, feeling
strangely stimulated, spurred on to new deeds. In the library,
he picked volumes from the shelves almost at random. Like a
drowning man, the phrase occurred to him, although the simile
did not hold up to further inspection. Did he simply have to do
something else before Else joined him? He had to gain control
of the ideas that had taken possession of him during the
Greenlandic winter. The impression of breaking into pieces. The
lack of cohesion.

After six hours of uninterrupted reading he came across a
piece by a certain Doctor Keilhack in an edited volume that had
drawn his attention through its title, Sky and Earth. The paper
dated back to the previous century, but that applied equally to himself. It was about plants on either side of the Atlantic. That was
what he clung to.

Wegener found no sleep that night. What if his feverish imaginings in Greenland did bear some connection to the real world? The tearing and drifting?

It was still dark when he decided there was no point trying to sleep. He poured himself a glass of wine and placed his pipe at arm's reach. Then he reached for a sheet of paper and began a letter to Hamburg, without an addressee, not knowing whether he was writing to Köppen or to his fiancée. 'Have you ever,' he wrote, 'been surprised by the congruence of the Atlantic coasts?' He lit his pipe. 'Not only the large right-angled bend that the Brazilian coast takes at Cape San Roque finds its loyal negative in the African coastal bend at Cameroon, but also south of these two points, every protrusion on the Brazilian side conforms to a like-shaped bay on the African side, and vice versa every bay on the Brazilian to a protrusion on the African side. As an experiment with compasses on the globe shows, the sizes are precisely matching.'

'Why,' Wegener wrote, firing himself on as he continued, 'is there flora proven to exist on opposite coasts of an ocean but otherwise nowhere on the entire planet?' He took a sip. 'What about the primeval earthworm, fossils of which are found on both sides of the Atlantic, and only there?' How was he to explain what was moving within him? 'Certainly, it could have been the land bridges that everyone suspects. Yet I cannot believe this theory merely because it is the predominant belief. It is such a far-fetched idea.' He mustn't get caught up in petty matters now. 'I spent all of today between bookshelves, which is not peculiar in itself.' He narrowed his eyes. He was aware what was needed now was to focus his thoughts before they slipped away from him. 'But even the friendly library steward found it rather uncanny that I was constantly moving between departments. Today,' he took another mouthful of wine, 'I was unfaithful to my traditional field of meteorology, trespassing in the stacks of palaeontology, glaciology, botany, zoology and especially geology. There is evidence to be found everywhere.'

Wegener unbuttoned his shirt, having grown unbearably warm. 'I could not have borne to spend all day at a desk,' he wrote, 'without the continuing habituation during the long Greenlandic winter, during which I did nothing but sit in my confined study.'

'But that,' he ran a hand across his brow, 'is of no concern here.' He filled his glass anew; he could have gone on drinking endlessly. 'Why,' he wrote, 'are earthquakes not distributed evenly across Earth? Why are they more frequent on the edges of the continents?' He wrote, 'Why do scars left by the large glaciers point in the same direction on one and the other side of the ocean?' He tapped out his pipe although it was already empty. 'Bacon noticed the similarity of the coastal shapes 300 years ago, but drew no conclusions.' He started a new paragraph and then added: 'Even Humboldt noted it.' And after a pause, 'I ought to know; my great-great uncle was a friend of his.' He wanted to take another mouthful but the bottle was empty. He wrote, 'There is no other option.' At the foot of the page, he noted, 'I should like to pursue these ideas further.' He looked out of the window for a while, gazing at nothing but black. Then he added the final sentence: 'Perhaps it is the other way around, and they are pursuing me.'

In the end he tore the pages to shreds and lay down to sleep. Before dawn, he woke and returned to the books he had brought home. By the time the library opened for the day he was standing outside the door, looking so lost that the young woman who had unlocked the entrance for him brought a cup of rosehip tea to his desk, although consuming food and drink was not usually permitted in the reading room. Her name was Gertrud, and she and Wegener almost became friends over the next few weeks.

The murmuring in the Senckenberg Museum had meanwhile subsided at last. Wegener removed his hand from his mouth, took a deep breath and spoke the words out loud: 'For this one and sole principle, nothing comes into question other than the horizontal movement of the continental floes.'

It was out. It was only the second sentence he had spoken in his lecture but the murmuring had already returned, grown to a chuntering and finally increased to a veritable rumbling. His listeners talked to their neighbours, someone called out, some slapped their thighs in laughter.

Wegener had taken the first hurdle. Had silence prevailed after that sentence, he would have done something wrong. It would have meant nothing other than that they considered him not worthy of a murmur. Precisely for that reason, he had practiced the sentence over and over, during his morning shave, on the way to the institute and at night, whispered, as he tossed and turned on his pillow.

What he purported in that sentence was nothing less than a subversion of all thought structures. And that from him, a weather man and a polar explorer. He didn't expect them to eat out of his hand. He was entitled to respect, however.

Directly in front of him, Wegener recognized the association chairman, Emanuel Kayser. He had always wondered what the old man with the harelip reminded him of, and all at once it occurred to him—a seal. To be precise, a dying seal. White sideburns drooped on either side of his face. He had his black cap on his lap, his hands folded over it. He looked sad. Wegener knew Kayser from Marburg where he taught stratigraphy, his hobbyhorse being Bohemian fossils. Wegener had read his Outline of Geology to no noteworthy gain. He did not value his colleague as a scientist but he was grateful to him for the invitation. Whatever Kayser had hoped for his newly founded association from the lecture, this was not it. Such an éclat during the conference was clearly unpleasant for him, but it did not look like he intended to intervene in an argument.

Next to Kayser, a gentleman issued dismissive grunts. It took Wegener a moment to recognize him as Albert Heim, the eminent authority on the Earth's crust travelled especially from Switzerland, the living representative of the vanishing land bridge theory. Let it vanish, and Heim along with it.

They still believed the species had spread via narrow runways that once linked the continents. Driven into a corner by related fossils found in the most different parts of the world, they had postulated the existence of land bridges and pointed triumphantly at the narrow waist of Panama, which still held the Americas together. So far, so good. But what had become of those links? They had vanished quietly into the ocean after the species had finished migrating. An absurd idea.

'I do not know,' Wegener began his actual lecture, 'which of my honoured listeners has ever had the pleasure of watching a floating iceberg.' He lifted his head. No one raised a hand, so he went on. 'The opportunity of a cartographical expedition a few years ago took me to Greenland, where I witnessed just such a monstrous block breaking off from its shelf ice base. Those who have not been present, gentlemen, can barely envisage the spectacle accompanying the calving of a glacier. The crash as the ice tears, the noise when such a chunk falls into the water, causing fountains to spray in all directions. I ask you to imagine the glow of the breaking-off ice as it shimmers pale blue, as delicate as a new-born child entering the world.'

Perhaps he was taking it too far. The first hisses sounded out, along with only apparently suppressed coughs.

'What happens to this colossus? Does it sink in the water? Of course not; you know that as well as I do. And why not? That too is a known fact—because ice is lighter than water. You may be wondering why I am beginning with a travel report and what it has to do with the subject of my explanations. Let me tell you. The past century taught us that continents consist largely of granite-based material. It was Eduard Suess himself who gave it the name sial; we paid tribute to his achievements only this morning. This sial, however, is lighter than the mainly basalt floors of the oceans, for which Suess coined the term sima. As much as I respect Suess, at this point he did not think his idea through to its end. For what happens when lighter material comes to rest on heavier matter? The iceberg shows us—it floats. What follows from that cannot be overestimated in the decisiveness of its nature. The vanishing theory cherished by many in this room no longer holds, for the simple reason that an imagined land bridge can never sink into heavier material.'

There were various interjections, to which Wegener paid no attention. He had talked himself into too much of a fury.

'Let us take the example of Scandinavia. Since the end of the last ice age, the inland glaciers have retreated and freed the land from their weight. What is happening now? If you only stand long enough by the edge of a sea there, you can watch the coastlines falling. The heavy ice masses pressed the land deep into the basalt subsurface, out of which, after liberation from this nightmare, it is gradually rising of its own accord, unstoppably, like a truth whose time has come.'

Wegener may not have been a geologist. But he felt he had inherited the art of the sermon from his ancestors. Anyone unconvinced by his argumentation was lost to science anyway. What would his father have said if he had heard him speaking this way? Would it have seemed heretical to him? Yet when Wegener looked up it was clear that his sermon was not having the desired effect. The gulf between the auditorium and him was as insurmountable as the widest ocean. And there was no bridge connecting their coasts.

A thin voice called from the back of the room, 'What would Suess say to that?' It sounded like a frightened child. Eduard Suess had just been elected honorary chairman of the association, in absentia. His core statement was engraved into the marble above the hall's entrance: It is the collapse of the globe we are experiencing. Wegener revered him despite his obvious mistakes. It was in Suess that he had first read about Glossopteris, the fern that had spread across the landmasses during the Permian period. Its stone imprints were now found on all southern continents. How would it have spread so far if unchanging oceans had separated the landmasses? The Marburg institute had one of the fossils in its mineralogical collection; the reddish grain, the tongue-like shape, the mesh of its nerves were more reminiscent of a feather than a leaf. Wegener had stood gazing at it like at the plaster cast of a Greek statue—it was all there, the copy sufficient to understand the idea of the original. Standing there between the cases in the exhibition room, he had closed his eyes and instantly seen forests of these ferns, a primeval wind rippling through the leaves, impossible to tell whether it was warm or cold.

The dead of Pompeii had also left hollows in hardened stone. Casts had been made of them like of ancient sculptures. Years ago, Wegener had once come across illustrations of the plaster figures, their faces contorted by their struggle with death or peaceful in sleep. It was so easy to envisage it all if only one looked. There was nothing more to do than interlock the existing material so that the individual observations formed a whole. A gigantic jigsaw of the world. It was all there; he had gathered it together in a matter of weeks. Was he to close his eyes to the truth merely because sleep promised such bliss?

Yet Suess too still adhered to fixism, no different from every other man here in the room. The belief in a world fixed in place. The great man of geology had quite simply not trusted his own observations. Yet it was he who had first voiced the idea that the southern continents had once formed a single landmass. It was only their movement he had been unable to imagine, their drifting apart into their present forms. He still maintained there

120

had been simply a large plate, the middle of which had sunk until it filled with the water now referred to as oceans.

Suess and his apple story. Half a century ago, he had claimed the shape of the planet's surface, from the peaks of the Alps down to the deepest of valleys, had formed through the gradual shrinking of the cooling Earth's crust. Like wrinkles on the skin of an apple. Wegener found the comparison abhorrent. He would never eat of that fruit.

He brushed his hair from his forehead and continued. 'You may begin wherever you choose. Take the manatee, a sea cow. Manatees belong to the Sirenia order. They appeared at the end of the Eocene and have proved extremely successful over the subsequent millions of years. They are lone animals. Closely related to Steller's sea cow, which weighed several tonnes and survived its discovery by man by only a few years. Since then, their closest living relative has been the elephant. The manatee's upper lip is split; each half can be moved independently. The manatee lives alone. Should they happen to come into contact with their fellows, social ties are barely formed. In contrast to the seal, of which it is reminiscent, the manatee is unable to come to land. The animals inhabit shallow coastal waters, brackish water and estuaries, where they float along at a slow pace; they are unusually sluggish animals. Why am I telling you about them? We find these sea cows today in two far distant places in the world: in Africa and South America, in both cases on the Atlantic coast. Do you have an idea of where I am heading? The manatee looks upon us, questioning. It poses a riddle for us. We may not rest until it is solved. No other mammal possesses such a tiny brain in comparison with such a huge body. I find it hard to imagine how it should have crawled along one of your land bridges.' Laughter, more derisive than amused. 'I'm glad my thoughts give you such pleasure.' There was a snorting sound from the front row. Kayser of course, and now it occurred to Wegener what he reminded him of even more than a seal. But it was not the time for malice.

An interjection from the floor: 'You've never set foot on African soil!' Wegener recognized Professor Rettler, who that morning had held out his giant hands in greeting, hands with which he had ploughed the Congo delta for half his life as a scientist. Wegener closed the folder on his prepared manuscript once and for all and moved straight to West Africa's diamond deposits and their geological similarities with those of South America. He knew he was not at home in the field and in fact a storm of heckles descended on him, the separate objections impossible to understand; probably for the best. Wegener retreated to the earthworm, which existed on both sides of the Atlantic, reminded the gentlemen of the Mesosaurus fossils and asked where the remains of this primeval reptile had been found. 'As you will imagine, in Africa and South America—but where exactly? In freshwater deposits! The Mesosaurus was capable neither of crossing a land bridge nor of swimming across the saltwater ocean. How did it nevertheless succeed in moving from Africa to South America? It did not. It was the continents that moved; it was nothing but a stowaway.' Once again, Wegener brushed his hair back from his brow, now wet with perspiration. 'The contraction theory attempts to explain earthquakes through the contraction of the Earth's crust. Why, though, do reports of earthquakes always reach us from the very same zones? Why are they more frequent on the margins of the continents? You know as well as I do that these findings cannot be reconciled with the theory of the fixed Earth's crust. If we assume, however, a splitting and drifting of the continental floes, we finally obtain a new and coherent image.'

A single interjection sounded from the floor: 'Every schoolchild knows that the Earth's form is unchangeable.'

Wegener called back: 'As unchangeable as the crystal sphere to which the stars are attached?' He held onto the lectern. 'If we believe that, we can forget the past decades' research and start from the beginning! Shall we continue to feed our children poisoned apples that will put them into another hundred-year sleep?'

'Humbug!' they were calling. Some of his listeners had risen to their feet. 'Anyone who supports such a thing is not of sound mind!' Wegener stood at his lectern and filled his pipe, holding his tongue. What were a few stirring minutes compared with the longanimity of the periods at stake? The record of the session noted that the advanced time left no opportunity for discussion.

On the Flight Path of the Registration Balloon Launched in Lindenberg on 4 January

'Do you believe me, Else?' Wegener noticed his lips playing with the nib of his pen. They must be quite blue, as if frozen. He would wash them later. He was sitting at the table in his kitchen; night had fallen. His half-eaten supper was pushed aside.

He had spent the entire evening summoning up the course of that confounded day, and all that came out of it was the question of who believed him. Was it nothing but a question of faith?

What he would have given to ask Else that question directly, not merely in a letter. Or to ask her father whether he believed him. Simply to hear a human voice to drown out all the sneers from the audience, which were still darting about his head, their questions as impossible to shoo away as midges before a storm. Doubts were a swarm of insects that could not be mastered, simply because they were everywhere. Once one was swatted, another appeared in its place. Did he believe himself? He thought he heard laughter coming from inside his own head. His father's quiet, unvoiced laugh.

The climates of prehistory were the thing to concentrate on; that would bury their land bridges once and for all. Coal deposits had been found in the Antarctic, yet they could only be formed under tropical conditions. There were fossilized trees on Spitzbergen, trees that now only grew on the Mediterranean. How did that fit together with an unmoveable Earth's crust? It was a riddle posed to him by the world, and he could think of no other solution but to free the continents from their chains. He would not retract, never. They had rejected him; he rejected them. Sooner or later he would have to return to Greenland to determine positions. Nowhere else could the drift be observed at such speed.

Wegener dipped his pen in the ink jar again. He could see it drawing up the blue, a bloodsucking insect.

'I believe,' he wrote, 'you consider my ur-continent more fantastic than it is. If it becomes apparent that it brings rhyme and reason into the entire history of the Earth's development, why should we hesitate to jettison old ideas? Why hold back with this idea for ten or even thirty years? I don't believe the old ideas have even ten years left to live.'

He looked out of the window, darkness behind it. What did anyone know how long anything had left to live? Had the Mesosaurus sensed its end before it became extinct?

When Wegener woke up his head was on the kitchen table, his hair soaked in sweat. The margins of the notepaper on which he had fallen asleep were wavy with moisture.

He needed more colours. More pink. Wegener put down the knife. It was no use; his plan would stay pale. It had grown dark outside again—the winter with its incessant lack of light.

Wegener sat at the kitchen table, bent over his papers. He had moved in there for the space but now the chaos on the worktop was no less complete than in his study. Around him were sketchbooks, a sea of drawings, ripped paper, between them the stumps of pencils and crayons, the broken ends of leads, pink, pale green, blue, and the knife to sharpen them, although there was little left to sharpen by this point.

He looked through the sheets one by one, then crumpled each piece and tossed them over to the cold fireplace. He missed it every single time. The white paper balls bounced off the surrounds and rolled briefly across the kitchen floor before coming to rest. He kept the four best drafts. The tool chest contained a few nails and a hammer, and Wegener used them to affix the pictures to the wall above the fireplace, next to the cast-iron pokers.

They showed the prehistoric face of the Earth. Wegener had spent the day cutting continents out of stiff card and transferring the most important characteristics to them: directions of the glaciers' motion, occurrence of rare species of flora and fauna. Then he had pushed the pieces to and fro on the tabletop like glasses at one of those seances all the world was talking about. What ghosts was he trying to summon? When the pieces refused to fit he had cut, torn and folded them until everything finally tessellated: abrasions, habitats, coasts. Then he had constantly retraced the continents' paths, how they split, divided, separated off and drifted into their present positions. He had repeated the movement until his hands knew them by rote, forwards and backwards, in a single moment overcoming distances for which the continents had taken millennia.

Then he had traced the various phases onto new sheets and finally coloured the surfaces of the continents as far as the pencil stumps had allowed. He had chosen a pink pencil for the ur-continent, because it was closest at hand. While the ur-continent was still a single mass in the first picture, in the consecutive sketches it separated ever further, each surface drifting gradually away towards its present position.

Only now that the series of pictures was on the wall did it occur to him that their course looked like a flower slowly opening its pink blossom. Or a plate breaking very gradually. No, thinking about it, it was an embryo, lying curled in the first picture and then growing continually, the little head rising, the foetus stretching out arms and legs and taking ever greater shape. As long as one did not get confused by the head and limbs gradually separating off from the rump. Wegener picked up the last piece of pink and wrote beneath the first picture: All the Land.

The last of that day's letters to Vladimir Köppen ended in a long series of addenda, supplements and appendices with one more postscript: 'Tell Else not to hang her head, I can't help being such a vagabond.'

He was planning another trip to the north and he feared his fiancée did not approve. Still, she was supporting him in every conceivable way with the preparations—and in fact it may have been him imagining she found it hard to imagine letting him go. He had simply not dared to ask whether she minded him leaving her alone. He wouldn't have known how to respond if she'd asked him to stay.

It was to be a second trip to Greenland. The first crossing of the island's entire breadth, after Nansen's shorter passage across the southern end. An unheard-of undertaking. Captain Koch, his former cabinmate, was preparing the voyage. They wanted to tackle the challenge with a small crew, four men and a few dogs. He could take care of the necessary science himself. Exner's unfriendly paper in the Meteorologische Zeitschrift had meanwhile destroyed his immediate prospects of a professorship. What did he have to lose here, among people?

Apart from Else. But then she and he would simply wait before marrying. They could take care of it straight away upon his return, in November 1913.

For the time being, however, he wrote to his fiancée: 'There is little positive news from me. I believe I will perish in the near future.' He considered adding an exclamation mark to the latter sentence but that seemed too dramatic. 'On Wednesday I held an unscripted lecture on cloud formation, which was so pleasing—at least to me—that I dictated the whole thing to a typist the next day. The next will be a lecture on airship travel and one on our expedition including the kite ascents, the day after the same thing again without the inclusion but with colour photographs, later in Kassel a lecture on flying with untethered balloons. Shall I survive it all?'

He was getting around a great deal now. How astounded the towns seemed when a stranger interrupted their orderly way of life. A rag picker, a basket weaver outside his workshop, even a dog stopping at a lamppost, they all looked caught out, as though he had disturbed them in the midst of some indecent act.

Wegener had grown accustomed to walking from the stations on the edge of town to the market square, where he would take accommodation. And whereas in Marburg, he barely looked up now on his short paths to the institute, the lecture theatre and the library, here he absorbed everything: the blond manes of the brewery horses, the sharp beats of their hooves on the cobbles and the smell they left behind. The jangle of an electric tram shooting around a corner. Two jovial military policemen in brightly coloured uniforms. A veteran begging for alms on his board of wood.

Wegener stopped at every posted bill and read what it was announcing. A tea dance, an exposition—all the many options for passing one's time. On one occasion, he came across an announcement for a talk to be held that same evening in the premises of the Geological Association and regretted being unable to participate. Then he noticed the bill was advertising his own lecture. How unfamiliar his name looked in its small print. That Dr. rer. nat. Wegener, was that really him?

Later he sat in his accommodation, tidied his few things into the wardrobe and then sat a while on the edge of the bed, his chin resting on his hands, while his good lecture shirt aired on its hanger beside him.

The Geologische Rundschau printed Wegener's revised theses on the ur-continent in three successive issues. They caused a stir. His most vehement opponents became, in this order, Soergel, Diener and Semper, all geologists. Semper entreated in the Zentralblatt für Mineralogie, Geologie und Paläontologie 'for the maintenance of the necessary distance'. Wegener should 'not honour geology any further but, rather, seek out subject areas that have neglected to write above their doors: Oh holy Saint Florian, please spare my house and set fire to another!'

As a farewell gesture, Wegener invited his fiancée to a long-promised hot-air-balloon ride. They set off from the meadows behind the institute. As soon as they were up in the air, Else began to squeak with excitement, sounding like a small rodent. She took his hand for a moment. How long had she yearned for that moment. And so they stood facing each other, Else beaming at him, and neither of them spoke until Wegener had to take a look at the map.

In pleasant weather, they floated calmly north, 2,000 metres above ground. No tremors, no engine roars disturbed them up there. Only rarely did dogs' barks from the villages interrupt their silence—like a memory, an illusion, a fata morgana. They simply stood at the edge of the basket and looked out above it, as though inspecting a parade of the landscape arranged for their benefit by a well-meaning creator. Whoever might have painted such an impressive tableau, using a palette full of leafy and grassy green, full of corn yellow and earth brown and light, light, light. And a giant tube of sky blue that ran darker towards the zenith, as though the picture's creator had mixed in a tiny blob of the black of space up there. Wegener was glad not to have his father on board, not wanting to clash with him now on the question of whom to credit with the whole matter. He tried to continue simply enjoying the artwork but he had to muster his full concentration to push the questions on the cause of this beauty out of the golden frame that opened up before them.

Wegener at least was looking out, then. Whenever he turned to Else, however, he noticed she was looking at him. They both smiled briefly on those occasions, Else with her whole face, he himself no doubt a little cautiously. Was it because of the silence all around that they did not speak? Sometimes Wegener pointed out a range of hills, a settlement, a cloud formation and explained everything while Else said nothing. Could she not see these things, due to her eye problem? Did she expect something from him? An explanation, a deed? Wegener smoked an entire pipe, which required a great deal of attention at this altitude. After that he carefully cleaned his smoking equipment and returned it all to his bag, discovering as he did the bundle of provisions his landlady had set out for him that morning and unwrapping it with a triumphant gesture.

Else took only a sip of the cider. After the picnic, Wegener dumped a little sand to take them up higher. Then they stood side by side again and stared out ahead, their faces concealed by the brims of their hats. Else gripped the edge of the basket.

They flew over the margins of the Teutoburg Forest, the wind now abated. It would be a while before they sighted open fields again.

Wegener stared out at the distance.

It was only once they had begun losing altitude, the ballast long gone and their landing no longer possible to postpone, that Else began to speak.

'Is it hard for you to leave me behind?'

Wegener wished he had his pipe back. When he failed to answer, she went on.

'I've been thinking. So as not to stay here with nothing to do, I'd like to go abroad for a time. I'd like to see something of the world.' She held onto the edge of the basket. 'Would that be agreeable for you? I was thinking of Scandinavia. We'd be a little closer to one another then.'

Wegener was already holding the anchor and didn't know how to respond. What was she looking for in Scandinavia that couldn't be found at home? What use was it to them that they'd be closer to one another? But then, the Scandinavian countries did have a good heritage. And the land mass there was rising. Only gradually, but it was a good sign.

He asked, 'Are you familiar with Oslo?'

Else shrugged.

A clearing opened up suddenly below them and Wegener quickly cast the anchor, calling to Else to secure the end of the rope. Never having flown before, though, she didn't hold fast enough to it; the rope slipped through her hands and was lost. Wegener saw the anchor submerge in the dark forest, the rope twirling between the uppermost branches for a moment and then disappearing like a snake into the leaves.

All they had now was the balloon and themselves. While Wegener thought about how to master the situation, Else stood behind him and asked: 'And after your return?'

He really didn't know an answer to that up here. Wegener stood at the edge of the basket and saw the tips of the trees passing close beneath him. There could be no thought of landing. He gathered everything of any weight, the remaining provisions, every inessential item of clothing, his umbrella, and sent it overboard. That gave them a few metres' height but it wouldn't last long.

He had a choice of sacrificing the balloon or his companion. When he looked around for Else he was shocked at her pale face. Once again she smiled but this time it seemed she meant to keep on the right side of someone she was afraid of. Wegener begged her forgiveness, lifted her onto the edge of the basket, threw the loose end of the tow tope overboard and showed her how to let herself down by it. He did not look her in the eye. What choice did he have?

She slid down, terribly slowly. A hesitant ballast. Wegener was glad the wind had subsided and they weren't moving quite as fast now.

The trees were sparser here too. Else slid a little and then held on again, swayed a moment and then slid some more. Wegener had a sense of how she might be feeling. At last she reached the treetops and sank between the trunks. In the end the rope was a metre short so she had to jump the last stretch; he watched her fall and roll to one side on the ground.

His heart almost stopped but at the moment she let go, the balloon gained height and he lost sight of Else. Wegener flew over a crest behind which the forest thinned out, a road passed beneath him and he almost touched a telegraph line before he finally managed to set down on fallow land.

His legs trembling, he ran back into the woods, panting self-accusations over what he'd done to his fiancée.

Once he reached the forest she came walking towards him, almost unrecognizable. Her skirt torn, her hair tangled; he had never seen her like this before. She held out her hands to him even from a distance, bloody with scrapes. Her eyes shone; she looked terrifyingly beautiful to him in her shock. Then he heard that she was laughing.

Wegener ran to her. She patted a last few leaves from her clothing and then raised her head, looked at him impishly and exclaimed, one finger threatening: 'That was not a smooth ladies' landing, my good sir!'

Wegener, relieved beyond measure that she was in one piece on the ground and not angry, couldn't help taking his fiancée in his arms. He whispered in her ear, not even knowing what he was saying. He closed his eyes and went on talking into her hair. What a marvellous fellow he had by his side. It felt as though a weight had lifted from his chest, as though someone had taken one sack of ballast after another and emptied the sand into the wind. Else too grew light in his arms as he lifted her up and then clasped her to him by turns, until they fell and rolled together through the late autumn leaves on the ground, he for the first time while Else had just done the very same thing.

They lay for a long time where they had come to a standstill, pressed closely together. Wegener wrapped his arms around his bride from behind and held her tight, not intending ever to let her go again. It was no more than that, and yet it robbed them both of breath.

They lay like that, his chest pressed against her warm back, hips and all else, his legs against the backs of her knees. How well it all fitted. They lay side by side like continents once torn apart, still knowing they belonged together. A force pushed them towards one another, back into a togetherness before the beginning of time, to the feeling of being everything there was in the world.

But Wegener could think of no way that would lead them back. At last Else turned around to him, put one finger on his mouth and left it there, while her other hand pulled at the knot of his tie. She looked him in the eye. The knot was tight and Wegener had to swallow hard, several times.

It was a righteous struggle; it almost cut off his breath but he held still. He was now glad of her finger on his lips and he kept to her command for silence even long after her hand was gone from there. During everything she did to him, he wouldn't have known what to say.

And while leaves floated down from the trees around them at the same calm pace as the sun gradually descending between the trunks, the two of them made use of the opportunity to be entirely undisturbed for the first time in a long while, there on the margins of the Teutoburg Forest.

Then they lay there, still out of breath. On their backs this time and side by side, their eyes focused on the last of the light, where it was impossible to say whether it was the treetops swaying or the sky. Wegener brushed a leaf from his cheek; they were all over him now. Everything smelt of dried leaves, worms and earth, a scent of decay. Wegener thought he could smell the leaves decomposing beneath him, countless tiny creatures going about their work in and among them, all the fallen foliage breaking down and moul-dering until it became new earth, from which in turn new life came about. He tasted sebum on his tongue and realized it was a hair. He immediately felt for it to pluck it out and was surprised by how long he had to pull. It was clearly one of Else's. How strange women were. Even their many types of hosiery and fas-teners, their garters, hair clips, ribbons, hooks and eyes; though he had learnt a great deal in that area that day.

Confidential Report on the Greenland Expedition

Everything was different on this trip, but what exactly was it? The sacks of hay all over the ship? They had made a stop at Iceland to load a few of the small horses, hoping for good work from them. With their aid, they'd be able to carry the expedition baggage along the snow-free coast to the glaciers and up over the steep walls of the inland ice, where dogs were no use.

Koch had come to value the horses' tenacity during his measurements of Icelandic glaciers completed the previous year, and on the crossing to Danmarkshavn Wegener too sometimes went down to the hold where they stood side by side in the dark, trembling with tension. He wondered whether this nervousness was part of their nature or a reaction to his arrival. There was little more to see than their black silhouettes in the light from the dirty portholes. Damp clouds of breath surrounded their nostrils.

Wegener put his hand on one horse's side and it snorted once, its flanks trembling. No comparison to the skittish, howling pack of sled dogs.

They had a single dog with them, which had run between their legs on Iceland for so long that they eventually came up with a use for him. He could sound the alarm if a bear or a wolf approached the horses at night. The dog was as black as night. They named him Gloë.

Four walruses were waiting for them as they went ashore not far from their previous anchoring place at the entrance to Dove Bay.

They were choice fat specimens, their lethargy outweighing any possible stirrings of fear. Koch unloaded the camera from the ship and asked the four of them to put on a friendly face. The team joked about sending the photograph as a Christmas card, each of them signing his name under the walrus that most resembled him. It wasn't hard to decide. The old one with the smooth skull was Vigfus, Larsen had the sad look on his face, the bull with his eyes screwed up was Koch. Wegener could be spotted by his thin moustache, and he was also the one with the most delicate build.

Perhaps that was the most palpable deviation from the first trip—that there were only four of them. Koch of course, his comrade from the past expedition. It was good to know he was there; his blond beard and flashing eyes imparted a feeling of safety.

Originally, Lundager would have been part of the group, the botanist both men recalled fondly as a single-minded companion. During the preparations in Iceland, however, it became clear that at forty-four, he was no longer up to the trials of such an undertaking. He had proved sensible enough to draw the consequences of his own accord.

Vigfus had joined them in his place, a strong, supple student of economics who spoke little. They had been impressed by how quickly he'd climbed Kverkfjöll when they were viewing the sulphurous springs. There was always a use for a good pair of legs. The fourth man was Lars Larsen, a twenty-six-year-old sailor who had seemed so fit for the expedition during the crossing that they'd hired him on the spot.

Or was it merely the prospect of being underway that was new? Their plan to cross the island's ice ridge, from sea to sea, a march of 1,200 kilometres, instead of simply sitting in one place like the last time.

Whenever Wegener thought back to his Pustervig exile, to the constricted space of his room, to his apparitions, as he meanwhile chose to call what had happened to him, a shudder came over him. The trembling came from his back, a tiny tremor that he didn't take seriously, that he only noticed because it set in so reliably and fascinated him, as a phenomenon. It was not as if Wegener felt no fear of returning to the land in which he had come too close to himself.

To get the horses moving somewhat after the long crossing to Greenland, they were let loose as soon as they had firm ground beneath their hooves. A mistake, it soon proved. The attempt to bring them in again was abandoned that evening; the horses were lost without trace.

It was almost a week before they were found. Gloë tracked three of them to a small lake behind the coastal hills, and another five to a hollow further inland. Then Koch's black riding horse and the three missing packhorses appeared, one per day.

To avoid similar incidents, Larsen developed a system of tying two horses together during their rests, one's head to another's tail. That way, they could move around without doing any major damage.

Once the hay sacks were loaded they set out, following the course of the bay inland. How small their baggage train looked. Having brought up the rear for a while, Wegener asked to ride ahead so as not to have their paltry caravan in view.

They pitched camp in the open air. While the others took care of the horses, Vigfus prepared their meal. He was a passable cook, though it was their habit to claim otherwise. He made a variety of evening meals out of peasemeal and bread, and the same porridge every morning. Sometimes Wegener thought he saw Koch looking over at the horses' hay sacks in envy.

Larsen's new tying technique meant the pairs of horses spent all night circling one another but did not cross much ground. Not unlike people, thought Wegener. The horse named Grauni proved to be a particular miscreant, encouraging each of his partners to dance over to the hay sacks with him. Once there, he opened the sacks with a single strong bite.

The transport along the banks of Dove Bay took them three weeks; then they'd reached Cape Stop. As they set out each morning, Wegener took one last look around to check nothing had been forgotten, and every morning the only thing left at their camp was Gloë, as though he found it hard to leave his newly claimed home. How quickly he gave his heart away. Wegener whistled for the dog; one could see the constancy and lust for adventure wrestling in his small black body, and then he would leap up and run after them, barking.

They had passed Pustervig halfway. Wegener spotted the remains of his hut as they rode by, collapsed and nothing more to see than a few boards, rubble, cloud shadows. The bent rods of the thermometer hut protruded like flagstaffs without flags. A picture of misery. As though none of it had ever existed. Wegener turned away, even more taciturn that day than usual.

Cape Stop marked the end of Dove Bay. For days, they had seen Queen Louise Land above them at sunset. The evening dabbed the ground beyond the glacier with dots of violet, red and blue light, which began to glow beneath a pink sky, and the whole spectacle reflected marvellously off the frozen Jarner Bay. It seemed to them like the Promised Land.

Yet, before they reached the glacier to make their ascent, there was the Borg Fjord to cross. To get from the land to the ice, the horses had to overcome the tidal gap and then a water-filled ditch. Koch's black horse plodded willingly straight into the latter, vanishing almost entirely. Larsen held its head above water until the others reached them with ropes and dragged the horse aside onto the ice. The red horse went in too but found the bottom. Once it was relieved of its load it let them heave it out without a struggle.

The expedition set up quarters in the shade of the glacier. The evening conversations revolved around the horses' harnesses for pulling the large sled up onto the inland ice. It was its own branch of science.

The next few days passed with exploratory walks to find a good way into the glacier. They hammered horseshoe nails into their soles. Now and then, thunder echoed for minutes at a time through the otherwise absolutely peaceful air; a piece of ice had broken off somewhere or one of the giants had turned in the water. They photographed a number of interesting melt forms at the foot of the steep wall. When they finally found a way up, that part proved to be already separated from the inland ice by a massive cleft, and they soon turned back.

On the way back they had a wondrous experience. They passed a bear that had caught a seal, a trail of blood showing where it had dragged its prey onto land from its hunting channel. The bear had already stuffed its belly and was digesting in the protective shade of a rock. On its right perched a raven, on its left a white fox, having invited themselves to the feast and now gorging on the leftovers. The fox with gusto, the raven hesitantly eyeing its prey from one side before every bite. None of the three creatures took the slightest notice of the silent observers. It was like in a fable, just that nobody spoke.

That evening they had bear soup, a rather oily treat. The amazement every time at the skin beneath the white fur being entirely black. Like discovering a polar bear's little secret in its death.

The next attempt fared no better. Larsen and Wegener set out bright and early to look for a way through at the south end of the Borg Jøkel.

Larsen went ahead with a walking stick, Wegener following him and carrying the theodolite but no stick. They reached the actual glacier after a good hour, then walked along the increasingly impressive wall of inland ice until they came across a point where they might climb it. They broke through the surface at the very first crevasse, but no damage was done. The second crevasse, likewise covered by snow, showed up as a recess, the hint of a shadow beneath it like dark rings below a pair of tired eyes. Larsen walked across slowly, not breaking through. Wegener followed him with caution.

Later, the others estimated he had fallen a total of eight metres. Wegener's own estimate was far higher. It seemed to him as though time stood still while he fell. While the wall of ice slid past his eyes, as clean and shiny as porcelain, he found time to formulate a farewell letter to Else. Not a weighty matter, simply the news of how sad he was at having to die without having made her his wife. For the rest of the way, he wondered at how it had been more important to him to leave a message for Else than to make the final mental additions to his manuscript on the ur-continent.

His head hit a protruding piece of ice, his hip was gashed open and he landed at last on a leaf-shaped ridge of ice split away from the wall, damaging one finger of his right hand. His feet too were affected. The theodolite was still gripped in both his hands.

Far above him, Larsen's face jutted into the opening. He looked like a head in a picture frame of light. Wegener heard his name, like a question called far louder than circumstances required. Eight metres might be a considerable distance to fall, but they did not render particular difficulties for communication.

Wegener wanted to call up that everything was fine, but when he opened his mouth nothing came out but a hoarse croak. He cleared his throat and then made his report, checking all his body parts in turn and informing Larsen of their state.

They discussed what to do. Larsen threw down his hat and gloves and then turned back to fetch help.

Koch was just tracking down a few horses that had danced off overnight when Larsen arrived with the catastrophic news. They agreed that Vigfus and Koch would go ahead on skis with rope ladders, a cable and the ice axe, while Larsen followed them with the hand sled and Wegener's sleeping bag. He was angry with himself for not leaving his coat there.

In the dawn light, it was hard for the two men to retain control of their skis, and their impatience made it no easier. Was it possible for Wegener to hold out motionless in the cold of a crevasse for two hours without freezing to death?

Wegener was by no means motionless, however. He had come round completely at the foot of his hole, sucked a few cola pastilles, sung a little and was now doing what he did best—keeping himself mentally agile.

In the sparse light that reached him from above, he examined the icy walls around him. He was clearly still above the dirty subglacial till; the walls exhibited a smooth, clean fracture that had brought forth basalt-like structures in places, in others the walls had lines of a shell-like structure. Wegener sought an appropriate word for this hollow form but he could not find one and suddenly feared his brain might have been damaged during the fall after all, and might fail entirely if he went on thinking.

He reached out a hand to get at least an approximate temperature for this depth of ice, but did not come to any finding. After a while he realized he'd have to remove his glove first to do so. But even his bare fingers were no further use, having grown entirely numb. The only result of the idea was the stimulating challenge of having to fight his way back into the glove for several minutes.

141

His eyes grew accustomed to the dusky light, at least. A melt hole had formed on a level with his knee, presumably through water dripping from the edge of the crevasse. Wegener enjoyed studying it in peace; it did not yet seem to have suffered any evaporation. On the bottom of the melt hole was a first layer of dust, displaying astounding patterns. What manner of things one might read from it, if only one ruminated on it precisely. Wegener tried to memorize the image, for a minor publication. Small publications added up too. All he needed was a concise title. A formulation that would illustrate the unique situation of its finding but not sound foolish. Such a shame that all that came to mind was foolish titles.

It was only when Wegener noticed the pattern altering every time he blinked, like a kaleidoscope shaken over and over, that he resorted to mere waiting. Presumably he was more affected than he'd assumed.

Doing nothing, however, had the disadvantage that it left considerable scope for the perception of cold. And cold carried fear along with it. Both were equally unwelcome for Wegener.

He shook himself. That was no good. He had to keep himself alive, he had to stay warm, he mustn't lose courage. He had promised his bride he'd take care of himself. There was no reneging on that.

Only, with the best will in the world, he could think of nothing he could do down there to save himself. He discarded the option of praying. In the end each of his ideas led to the plan to light as large a fire as conceivable, as soon as possible. In the midst of his joy at this idea, however, he realized every time that the melting ice would soon extinguish the flames. Wegener was too weak to decide whether to be proud of coming up with this objection or despondent. Possibly, it was the fault of his already sinking body temperature, which commanded him to concentrate all remaining energy on what had to be done now: freezing, trembling, breathing.

Thus reduced to animal survival, one possibility to keep warm did occur to him. He called to mind the thoughts that had served him so well in his Pustervig hut. He closed his eyes and little by little his icy crevasse filled up with images of women, some of them even strangely familiar after all the time gone by. To begin with, he thought he could tell they were cold, being anything but protected from the weather. Then he concentrated entirely on making their acquaintance in as many ways as was mentally possible.

In the meantime, his rescuers were approaching the incline. Koch called from some distance so that Wegener heard them coming and wouldn't give up. Hullo and hullo again, over and over, and when the marked spot was finally visible he went ahead of his companion, still calling hullo, only ever that one word, but no answer came. Not until he had almost reached the end of the footprints did a sound suddenly rise from the depths, a noise he could not quite classify, a grunt or a snort, and for a moment Koch thought it might be one of those mythical creatures the Greenlanders believed lived in the inland ice.

Koch's face appeared above Wegener like an apparition, only now hearing the calls. He had rarely been so happy to see a fellow human being. From his low vantage point, Koch looked like a Viking with his blond beard. Wegener, responding to his question, tried to put as much strength in his voice as possible. Yes, he was alive. He may have sprained his ankles slightly. But he hadn't frozen to death at any rate.

In the crevasse's opening, Vigfus' face joined Koch's. He let down the rope ladder and a torch.

Wegener managed most of the way up of his own accord, until his strength threatened to abandon him just before the edge. The other two handed him a rope and pulled him up the last section.

Koch looked concerned. Wegener asked what was the matter, so Koch described what he saw, the grey of his face and the dried blood crossing it from a wound on his forehead. He showed him where it ran down his collar, but when Wegener tried to turn his head to look at the mess, the pain held him back. He was also struggling not to faint.

They led him to the sled, with which Larsen had meanwhile arrived. Wegener retained no memory of his return transport to the camp.

Only Gloë managed to recall him to brief consciousness. The dog barked so long and loud for joy at his master's return that Wegener awoke from his immersion. Then he fell into a feverish glimmer for the rest of the day and the entire night that followed.

The three unharmed men spent the next morning building a stall in the ice for the horses. There was no avoiding several extra days at the camp. The floor consisted of a recess in the glacier, the upper structure of empty provisions crates, with horse blankets for a roof. Koch brought Wegener's tea into the tent, reporting that the horses even had a manger hacked into the ice so that they could nibble fresh water whenever they felt like it.

The examination revealed Wegener's injuries to be modest by the light of day. The bruises changed colour beautifully with time. Like the Northern Lights, Koch joked as he washed him. His comrades visited his sickbed every morning and made bets on what colour to expect that day.

His finger was splinted to a tent peg. Koch thought his foot bones had probably sustained a few hairline fractures, which would no doubt remain painful and cause complications at a later date. As the damage could be neither verified nor treated, however, they decided they might as well ignore it for the time being.

Over the next few days, Wegener led the life of a robber baron. He could only make himself useful by cooking and doing other domestic tasks. He performed well in these areas, however, although the others passed no comment on his creation 'single tinned sardine in bread soup'. Breakfast was the last of the seal meat. Otherwise, he lay and stared at the tent roof a great deal. The way the light changed upon it. Sometimes Gloë lay with him and they warmed one another.

With nothing else to do, Wegener tended his science. He read Suess. The old man actually tried to find an explanation for the Great Flood. As though there were no more urgent question in natural science, every theory now had to be brought in line with the Bible as well. Wegener was reminded of his lecture at the Senckenberg Museum, how respect for the absent honorary chairman had culminated in the interjection 'What would Suess have to say?' Not a pleasant memory.

From his disputes with his father, he knew making admissions to the church bore no fruit. What use was proof of the Great Flood to believers? It would never make the scientists' activities any godlier.

Suess attempted it nevertheless. Wegener marked the more absurd passages in his argumentation with a vertical line in the margin. The extremely absurd ones with a double line. Suess considered the biblical flood a tragic correlation of two incidents in the south of the Gulf of Persia, where the destructive force of an undersea earthquake and a tropical storm had exacerbated one another. In his opinion, the wave washed the crews of seaworthy boats all the way into the mountainous lands of the Euphrates. Wegener imagined them leaving the ships, swaying slightly, holding hands two by two, like children. Suess failed to provide an answer for the animals on board, however.

The breaking up of the fountains of the great deep in Genesis, Suess put down to the well-known phenomenon of springs in

145

floodplains that disgorge water during an earthquake. Wegener was by no means what one called a religious man. But he did not want to have the stories of his childhood destroyed. It was no use robbing the old stories of their mythical elements, or equally of their moral side. The next thing Suess would want to do was explain the disappearance of Atlantis with his vanishing theory.

Wegener put the book aside. He would leave it here. No matter how little its weight, it was not worth its holding back their progress.

On the third day, he'd had enough of the jeremiad of his sickbed, and got up. He still walked with a stick but he could accompany his comrades as they made an initial transport to push the depot forwards. Wegener was impressed by the engineering work they had undertaken during his indisposition. Several small cracks had been filled from the ground up, and they had bridged another with two huge blocks of ice. In some places, the path had been carved half a metre deep into the ice, otherwise the sleds would have slipped on the steep acclivity and disappeared into one of the chasms.

They could only hope not to be embarrassed on their way by new crevasses forming. The ice all around them crackled with life.

By early May, with the aid of much 'Come now!' and 'Whoa', Gloë's barking and a good few jabs in the ribs, they finally had the entire baggage up on the inland ice. Koch had gone back down to Cape Stop on skis to leave behind a report. It was good to know that a search party would know where to look, if the expedition members were to perish on their long trip.

They rested one more day to distribute the load. Then there was nothing more to do but shoot the weakest horses. Wegener did it in a hollow at some distance from the tent, and was in a foul mood all evening because his previous riding horse was among them. They kept only five—Red, Lady, Cavalier, Polaris and Grauni—from which they expected the greatest use. The horses were also unsettled by the loss of their companions. How small they looked all at once. Their low withers would help them to come through the driving with less damage.

Only Gloë was glad. He was given a black pudding so huge that even he, always a greedy creature, rolled up in submission after a while, merely tapping a paw now and then at the tempting bowl.

The Stopping of Chronographs in Cold Temperatures

Driving snow. Entry into the great wild plains. Endless as a sea was the surface ahead of them, stretching likewise from coast to coast. All around them it touched the sky. They were the only boatmen on this ocean.

Watching from above the army of shining white snakes of snow speeding across the firn in a restless chase, one would feel like a fakir in a story, whom all this obeyed. Wegener sat cross-legged on the first sled's hay sacks, Gloë on his lap, and looked ahead into the stormy distance. They were on the move at last. Now they had to press onward, ever onward, all the way to the other side where a small emergency depot awaited them, set up by Koch the previous year.

It was not friendly ground they were travelling on. The surface proved hard as glass, whipped by storms. Furrows lined up in low waves, carved by the wind; no one would ever count them. The sleds danced across them like fast-sailing boats.

All the land was vanished; even the last pointed peaks at the southern end of Queen Louise Land were behind them now. They were on the high seas.

Twenty degrees below freezing. One didn't know what was more cruel, the never-ending march against the driving snow, during which their faces grew stiff with ice, or the time in the tent too small for four people, its walls covered in finger-thick frost. And everything, literally everything in it was filled with driven snow, the sacks, the instrument cases, their journals. Even Gloë, whom they let huddle at the entrance, had to be brushed free of snow in the morning. Heaven knew how things would go on.

Each of their sleds carried 700 pounds. How long would the horses be able to pull that burden? They were still walking uphill and the biting wind did not make matters easier.

They soon had to shoot Polaris. They had pushed him on mile for mile by the skin of his teeth, until he finally gave up entirely. The load on his sled was laughably small by that point, far less than that of the equally-tired-looking Cavalier, who marched on obediently. They would have to lumber Grauni with most of the baggage, the only one not to have shown any sign of exhaustion so far.

Once again it was Wegener who took care of the business of death; that was how they had come to do things. He led the horse a little way off so that the tent was between him and the other animals. The large, luminous red stain on the snow like an assault of colour on their lives, lives in which colour barely existed now. On his way back to the tent, carrying a pail of meat for Gloë, Wegener looked around one last time and then saw the outlines of the bloody pool before him whenever he closed his eyes, until he slept.

Usually he was the first to wake in the morning, sitting up and putting an end to their night's rest in the cramped tent. He crawled out of his cold sleeping bag and knotted it together in a bundle, paying no mind to the men lying curled up around him. They had agreed that anyone driven from his bed by the cold was allowed to wake the others, so that they'd make progress as soon as possible. But when Wegener banged about the tent in the early morning, none of them wanted to hear about their agreement.

It annoyed Wegener when Larsen, directly next to him, turned on his side with a dramatic gesture; he knew the sound of

149

the great yawn he emitted as he did so, and all too well the stench that came with it and lay suspended beneath the low tent roof for a moment, the poison of the new day.

Had someone prophesied that he'd have to spend his dotage with these three men in a space as cramped as this, he would not have hesitated to run out alone, to lie down in the firn somewhere at the end of his strength and wait to be relieved from the situation. As it was, though, he still had the hope of being by Else's side by the autumn. With the best will in the world, he couldn't imagine how it might be to wake up next to her. He envisaged it would be pleasant but sometimes, when Larsen pressed up against him in his sleep and rubbed his sticky hair across his face, he was overcome by panic, forcing him to sit up and simply breathe in and out for a while.

Once he'd calmed down sufficiently to try sleeping again, he reached for the slumbering Gloë, draped him over himself as a warm cover and lay there, his eyes on the canvas lit up by the night sun, waiting for sleep to take him.

Their provisions now consisted mainly of pemmican.

There was baggage to be redistributed the very next day. Barely a mile from Polaris' no-doubt-snow-covered cadaver, they had to make use of a pause in their march to shoot Cavalier. They drove Gloë on to hurry with his share, and then tried in vain all afternoon to make up the time lost on their planned leg of the journey.

Larsen and Wegener travelled on skis from then on. Directly behind them Grauni, who thus got the most driving snow of all the horses. At the rear ran Gloë; they still had to check whether he came along every time they set out. Skiing did Wegener good; he was relieved that his injuries had meanwhile fully healed. They had now reached the upper section of the Greenlandic Ridge, with excellent pistes at this altitude.

Several times, however, they heard the sound the Danmark expedition had described in their report, a huge sigh when one of the gigantic snow floes collapsed beneath the weight of their small group. Lady was shocked every time and dashed forward.

Then the weather thwarted their planning once again. Wegener had stepped outside the tent in the morning and seen instantly that there would be no progress that day. What possessed him to spur his comrades on to set out nonetheless, perfectly aware they would recognize the impossibility at first glance? His unwillingness to spend another series of days lying tightly packed alongside them, not knowing when that enforced proximity would ever end. Why was Gloë exempt from this antipathy? The two of them lay together for hours and the dog let Wegener stroke his neck with a never-changing motion, lost in daydreams.

One might have spent the time thinking, but there was barely any subject upon which the mind was willing to remain. Only two questions ran constantly through Wegener's imagination during these hours, forwards and backwards—how he would set up home with Else and what kind of food they might cook there. The first question tended to arise after meals, and the second beforehand. He lacked courage, otherwise he could easily have written two articles, compared to which The Origin of the Continents would look like a sixth-form essay. How could he have left without marrying Else first! Once they had entered into matrimony he would never leave her side.

It was a dog's life they were leading. The weather refused to turn. By day they lay in their sleeping bags, uninterrupted. Wegener told the story of the Danish governor of Greenland who had been ordered to cross the island 200 years ago. He was to check whether any descendants of the Norwegians were still living anywhere. And whether the speculations about inland oases were true, where warm winds had melted the ice. The governor hadn't even made it to the edge of the inland ice.

Wegener opened the tent flap to see whether the weather had improved. One glance out scotched that hope. Nor was there any sign of oases.

As soon as conditions allowed, they made new attempts to move on. Usually, however, the brighter weather was merely temporary and the foray was soon abandoned. Every attempt to dry their belongings outside led without fail to them filling with snow. Their sleeping bags were sopping wet by now.

The tough days in the tent and the impossibility of changing anything about the conditions made Wegener irritable at times, Koch being his main victim. There was no objective reason for that; perhaps Wegener envied him his inner peace, perhaps he dared to abuse him where he would not have gone so far with the others. He felt imprisoned, flailing around at night in his tight sleeping bag, which prompted him to be allocated a space at the side of the tent. Snowflakes even penetrated through the gaps in the seams, as small and invincible as ants.

Koch generally accepted Wegener's expressions of inner dissatisfaction with admirable stoicism, as a necessary evil. Only now and then, when he did lose patience, did he cast Wegener a sharp look, which cured the latter for a while. He simply had to hope that any improvement in conditions would make him more sufferable again.

To their great relief, they at least got out of the wind zone and the snow grew lighter. Now and then Wegener unpacked the instruments, freed them from snow and made his measurements, in the hope that his findings might prove useful at a later point. For some matter that was impossible to envisage out here. Above all, though, it did him good to hold a hypsometer, a sextant or the good black ball thermometer in his hands rather than a horse's reins.

Their height was now 2,287 metres above sea level. Length, width and height were the most interesting things in their lives now. Alongside them only the endless white and the meanwhile almost permanently clear sky. Nature seemed unable to afford sights such as clouds or a deviation in the snow out here.

Larsen found a little mirror in his luggage, which instantly made the rounds out of joy at seeing a new face. They encountered themselves again, astounded by the meeting. The most affected was Wegener's nose, nothing but a frozen wound with tatters hanging from it. His chin fully frostbitten. Had he met such a person anywhere else, he would never have trusted him.

The sinking or, rather, the collapse of the firn beneath them had now become an everyday occurrence. It was no longer a sigh but more of a groan, a roar. A thundering that proceeded for a while before it echoed in the large, empty space in which they were living. They all knew it was them causing the phenomenon, through the weight of their caravan. At the same time, though, it sounded as though a maniac were trying to break free from his chains. Wegener thought: De profundis. It's the continents freeing themselves from their man-made confinement beneath us.

The horses had grown accustomed to the noise. Only Gloë was still shocked to the core every time anew, running over the skis in his desolation or between the horses' legs. To save himself, he would jump onto one of the sleds, once even getting in the way of the skids. He was not a heroic dog. Perhaps, Wegener thought, he was the only one of them to fully grasp the extent of their state.

The horses looked worse from day to day. In the mornings, while his comrades were struggling out of their sleep, Wegener's first act was to go to the animals, pat the snow from them and talk to them. Were these the conversations with himself he had known in Pustervig? Not as long as the horses listened to him, and so Wegener whispered directly into their erect ears.

They reduced the red horse's burden at Lady's expense. They now fed them generously at noon too. The red horse got through the afternoon better that way, while things often grew too much for Lady. And so Vigfus and Wegener harnessed themselves in front of her, on skis, which seemed to help a little. Nonetheless, the animals remained weak. The altitude affected them.

They tried this method for a few days and then had to admit they were simply demanding too much of the horses, the three of them now carrying the extra loads of their dead companions.

They ought to have fed them much more. Instead, all that happened was that the men grew tired faster from pulling the sleds, especially at this elevation.

They now began to carry out systematic measurements of the snow temperature down to several metres' depth, so as not to lose morale. Someone might be able to draw conclusions from the results: about the mean annual temperature here, about the conditions in the group. Whereas they measured about twenty-five degrees on the surface, the temperature fell to thirty even at the depth of an average grave.

When the time came to sleep, Wegener would stand outside the tent as his comrades readied themselves for the night inside. He tried to coax regularities out of the sky, announcing one of the sudden changes of weather, but every rule he found applied only to the moment in which he made it. In the end, he simply watched the gradual sinking of the sun until it had settled at its night level, close above the horizon.

It was incomprehensible to him where his pictures of Else had gone. He missed them both in equal part, the images and Else herself.

Then there was new strength, from wherever it came. A rest day strengthened Lady and she was able to bear her leg of twenty-two kilometres the next day with no sign of weakness. The horses now received double rations, ten pounds of hay each, plus four to six pounds of concentrated feed. They couldn't stomach more without getting diarrhoea.

Some of their feed pellets were therefore used as human provisions. The men ate them without batting an eyelid. Where they had once ended each meal still hungry, they now almost burst. They ate in the knowledge that every gram eaten would not have to be carried the next day.

They took their bearings by the sun; the compass deviation was too great here in the north, apart from which its alcoholic fluid was frozen anew every morning.

Koch designed a small azimuth table, with the aid of which they set the direction for the next half hour using the shadows of their ski poles during every five-minute break in their march. At night Wegener dreamt of the slim shadow revolving around the pole, their only signpost, gradually at first and then ever faster.

The cold was tremendous.

The red horse broke down at the beginning of June. Vigfus and Larsen unharnessed him and reined themselves to his sled. The horse trudged alongside them, unimpressed.

155

Grauni was still in possession of his normal vigour, but the more baggage he took on, the less likely it became that he'd make it through. Even now, he was doing the lion's share of the work.

Wegener's tobacco rations were also reaching their end.

The good news: the barometer had been rising since their midday break. Elsewhere, such news would have caused merely pleasure over an impending weather improvement. For them, however, it held a sweeter message. As barely anything would change about the weather—twenty or thirty degrees below freezing, twelve-metre winds, snowdrifts, not exactly what one called an idyllic summer, but at least stable—the rising air pressure could only mean they were walking downhill.

They had crawled across the ice panzer's back. The news sent them all into a rapture of relief, Vigfus throwing snow in the air, a cold firework display. Even Gloë leapt around them and barked with joy.

When they set out, Koch raised a laugh when he referred to the absolutely flat surface ahead of them as the western slope. All they had to do was slide down it. The snow did in fact grow softer. On one of their rest days for the sake of the animals, Koch remembered that horses back home were given wide shoes for marches on the moors. They now improvised something similar for Grauni and the red horse. Lady had not made it any further after one of their rest stops.

Wegener smoked his last pipe.

He had taken wise precautions for the possibility of a very last one, collecting the unburnt remains of the pipes he had smoked since they set off. Such long distances to the next tobacconist made a thrifty man of him.

To their regret, the barometer fell again, meaning they were still going uphill even though the surface of the snow looked absolutely level.

On leaving the tent one morning in mid-June, Wegener spotted a white rainbow. Must everything here be white, the land, the animals in their winter coats, their faces in the driving snow? That evening he shot the red horse; there was no food left for him. Gloë, having eyed the horse for some time with an apparently hungry look, rejoiced.

The next morning they dug a pit to measure the temperature of the firm layers. Up to a depth of three metres, it grew colder, then below that the temperature gradually rose again. What might that mean? Wegener was reminded of his discoveries of layer boundaries in the atmosphere. Larsen wanted to move on but Wegener commanded silence. He wished he could go on digging for ever.

They worked their way down to seven metres below ground. Koch's feet were so cold that he performed little dances at the bottom. From the edge of the hole, it looked like a baroque *danse macabre*. The measurements brought no further surprises.

They were now pulling the entirety of their baggage, along with Grauni, and still gaining altitude, now at 2,937 metres above sea level. It would have been easier if they hadn't previously persuaded themselves they were going downhill. Sometimes the wind came from the side and then they set sails and Grauni ran like a sailor. It was a joy to see him like that. The sled tipped over several times, however.

Grauni's left eye became stricken; he was probably snow blind. The changing colours of the pus presented them with new mysteries every morning. If only he'd hold out. He had barely anything to pull by now, as they all helped out. Even the wind pushed steadily.

Gloë too suffered from snow blindness. They had to keep a constant eye out during the day so as not to lose him. In the evenings he ran zigzags between the sled and the tent, making them sorry for him. Wegener covered the dog's eyes with his hand at night to protect them from the cold breeze sweeping the tent. How chapped his skin had grown.

At the end of June the snow became harder and they were able to liberate Grauni from his shoes, which brought him temporary relief. Soon, though, the effect wore off and the grey horse could barely summon the strength to lug himself along. By the afternoon he was close to exhaustion, and so they gave up and pitched their tent without completing the planned leg.

A further rest day was necessary to delay Grauni's collapse. The next day, they managed a pleasing twenty-five kilometres again. In the end, though, Grauni simply threw himself down on the snow and was not to be persuaded to stand up again. They had to set up the tent.

At every stop they left behind items of baggage that seemed expendable. How many things suddenly seemed expendable.

The following day, Grauni walked behind the sled, his reins tied to the back struts. Sometimes he cast himself to the ground without notice, like an anchor that stopped their ship mid-motion. It was usually Wegener who then went to the horse, simply because he was walking closest to him. He spoke words of encouragement, which sometimes helped and sometimes didn't; there was no pattern to be established.

When words didn't help they simply determined their position for a while, took the sun's height, measured the sky's brightness at the zenith. In this manner, the question of breaks, which had previously given cause for dispute, was regulated by Grauni. At some point he was ready to set off again and they'd move on.

It was only another hundred kilometres to the depot. They would find it, with God's help.

They invented a new form of forward motion. Vigfus and Larsen loaded Grauni onto the sled and tied him down firmly, then they pulled him together. It was only a trial, yet with a stronger wind at their backs it might become an actual possibility in an emergency. There was not enough wind that day, and so they unleashed their companion after a few kilometres. Gloë had danced barking around the sled the whole stretch, out of jealousy or confusion over this role reversal.

That day, Grauni managed the rest of the leg without protest, seeming relieved indeed to be back on his feet.

If only he held out a little longer, they could reach the emergency depot in three days' march. The feed would probably last that long if they helped out with bread, peasemeal and meat chocolate from their own provisions.

In the meantime, they had grown accustomed to taking a three-hour break with the tent after a leg of around seventeen kilometres and then continuing during the second half of the night. Sometimes they also agreed, after some dispute between Wegener and Koch, to pitch the tent definitively at the end of the morning's leg and only to set out anew at the beginning of the night. In the past few days they had needed slightly over twenty-four hours to manage the day's leg, so that they set out later and later. At one point Koch calculated a longitude, according to which they were only sixty-three kilometres away from the depot. Yet there was not a trace of land and Wegener still measured a sea level of almost 2,200 metres. How did the two tally?

They were not to let such questions confuse them. And when Wegener stood outside the tent in the evenings he knew too that he must not risk his good understanding with Koch over their differences. He tended to do so, at times.

Wherever they might be exactly, without Grauni they would no doubt have covered the remaining distance to the depot in a day's march.

The majority of their conversations now revolved around the question of whether their longitude calculations were correct. Over and over, they made error estimations, measured anew, corrected one another. Once one began to consider what might be wrong, one soon got into a devil of a muddle. Wegener considered a number of times, in fact, whether a character like the devil might not take great pleasure in this world. He had previously thought of hell, in conformance with tradition, as a hot, constricted, dark place. The frost, the boundlessness, the dazzling brightness shook that image. Whereby the nocturnal cold meanwhile gained a surprising opponent—on some afternoons, the sun now heated their tent so much that it came frighteningly close to the occidental idea of Purgatory. Could nature never exercise moderation here?

Then new snow again, no wind. The snow stuck so fast to blades and soles that the sled could only be dragged along with great effort. They did not dare harness Grauni to it. Although he'd rested on the past few days and was visibly recovered, they had only scant food for two days, and that only if they scratched together all the sennegrass meant for their boots, all the bread from their provisions and whatever else he might want. So they could not put any further pressure on him until the depot.

They got no further than twenty-one kilometres that day.

When they set out again at midnight, it was the first of July. They exchanged glances and vowed by handshake to get as far that day as possible, in all circumstances. A look back at Gloë, a whistle, then off they went.

They covered forty kilometres, half of them with Grauni on the sled, travelling almost without pause.

When Koch measured the altitude they had only come 200 metres lower over all the distance, which did not indicate they had reached the steeper section near the west coast. Wordlessly, Wegener took the instruments out of his hands and measured for himself, with identical results.

They gathered together and took counsel. Gloë lay down in their midst, where he was best protected from the wind. They made assumptions and cast them aside, in the end agreeing on an estimate of forty kilometres remaining to the edge, whereas their map showed it ought only to be twelve.

The signs of land multiplied, at least. The ice grew uneven and they came across the waves they remembered from the eastern strand, now more and more frequent. How far behind them that lay. Koch spotted an irregular structure on the horizon, which they made out in great excitement to be snow-covered coastal fells, and Vigfus was back to throwing snow in the air.

As they continued, however, it emerged that their anticipation had been premature. The mountains proved to change their shape as they approached. The further they went, the clearer it became that the changes had nothing to do with their position. They were clouds.

Wegener suggested assuming until proof to the contrary that they were wave clouds, a sure sign of ground elevations. No one contradicted him.

How reliably the body reacted to depression with exhaustion and inertia. The only drive resulting from a disappointment may have been increased appetite to counter the annoyance. That was how they felt, at any rate. They had to postpone their hunger until they reached the depot, however, at an uncertain date.

They now took breaks whenever it suited them. When it was not Grauni who demanded them it was often Koch, whom Wegener accused in many words of not being genuinely exhausted but only wanting to spare himself; indeed he would soon spare them all to death. Wegener would have liked to go on walking until the expedition came to an end. Koch did not usually reply, merely looking at him, and sometimes Wegener went to him later and apologized with a nod.

At places where they wanted to stay for several hours, they first dug a makeshift stable into the firn to protect Grauni from the wind. Once, Larsen hit solid ice as he dug and threw the spade in the air for joy. The firn must have melted there last summer. They vied to interpret this as a sign they were approaching the coast.

The next day's march went downhill with jubilation, the entire expedition now on skis apart from Grauni, who lay on the sled. They had begun to put Gloë with him to spare him his jealousy.

They came across a series of small crevasses and across stretches where solid ice was covered by a thin layer of snow or even unadorned. Ahead of them a long chain of hills. Koch thought he recognized the peak where he had put down the emergency depot the previous year. After that it would only be a good twenty kilometres, perhaps thirty. They could only hope their perception conformed to reality. All measuring led to such varying results that they ended up arguing on every occasion, and soon decided to use the time they'd spend disputing to make progress. They had only one last batch of feed for Grauni.

A long half-day's journey later, they had still not reached the hills but they had come to a small river. On the last stretch, Koch and Larsen had joined Grauni on the sled and sped down the slopes at a rapid pace, while Wegener and Vigfus chased them on skis as fast as they could.

They reached the water almost simultaneously, and the mere sound of its babbling enchanted them—for the first time in months, the mercury was above freezing point.

Koch jokingly asked who had called a plumber to install running water out there. They now had plenty to drink. They were too weak to wash but they squatted down close together on the bank, six thirsty creatures—Larsen, Vigfus, Koch, Grauni, Wegener, Gloë—and drank as though they had no other destination.

Then they lay on the ground, each where he found himself, and it was a while before Vigfus was the first to get up to seek a possible crossing point. Yet even after some searching upstream and down, the river proved impassable.

So they camped on the ice intending to wait for midnight, in the hope that the meltwater might withdraw far enough for them to ford. They were too excited to sleep; the camera came back to life in the warmth and they took huge amounts of photographs.

They were able to cross without major effort during the night. The sled served as a bridge across the remaining water and they pulled Grauni through. Halfway, however, he fell and reached the opposite bank soaked to the skin. Wegener went on ahead with him so he wouldn't get too cold, while the others loaded the sled.

Wegener walked closely ahead of Grauni, pulling him along to keep him moving. He thought he could feel the horse trembling through the rope. Sometimes he stopped for a moment and looked Grauni in the eye but it barely seemed as though he looked back. His eyeballs were clouded, the pupils themselves black and empty.

Their walk harboured all the unpleasant surprises of the ridge zone they had encountered on the eastern coast: crevasses, streams, bulbs of melted ice, noon holes in the firn, everything that gladdened a glaciologist's heart but made sledging almost impossible.

Wegener rested at an overhanging rock until the others caught up, with the sled. They left Grauni there to spare him unnecessary torment on the difficult territory, and continued to the depot without baggage.

On the last stretch, they saw stones in their path. They touched the rocks incredulously—it really was no longer ice, it was all land they were walking over here, real land after all the snow and snow and snow.

And though it was nothing but a moraine landscape that more cossetted eyes would have considered dreary, for them it was sheer paradise. Between the pebbles huddled thin flowers, pale pink, pale blue and white. Bees chased one another through the clear air, a single bird called. Wegener rubbed his eyes, only then noticing he was still wearing gloves, for which it had now grown far too warm.

All the sights there were to see! The colours of the stones, grey and brown and grey-brown, plus the many shadows, the shapes, the unshakeable hardness of the ground. It was a marvellous riot for their eyes.

In the midst of this Elysium waited the depot. It was very easy to find, marked by three poles rising high into the sky as Koch had so often described.

Then they squatted down among the crates and ate in silence from the delicacies within, tinned fish, gooseberries in jars, cold beans, Gloë too getting his share, and Koch looked proudly from one to the next as though he had prepared it all himself and they were now his guests.

There was a cigar for each of the men afterwards. As they puffed away, the smoke going to their heads somewhat, they held a powwow. Koch and Vigfus were to go ahead in the hope of encountering Eskimos, while Larsen and Wegener would return to Grauni with all the available loaves of bread.

They found him dying, his mouth opened, his eyes wet, his neck oddly twisted. A mile away from the depot, which might have meant his rescue. After all the effort they had taken to get their comrade through in one piece.

He no longer touched the bread. Wegener had to fetch the pistol to put him out of his misery.

Exhausted, Grauni collapsed on the ground, barely losing blood from the wound as though all life had left him long ago.

Gloë circled the spectacle, barking but likewise dazed by the developments, by the many delicacies he had consumed and perhaps also a little by the prospect of a new treat, cut from the flesh perishing before his very eyes.

On the Cause of Optical Illusions during Sunsets

Rain and fog. How monotonous the sky had seemed to them up on the ice, and how they now longed for its former clarity. The ice was so poor that even a healthy horse would have had trouble crossing the leg to the depot. On the day after Grauni's death, Wegener and Larsen managed 300 metres with the sled in an hour. They could only hope Koch and Vigfus really did find people on their march ahead.-

Rocks, scree, broken ground; it was nothing but labour. As long as each of them pulled the sled in silence, it was bearable. When Larsen then came to him and they admitted how hard it was, they gave up. Where were the others? Everything was swathed in fog now; there was no point in looking for them.

The next morning, Wegener and Larsen had just packed every-thing together when they saw the advance party returning in the distance—without company. They immediately unloaded the sled, put water on to boil and laid out Koch and Vigfus' sleeping bags.

The two men were utterly exhausted. They had made it all the way to the Laxe fjord. Traces of Eskimos, tent rings and other remains, but not a living soul. They had deposited a letter to the colony board. With God's blessings it would be found in the next few days.

Otherwise they'd have to walk to the colony, which would take almost a week, if they managed somehow to cross the rivers along the way. They'd have to carry everything they wanted to take with them without the aid of the sled, without a horse. Koch and

Vigfus were not yet capable of walking again, so they re-pitched the tent. While the two of them slept, Larsen went in search of flammable material and Wegener sat on a rock and tried to envisage possible solutions to their fate. Whenever he came to a bad end, he quickly withdrew his thoughts like a snail its feelers, and headed in a different direction. They might well make it to the fjord. And then? How were they to get across it? They'd have to build a raft like on Wegener's way to Pustevig years before but, unlike then, they had no material to do so.

They struck camp the following afternoon, piling all their baggage in one place. Only standing together like that did it occur to Wegener what a small group they'd become, without the horses. The mountain of their burden seemed all the greater. They sat around the baggage in a circle and hoped for an idea, a plan for how to proceed. No one said a word, Gloë running to and fro between them, presumably thinking it a new game. He too missed Grauni.

Every choice might prove wrong, as ever.

Koch moved the sled aside first of all, to make the pile smaller. Then he sat back down on his stone.

After a while, Wegener shook his head and dragged the sled back. Larsen asked him what he was doing. Had Wegener not noticed the day before that their vehicle could not be pulled over stones? Then they'd just have to carry the sled, Wegener responded. No reply from Larsen, who looked as though he wished he could set off alone. Vigfus suggested leaving the cooking utensils, as the provisions from the small depot wouldn't last long either way. That made sense to everyone. They set aside the pots and pans but it did nothing to reduce the size of the pile.

Larsen asked whether they couldn't fetch the documents and photographs later. Wegener merely stared at him and Larsen said no more.

Silence for a while and then Koch suggested they should reduce their clothing once more. It turned out they all possessed nothing but what they were wearing. In the end it was Wegener who decided they would do without sleeping bags. Even so, they still had 200 pounds to carry in all. When they distributed the load for a trial run, it emerged that there was no room left for the tent either.

Vigfus took the sled, a weight of seventy-five pounds. Each of the others got a load of forty to fifty pounds, made just as crushing by the uncomfortable way it was carried. Shouldering a crate, Wegener had only one thought in his mind on taking the first steps: how very much he had had enough of the wanderer's life. He longed for an ordered way of life, a fixed place. He was simply tired of travelling, terribly tired of it.

It began to snow before noon, continuing until the next morning. They had to cross another stream, the ice-grey water leaping past them hastily. Wegener laid the sled against the far bank as a bridge and balanced across the swaying gangplank. They wanted to pull the baggage across on a rope. First came the crate with the photographic plates, films, journals and diaries, their greatest treasure.

While the others placed the load on the bridge, Wegener stood alone on the other side of the water, holding the rope. Then he began to pull, carefully. When the crate was halfway across, Wegener's foot caught in a loop in the rope. As he freed himself his freight slid to the edge of the bridge, slithered, tipped and finally, as Wegener watched incapable of motion, plunged into the water.

The rapid stream carried it in a matter of moments to a nearby lake, where it would have sunk had Vigfus not instantly torn off his clothes and braved a jump into the ice-cold water. The lid opened, however, the whole crate filled up, and the tide stole away the black ball thermometer, its long wooden box soon visible floating far out on the water. They would measure no more temperatures now.

Fortunately, the sun had come out again by this point. The other three rubbed Vigfus down with the large sled sail, which they had brought along as a signal flag. They spent the rest of the day drying everything on the stones of the bank, the books, the documents and Vigfus too, who only stopped shivering a good hour later.

A series of photographic plates that Wegener spread out to dry showed Gloë on their arrival in Danmarkshavn, playing with abandon in the driving snow for the sheer joy of feeling land beneath his feet. Wegener had pursued him with the camera for a whole hour. How recklessly he had photographed back then, as though they wouldn't have to carry everything on their backs. How wildly Gloë had chased every single flake. How long ago all that was.

Wegener took one of the negatives and held it up against the light. This one too showed Gloë as a pale patch, as white as all the other animals they had come across here. He ought, Wegener considered, to be classified as a new species, a snow dog, the first and last example of his kind. Dark snowflakes contrasted with his white fur, Gloë batting at them with his alabaster paws but not hitting a single one. The rest of the picture was entirely black. Gloë danced through a night far more impenetrable than any they had seen in months.

They filled their bottles with water and continued towards the Laxe fjord. Even their rests barely reduced the weight on their backs, simply because they had barely anything left to eat that might be taken away by a meal. Gloë refused to believe they were setting out after a break without Wegener throwing a crust of bread for him or putting down his dish to lick, and he leapt yowling around his legs. They had to hope he would catch himself a ferret somewhere.

Once, they startled an auk, which came fluttering from between rocks. They immediately threw down their baggage and chased after the bird, stumbling, jumping, calling and barking, finally succeeding in encircling it. It must have been injured or it would have flown away; they had no other explanation for what it was doing all alone, away from its colony. It had just as little business out here as they did. Step by step, they cornered the auk. Wegener ahead, vowing to let Gloë have his share if the hunt went well. Its wings beating in agitation, the bird tried to take off but could not get high enough, plunging at Wegener, its bright beak, its sad eyes, the plump body at which Wegener tried to snatch. A collision, scratches at his face, Wegener started back in fear and then the bird was past him and escaped.

It had been a mistake after all, Wegener thought on the way back to their baggage, to leave the pistol at the depot.

His cheek stung where the beak had grazed him. Then that too faded.

Wegener could not have said how the land looked through which they passed in the next hours. He looked only at the ground ahead of him, at some stone on which his next step might find a hold. The others presumably did the same, sometimes at any rate growing so distant from each other in all the scree that they were close to losing sight of one another. Four lonely souls with no cohesion. Had Gloë not barked them together from time to time, they would have lost one another without as much as noticing. It was impossible to reach the fjord this way.

In the end, though, they came across a path, perhaps trodden by reindeer hunters. It brought immeasurable relief, for walking and for their peace of mind. Thus, they reached the northern bank of the Laxe fjord two days after leaving the depot. They cast down

170

their baggage, each of them lying on the ground next to his own pile and staying put. After a while Wegener closed his eyes so as not to stare all the time at the cold, empty sky. In his mind it was a grassy field where he lay resting, with Else by his side; it was that moment on the dyke again when she had taken his hand. He felt at the ground a little, first with one hand and then with the other, but nowhere did he find her; he called something and at last opened his eyes. Larsen was leaning over him, looking concerned. Wegener sat up. Vigfus brought him water.

Koch had meanwhile set off for the place where he and Vigfus had previously deposited the letter. Unfortunately, the envelope was untouched. They had to rely on themselves.

They began building a raft, in silence. The fjord was perhaps twenty metres wide at this spot, but its water stood perfectly calm, grey and motionless, only the wind casting a shiver on the surface from time to time.

Using the sled as a framework, they attempted to make it floatable with the aid of the covers of their sleeping bags brought along in wise foresight, the sled sail and a few empty petroleum canisters. Wegener took one last reading from the barometer and hypsometer. They all suffered severely from the midges comporting themselves with abandon here at sea level. It was evening before they launched their vessel.

Packed close together, they took seats in the middle of the raft, clinging to one another, between them the baggage and the yowling dog. Larsen paddled them out onto the water with a blade broken from the sled. And that was how they crossed the Laxe fjord at midnight between the 11th and 12th of July.

Their provisions were too scant for long breaks, so they set out immediately on the other side. Now, though, they possessed the certainty of having survived the greater danger, and they had no doubt that they would reach the bank opposite the colony in a few days' march, no matter how onerous the journey might be. From there, they would somehow manage to attract attention.

They walked fifty minutes and then rested ten minutes, day and night. Once they had made four hours' progress in this manner they boiled water, which was a long and complicated procedure without a stove. As they reached the basin dividing the southern part of the land from the interior, rain arrived. In a minimum of time, the fells they were to cross were swathed in fog. Using a pile of dry willow branches and heather collected before the rain, they cooked their last pemmican and shared a can of milk and the four remaining pieces of tack.

Then the ascent. It was more complicated than expected. Instead of a high plateau, a mountainous system of valleys and peaks led them up and downhill, the peaks causing them some trouble. It was now pouring with rain. Now and then they lay down beneath a stone offering protection from the weather, but they were so wet that the cold soon drove them onwards. Without the sun, it was hard to maintain their direction. Especially as the map proved unreliable, the mountains as charted there very misleading. Seeing the arm of another fjord ahead of them, they had no option but to climb down to its banks to identify it by its shape on the map. They failed to do so, however. The fjord was not on the map.

For a while they followed the coast, which had a pronounced wealth of embayments. The dear Lord knew where they were; they had not an inkling. At last Koch recognized a 500-metre peak included on the map, with steep slopes leading down to the sea. They proved impassable.

They would have to cross it, despite the fog. Without taking a prior rest, they set about the ascent but it soon emerged that their strength would not suffice.

Vigfus' face was growing increasingly pale, which Wegener initially wanted to blame on the fog until Vigfus said he could go no further. He was close to fainting, he told them.

And so they stopped at half the height, in an exposed position, which was fine by all of them. Having fortified themselves with camphor drops, they managed with some effort to warm a little water, to which they added the remaining condensed milk. It was here, halfway between earth and sky, that they consumed the last of their provisions. The firewood was so wet that preparing the meal bought them an hour's rest. None of them felt any desire to hurry. Only the cold drove them on.

The rain had meanwhile turned to snow. They used every overhanging rock to recover and made so little progress between them that they sometimes rested twice beneath the same rock.

At last Koch decided they should build themselves a shelter to await better weather. They sat in a line below an overhanging wall of rock; from time to time someone got up to fetch another stone. In this way, they erected a half-metre parapet over the course of the evening, behind which, once it was sealed with heather and covered with the sail, all four of them could lie in severely hunched positions.

They lay there in their sopping clothes from midnight of the 13th to the 14th of July for the rest of the night, the following day and the whole next night, while outside it snowed and snowed.

The others slept a great deal in that time, while Wegener could not sleep for the cold, even though Gloë lay on top of him and warmed him a little. Food would have provided distraction. Vigfus sang quietly with hunger. Koch, who otherwise needed so little, asked from behind closed eyes whether he might have a veal cutlet with asparagus.

Wegener simply lay there and looked out at the series of snowflakes falling, according to the angle of the light, either dark before a pale sky or pale before dark. He did not ask himself what they were doing there, how they came to be lying there and where they ought to go from there, but he'd have liked to do so, had he been strong enough. Sometimes Gloë trembled in his sleep and whined. Wegener did not allow himself to think of what feasts his dog might be dreaming of, what hunts and what prey. He spent hours stroking the dog's fur.

Only by his own dreams could he tell he must be drifting off for moments himself. Wild visions in which he walked along the flat shore of an ocean, his eyes fixed on the edge of a grey sea. He knew that his happiness lay on the other side of the water, consisting in this case of a carousel rising above the horizon from time to time, a children's carousel as seen at fairgrounds, turning and turning in the distance, and Wegener saw that all the black and white horses, lions and coaches would never catch up on one another. Waking, he wondered whether he'd ever dreamt in colour and when that might have been, and he couldn't remember with the best will in the world.

On the morning of the 15th of July, the snowfall came to an end. The heavens too had at last run out of provisions. The fog parted now and then and for moments they could make out the new fjord below them—cold and black and smooth in its ragged picture frame of cloud. They decided to set off. Wegener considered singing a hiking song but could not think of one.

It might have been thirty metres they had climbed from their hut, perhaps twenty, perhaps more, when one after the other gave up. Koch had to sit down and even then could not fight off his weakness. Wegener gave him camphor drops but Koch could no longer see the spoon, so Wegener had to dribble them into his mouth. Koch stared at him but Wegener was not sure he recognized him.

He stayed on the grass next to Koch and held his hand, the other still clutching the spoon. If Wegener didn't look he had no idea which side was holding the spoon and which side Koch's cold fingers.

Horror at realizing they had come to the end of their strength. It entered his consciousness with merciless patience, like driving snow through the gaps in a tent.

It was a mild form of horror. He had no energy for anything more.

The fjord now lay clear before them; they might have dived into it.

Where were they to find the strength to carry on? Wegener wished for the carousel he had dreamt of. He would be sitting in one of the coaches and it would take him wherever he wished. When he closed his eyes he saw the horses again, rocking back and forth as they turned in their circle. They were small horses, like the ones they'd had with them once that now lay scattered across the land, covered over by snow. He heard the music of the carousel quite clearly now.

They were incapable of going on. This, then, was the tribute for the long rest they had hoped would strengthen them. Koch had meanwhile fallen onto his side; Wegener spotted Vigfus and Larsen some distance away, they too sprawled along the rocky ground. He seemed to be the least affected, heaven knew why. Looking at his comrades lying motionless, everything inside him was appalled. His existence cried mutiny, his very life perhaps. Or perhaps only his lack of recognition. Or his fear. What would his father have done? Prayed? And if he did the same? It didn't matter now. How would the hero Nansen have acted in his place? Did Vladimir Köppen know what to do in such a situation? How had Mylius-Erichsen felt at this moment in his life? Would Suess be strong enough to master such a challenge? The frost giants on their ship with the strange name—had they ever been in such an emergency? The Kaiser? Else? Or Kurt and his other siblings, might they have been able to help?

Else would surely have touched his arm and looked at him, as was her way, through her eyelashes with her head imperceptibly cocked, so that one never knew whether she was looking from below or the side. His brothers and sister would at least have been able to warm him. And his mother? All at once Wegener saw them all standing around him, his father, Mylius-Erichsen, more than ever resembling a troll, the frost giants, blurred by the fog but by his side. He swallowed. It did him good to know they were close by. He had companions.

The outrage that now rose within him. Were they to perish here like wild animals, at the end of such a long and dangerous journey? Not two miles away from the colony? In the month of July? Was there even a trace of sense in it? Wegener could see his nebulous companions were not agreed with this exit either, neither the living nor the dead. How enraged they now looked. Else had clenched her little fists. When the crowd of his siblings saw that they did likewise. Some of the frost giants stamped their feet. And Suess frowned as angrily as on his bronze plaque in the Senckenberg Museum. Wegener could not hear it but he could read from his companions' lips that they were calling something. Don't give up. You want to stay alive. He was not certain they were right but he decided to believe them.

And thus his entire mind revolted against the prospect that this should be his last hour and his last resting place.

He led his comrades the few steps back to their shelter, where they slaughtered Gloë. They had not eaten for thirty-seven hours. It was not easy to apply the knife. Gloë's uncomprehending look as the blade pierced his throat. It was the only hope left to them.

They had boiled almost half of his flesh and were portioning it up when Wegener spotted a sailing boat on the fjord below them. The distance was quite great and he would have taken it for an ice floe, had its rapid motion not caught his eye.

One look through the telescope taught them it really was a boat, and they immediately began to attract its attention by calling and waving the sail. To their joy, the boat turned and headed towards them. Wegener helped Koch onto his feet and then the two of them instantly began their descent, not waiting for the shared meal. Each of them only took along a cup full of the hot, sinewy meat, stuffing it into their mouths as they climbed down. Soon they saw Vigfus and Larsen above them, following fast behind them.

They were all seized by a powerful tension, the same men who had barely been able to lift their legs now leaping from stone to stone towards their rescuers. Like animals that belonged here in this world of rock, scree and abyss.

Not until they reached the Eskimos, who came climbing towards them up the steep slope, did calm come over Wegener. How slowly their contours grew clearer, the outlines of their hoods, the faces, in the end their narrow eyes, pleased at the meeting yet presumably not knowing who they were encountering here on the mountainside.

Their rescuer proved to be Pastor Chemnitz from Upernivik, the last to come panting up. He had been travelling the country to gather souls for confirmation. He immediately offered to take them to Pröven, and when he heard what a state they were in he had a breakfast made for them of black bread, auk eggs and coffee. The

Eskimos gave them their hooded coats and generously offered tobacco, and the rescued men were so overwhelmed by the sudden reversal of their fortunes that they were barely capable of following the amiable pastor's conversation.

Three hours later, their ship arrived in Pröven harbour with its flag raised and alarmed the entire colony. The expedition had been expected to arrive weeks ago. The portly colony chairman welcomed them on the jetty, leaping aboard and almost smothering them with his greetings. One after another, they climbed cautiously on land, as if after a long, long crossing. And not until Wegener, the last to leave the ship, looked back one last time out of habit, did he remember that their dog was no longer with them.

Proliferation of Sound

On his return, he married Else. That was all he'd been waiting for. In August 1913, she had gone to Zechlinerhütte to be with her fiancé's parents when the first post ship brought the news of whether the crossing had been a success. It was Else who accepted the telegram and read it aloud to the Wegeners. His mother's quiet joy, his father's silence. And Else herself? Not until that night, in his childhood bedroom in the attic, did the tears come to her eyes and not stop flowing. Her long conversations with his pillow, in which she told him everything. And he? Had remained silent, as so often.

The image of his unspeaking mother accompanied Else into her sleep. Anna Wegener had suffered a stroke during her son's absence and was now half lamed. When Else read the telegram from Copenhagen, her mouth had smiled on one side, happy and light, while the other side hung down unaffected.

Soon after that, Wegener himself finally arrived in Zechlinerhütte. He had been on the way to a banquet held in honour of the expedition participants by the Danish interior minister when he received the news of his mother's stroke. He excused himself from the meal; they would have to send the medal on after him. It was late at night by the time he arrived in Berlin. Else welcomed him as warmly as possible in view of the circumstances. How often he had imagined this meeting, and now he almost hastened past her to his mother.

179

She raised her head as he came in. A sign of recognition, at least. His father watching over her. Then they sat around the bed and looked at his mother's hands, resting motionless on the flowered counterpane.

The next morning, Wegener walked with Else to the neighbouring village to publish the banns. They found the registrar in his potato field. He leant on his rake and asked whether they could prove they hadn't married any other person during their long separation. Else looked over at her fiancé; she had her papers with her but Wegener had thought of all kinds of things in Pröven, except for having such a thing officially confirmed. The registrar pushed his hat to the back of his neck and said, 'That you were in Greenland, Doctor, that I read in the newspaper. And that you wouldn't go marrying an Eskimo girl when you've got such a pretty bride waiting for you, that I'm willing to believe.' Wegener refrained from commenting that there had hardly been a ready supply of Eskimo girls where he'd been. The registrar continued that he did not need to read them any instructions on love and loyalty, they'd know all that already after such a long time apart. They were man and wife by noon.

They moved into a small, cheap flat on Biegenstrasse, at the foot of Marburg's upper town. Else climbed the hill every morning to the market, bought cabbage from the farmer's wives, understood not a word of what they called after her in amusement, and secretly admired their brightly embroidered black dresses.

During her time in Oslo, Else had boarded with a family of hatmakers and had learnt the trade almost in passing. She had been there in the summer when the fashionable ladies were wearing wagon wheels, flat hats of a monstrous diameter, so every deft hand was a welcome addition to the family. Along with their enormous head coverings, the customers wore hobble skirts so tightly cut they could barely make it into the shop. How awk-wardly the women had turned in front of the small mirror, Else said after dinner; she had always stood nearby in case one of them lost her balance. They had added additional steps at Oslo station that year to help the ladies disembark from the trains.

All the things he'd missed. Wegener was glad to have been out of the world for that time.

Then, said Else, they had read about the suffragettes smash-ing London's shop windows. 'To begin with I thought it was a Norwegian word I simply didn't understand. The papers were full of them. Angry women, cigarette-smoking women, hatless women. Concerned glances were exchanged at the hatmaker's breakfast table. No one could imagine that fashion would make it all the way to Oslo, but we had to be prepared for anything. The master decided to make his hats a little more expansive and expensive from then on so as to put some money aside.'

Else said it hadn't been quite clear to her to begin with what the suffragettes were fighting for or against. It was about equal rights and suffrage; they were as if intoxicated, but it was obviously more than that. In the end one of them threw herself in front of the English king's horse, which had killed the both of them.

'The king?' Wegener asked. He really had been cut off from the world.

'No,' said Else, 'the horse.' She took a drag on her cigarette. 'And the woman.'

Else smoked now too. As a trial, as she called it. When they sat in their tiny salon in the evenings, he with his pipe, she with her small cigarette holder, the air was soon as thick as in a seedy back room.

If they were honest, the whole flat looked like a back room. Laundry dried by the kitchen window. Their shared bed was

181

walled in by piles of Wegener's books, a yellowed polar-bear pelt hanging on the opposite wall. What they called a salon was in truth not a salon but the hallway. The place was too constricted. As often as possible, Wegener therefore vanished to the institute library above the Lahn River, while Else withdrew with her needlework.

She was nurturing a plan to earn a little on the side as a milliner, for which the skills learnt abroad would come in handy. Wegener objected to begin with, but then he admitted it might help to improve their slim marital budget somewhat. Along with their bedroom, the tiny flat on Biegenstrasse boasted a small box room that the plump landlady insisted on calling the 'nursery'. Else began to set up a small workshop in there. Her parents-in-law had given her a sewing box as a wedding present, and Wegener purchased the first lengths of fabric and a selection of ostrich feathers and veils out of his savings. He had nailed a holder to the wall above her little desk for the two dozen reels of thread. Now the spools glowed in all hues and Else now and then rearranged them, every time producing a brand-new picture.

Despite their limited possibilities, they managed to make their life rich in variety. At weekends they skated on the frozen river or stomped through the snow up to Amöneburg Castle. Sometimes they took the train to the Sauerland and skied cross-country. How his memory returned with the bodily motions. When they picked up speed with fast thrusts of their poles he thought of the hopeful outset of the Greenland crossing. As soon as Else grew slower alongside him, however, and the gliding gave way to an effortful shuffle, Wegener sensed once again the exhaustion at the end of the journey, the feeling of being abandoned and lost.

In March 1914, Wegener was drafted for a military exercise. Crammed onto crowded benches, the officer cadets studied the art of ruse de guerre. Clausewitz wrote that battle was incalculable. Until the opponent was defeated, one could be defeated oneself. Wegener learnt that war was a question of determination. If no one knew how determined the opponent was, the trick was to appear as determined as possible. That made sense to him.

After their lessons they were made to run across harvested potato fields for hours, stand mutely in a column by the edge of a forest, duck motionless in the protection of a rampart. When the unit returned to base deaf from shooting, each man sat perched on the edge of his field bed, chin resting on his hands. His combatants' faces were pale beneath the dirt.

When he returned home some weeks later there was a new sign on the gate: Else Wegener. Hat fashion and head décor en détail—white letters on an oxblood background. She had installed it with her own hands.

To begin with, the customers came mainly to have pennants in the national colours sewn onto their caps and lapels—not really Else's profession, and for only two pfennigs it seemed to Wegener such an un-lucrative business that he advised her to give it up. But it was done so quickly that the clients' patriotic passion soon began to turn a profit. A few weeks after opening her trade, Else could pay the first instalment for a used sewing machine, a silver-coloured Opel, a foldaway model with a vibrating shuttle.

Then the newspaper boys began to shout louder, the headlines grew shorter, and young men were gathered up on the streets. The whalers' spoils no longer went to make soap, but nitro-glycerine.

Wegener too received his draft notice. Else accompanied him to the station. It was August; only on seeing the other soldiers did Wegener button his uniform jacket. Then he kissed Else's forehead and stroked her belly. She was not allowed onto the platform.

When he turned around to her as he embarked, she was still standing there at the barrier. Beneath her pale summer hat, she looked like a small fat child. She was nine-months pregnant.

The train took them via Kassel to Apolda, where his regiment came together, and then it was on to Belgium. The slate-roofed churches, the low horizon. The forces' postal service was not yet working, so quickly did they advance. A shot straight through the lower arm in his first battle, his thumb unfortunately remaining stiff. The look on the doctor's face when Wegener asked to be allowed to lie on the edge in the military hospital; his comrades' moans kept him from sleeping. He was put in the care of a nun from the Bergisches Land and spent long nights imagining what colour her hair might be beneath her wimple.

He found his regiment again outside Reims. The cathedral, the chalky ground into which they dug, man-deep. At the foot of the trench, they hollowed out niches facing the enemy. They lay down in them when the first grenades hit at three in the afternoon. Wegener pressed his hands to his ears. After the end of the battle, nothing but an unclaimed helmet had been hit—but a severe moral impression had been made. The Red Cross flag still flew from the bell tower.

Wegener did not immediately manage to develop a passion for the war. He put it down to being less susceptible to mass suggestion. Nevertheless, he made an effort to be a good soldier. They were transferred further west, where he received a card informing him his child had been born. A daughter, named Hilde. The comrades raised their glasses with him during a break in battle. One of them, a thin streak of a lad from the Pfalz called Googly for his protruding eyes, couldn't resist firing a salute into the unclouded French sky, which the enemy instantly answered with a hail of shrapnel.

Lying flat on the ground of his trench, face pressed to the inside of his elbow, Wegener recited her name, Hilde. A beautiful name.

A card with the news that Hilde had inherited his small mouth. She was slow to drink and sleeping a great deal.

Weeks in trenches ever further westwards, the scent of burning, decay and carbolic.

A card reporting that the demand for appliquéd flags was tailing off.

Another card informing him that Hilde had suffered from bad diarrhoea for several days but was now on the path back to health.

He too had diarrhoea, but that in itself was not enough for a reply.

A new card—business was now going badly. The picture was a view from Marburg Castle to the south, the prospect he had enjoyed from the window of the institute library. At the foot of the hill, Wegener thought he recognized their house. He picked up his pencil, wrote 'My dear, dear Else' on his blank field postcard, looked for words, waited, and as he went on seeking he marked the lines of his salutation deeper and deeper, until in the end the lead broke.

The road to Achiet le Petit on which they were marching, the starry sky between the leaves as cold and clear as during a polar night. The village still in deepest peace. Past several horse cadavers to a steep slope where they took up position. Day dawned gradually. A foray towards the village and the response from the hedges opposite. Hornbeam hedges mainly, also hawthorns and boxwood. The pale clouds of shrapnel at the level of the treetops, the brown clouds where the grenades hit the ground. The trees splintered all the way along. At dusk they stormed the village, whereupon the enemy artillery blasted it with fire. The descending darkness put an end to the horror. Undisturbed night on the eastern edge of the houses, where bales of straw were stacked under the open sky.

The next morning to Puisieux, under long fire. The bullets that sailed far above them caused a very pure, singing tone that resounded for a long time. The closer the bullets came to their ears, the shorter and sharper their whistle. The ricochets were quite different, coming dancing with a loud buzz that made the men instinctively look around for them. Here before Puisieux, Googly fell, awaiting the storm, his large eyes fixed on the sky.

At noon, the Eighth Company on their right switched to attack. They dropped like flies. Just as it was Wegener's company's turn to push after them, their own artillery cut in, its main achievement to date having also fired a load of shrapnel into the line of storming comrades at the end of the assault. When the gun smoke hung denser they ran forwards. When the clouds cleared again they squatted among the turnips. Into the village with hip, hip hurrah. Wherever a Frenchman showed his face in a bush, they shot him down. They were easily spotted by their red trousers. Human emotions now almost entirely subdued.

Then a shot came from a hedge and another, and all at once a blow hit Wegener in the neck, so hard he spun in a circle. He wondered why he could feel no blood, and thought a shot had merely hit his collar. He asked a comrade to check whether anything was broken, and he was astounded when the man pulled a bullet out of his neck.

In the military hospital, waiting to be transported back home, he read the Edda. 'Brothers feud as mutual enemies, sisters' sons deal death to one another. The world is in throes, misconduct runs rampant. Age of axes, age of swords, shields clashing. Time of wind, time of wolves, before the world collapses.' He could not have described the situation any better.

He received a card from Else with the news that business was picking up again. It was mainly mourning hats to be made. Wegener worried all that sewing of black fabric would be bad for her eyes.

He was back home by January. How unfamiliar the town looked from the train window. One step onto the platform, the few stairs down to the main road and across the river in the traces of the horse-drawn tram to the town. Dirty snow in the gutters, dark drawing in. At Saint Elisabeth's stood an old man, shouting to himself, shaking an enraged fist at the evening sky. Only then did Wegener understand what had changed—apart from the old man and himself, there were only women on the streets. None of them paid any attention to the dotard.

Beneath their window, Wegener gave the whistle to which they had grown accustomed. The light went on in the stairwell and Else's giant shadow darted across the hall walls. She opened the door, her child at her breast. He barely managed to embrace her.

Hilde. The child stared at him, eyes huge. As though she were looking at a stranger, thought Wegener. Her head was covered in red scabs. He would have wished his daughter to show clearer signs of joy at their first meeting. And her mother likewise.

Then he stood in the kitchen; Else had handed him the child while she went to ask the neighbours for coffee. He was not supposed to carry anything, with his injury. They had barely exchanged a word yet.

When he put the child on the settee she began to cry. When he lifted her up she didn't stop, so at last he bedded her back down in her cradle and gave her the end of his little finger to suck.

Else stopped in the doorway as she came back, looking over at him. He too stayed where he was, half-leaning over the cradle, one finger in his daughter's tiny mouth. Else looked serious, almost frightened.

After eating, Hilde screamed without pause. When she finally calmed down they pushed her cradle over into the workshop. Else turned away from him as she slipped into her nightshirt. Then they lay side by side, Wegener still in uniform. At last Else reached for his hand. He wanted to do something, so he stroked his thumb over the back of her hand, over and over.

'What's making you so dark?'

He didn't understand what she meant.

'Why didn't you write?'

His thumb interrupted its stroking. What should he reply? He had wanted to write to her, as he wanted to answer her now, but his thoughts dashed away in search of an explanation, losing themselves at ever-greater distances like a child playing in the woods. And when he realized with a shock a while later that he still hadn't responded, there could no longer be a simple answer.

In the end he noticed Else had fallen asleep next to him, and he succumbed likewise to his fatigue.

After his injury, Wegener was no longer declared fit for field and garrison service. He suffered from chronic cardiomyopathy and was considered permanently incapable of bearing even light physical exertion.

The other thing he was incapable of bearing: the memory of what the war had demanded from him. What had seemed perfectly normal in the garish light of battle now seemed, in the mild glow of his usual life, a monstrosity. How had he, a prudent middle-aged man, let himself get so carried away? He decided not to remember it any more. It was repulsive what existence in groups did to people.

Wegener was deployed to the Army Weather Service and had to travel now and then, from one weather station to the next. It took him all across Germany with a brief excursion to the Balkans, with the purpose of predicting when it was time for attack and when for defence.

He spent the majority of his days, however, in the Marburg library. He felt that nothing waited as urgently for him as science, especially now that it had become really rather cramped at home.

Gertrud was still working in the reading room and she still brought an occasional cup of forbidden fruit tea to his desk. When she made a whispered enquiry as to what he was working on, he answered just as quietly that he was in the process of pulling the ground out from beneath mankind's feet.

Gertrud looked disturbed.

He said, 'I'm sure you've seen the ice floes in the late winter, floating on the water down by the Weidenhaus weir.'

Gertrud nodded.

'We too,' Wegener continued, 'are floating no differently. What we call fixed continents are nothing but floes on a huge inner sea.'

Gertrud raised her eyebrows and took away his empty cup without further comment.

In letters to Köppen, Wegener charted maps of past epochs, traced, erased, shifted and connected, drew anew and in the end added ancient deserts, jungles and ice. When he entered the direction of long-melted glaciers, the marks of which were still engraved in the rock to that day, he saw that his jigsaw could only fit together in one way and in one place. And suddenly it became perfectly obvious why the Permo-Carboniferous Ice Age had only affected the southern hemisphere. There were marks left by gigantic glaciers on all southern landmasses and their directions fitted together precisely if one united all the continents—directly above the pole.

Wegener looked up at the library ceiling. He was triumphant. He wished he could immediately enlarge his drawings to an enormous format, as a monument to the truth. He imagined what it would be like to invite all his opponents to a lecture right then and there, a lecture that would leave each of them speechless, a general lecture to put an end to the nonsense once and for all. With the best will in the world, he could not envisage that the simple elegance of his sketches might leave any observer cold.

Then he thought of the faces at the Senckenberg Museum, the flushed cheeks, the mocking words. He could hear how they'd rather instantly pull this to pieces too than take time to study his illustrations. He saw them laughing and wished he could chase the scorn from their faces, by whatever means necessary. He still fell into a rage all too easily at the memory of that moment. But he needed to calm his temper if he were to achieve anything. Knowledge had to become a skill. That was Clausewitz. So the academy had been good for something after all.

He'd have to use a ruse de guerre. Isolation. An absolute battle wouldn't be an option, defeating the enemy on a single day. He had to choose a strategy of fatigue. Writing a book, that was the solution. Each of his opponents would have to read it alone, at home at his desk. He would present his argumentation step by step and they'd have nothing to counter it, without the power of their cliques. He had to get them separately; he was alone too. That way they wouldn't be able to sidestep him. Man against man.

A whole book, then. One for which there was no model. Wegener swallowed. 'Everything is very simple in war, but the simplest thing is difficult.' Clausewitz again.

There was the heather found only in Newfoundland and the adjacent areas, outside of Europe. There was a ribbon of marine layers in coal seams, stretching from the Donets valley through Upper Silesia, the Ruhr coal basin, Belgium and England all the way to the west of North America. And there was the garden snail—in southern Germany, on the British Isles, Iceland and Greenland and over on the American side, where it was only found in Labrador, Newfoundland and the east of the Union, however. How could anyone close his eyes to the garden snail? To its zoogeographical inescapability? Was there any healthy, right-minded individual who could really imagine the garden snail crossing via such a phantasmagorical land bridge?

And then Spitzbergen. It was under ice now but there were traces there of ivy, sloe, hazel, hawthorn and viburnum, even of such warmth-loving plants as water lily, walnut and cypress. There were once plane trees there, chestnuts, ginkgo and magnolia, even vines! It must once have been possible to lead a warm and heady life in Spitzbergen.

He noted down each of his arguments and divided them into groups. Geological arguments, geophysical arguments. Palaeontological, biological, palaeoclimatic arguments. The lists now filled an entire file.

When he came home in the evenings, Hilde had wind and screamed. Perhaps it was the cabbage. Wegener considered getting a dog so as to have an excuse to leave the house after dinner, but he had had no luck with dogs to date. Feldmann and Gloë had died in the ice. He discussed the matter with Else, who missed the goldfish from her parents' home. In the end they got a cat, which was no help to anyone. Hilde eyed the creature with undisguised horror.

In the institute library, Wegener came upon the expedition reports of one Edward Sabine, who had travelled to all corners of the world with his pendulum a hundred years previously. Wherever he went on land, he measured the thread length at which the pendulum took one second to swing, thus determining the local gravity. Wegener envied the man his small baggage. How marvellous was the task he had set for himself. How clear. He shuddered when he made a mental calculation of the mean error.

All at once he remembered where he had heard the man's name before. Had the Danmark not anchored at a Sabine Island on his first expedition? Excited, Wegener flicked through the pages and cursed quietly as they began to stick together from the sweat on his fingers. At last he reached the place. This Sabine had in fact sailed up the east coast of Greenland; the horrifically imprecise results of his pendulum were noted for every bay. Then he had reached the island so impressively located offshore, and even given it a name: Inner Pendulum Island. He had carried out a variety of experiments there. Wegener skimmed the columns of figures; what a lot the old fop had recorded. At the end of the page, Wegener finally found what he was looking for—a measurement of the geological position. His breath cut out for a moment.

Naturally, the determination might contain errors. But it was old. As old as a saga, that was how it seemed to Wegener, as old as continents. Anyone wanting to determine the movement of the Earth's floes had to compare time periods in which the landmasses had the opportunity to drift further apart. When had Sabine been on the island? 1823, more than eighty years before Wegener had determined its position. An eternity.

An hour later, he had found out that the Germania expedition had been there too, even spending the entire winter of 1869–70 on the island. They had of course taken a longitude measurement. It was Koldewey himself who gave the island its current name, Sabine Island, in honour of the scientist.

By the evening, Wegener had found the differences between the three measurement procedures, assessed errors, weighted and related them, and now the light of the setting sun fell upon two small numbers at the foot of the last sum: 11–21. They looked like dates of birth and death. Wegener imagined somebody one day chiselling the two figures into his gravestone, in memory of the outcome of his calculation. Year for year, Greenland, the largest island on Earth, drifted eleven to twenty-one metres westwards.

In absolute agreement with his theory.

The Detonating Meteor of 3 April 1916, ½ past 3 in the Afternoon in Kurhessen

The first edition of The Origin of Continents and Oceans was published by Vieweg in Braunschweig in 1915. Wegener tore open the parcel containing his author's copy and at last held the book in his hands. How light it was. What beautiful red linen they had chosen. He barely dared to open the pages, fearing he might come across a mistake.

He did so nonetheless. 'At a specified time the Earth can have had just one configuration. But the Earth supplies no direct information of this. We are like a judge confronted by a defendant who declines to testify.' Had he written that?

Wegener put the book on the mantelpiece so that he would always see his work, and to protect it from Hilde's malign hands. He moved a pair of candles aside to frame the event. They had never burnt since they moved in; now he lit them every time he was in the room.

Anyone could now read the truth. Shortly before printing, one last, deadly argument against the theory of intermediate continents had occurred to him and the typesetter had been so kind as to include the additional paragraph. No one had ever considered what huge amounts of water such land bridges would have displaced. Before they sank, the water level of the world's seas must have been far higher than now; the water would have flooded all the land. This already absurd theory therefore did not lead to the desired end of dry land bridges between dry continents.

With the best will in the world, Wegener could not imagine how anyone might elude such obvious truths. Over the following days, he read the entire red book several times over and made a considerable number of underlinings.

General interest in his publication remained minor, however.

'The people who insist on standing on solid factual ground and want nothing to do with hypotheses,' he wrote to Köppen, 'are all prey to a false hypothesis themselves.' How cold the rage that came over him when he thought of the few reviews of his volume. 'Such people,' he continued, 'are not to be had for a reorientation of ideas. Had they learnt the drift theory at school, they would advocate this view with the same lack of understanding in all details, including any incorrect aspects, their whole lives long, as they do now with the sinking of the continents.'

Köppen attempted to placate him in his answering letter, which Wegener began to resent until he read that his father-in-law had learnt to his joy that the transatlantic longitude measurement Borkum–Horta–New York was about to take place. So there was someone using his theory as an occasion to carry out his own studies! Though the Greenlandic floe was far more mobile, the much more accurate measurements now possible would doubtlessly provide evidence of drifts in this case, sufficient to pull the ground out from beneath his opponents' feet.

And there was no point, he wrote in response to Köppen, in fooling oneself. Although there was no geological difference, modern man felt far closer to the Borkum–Horta–New York longitude than to the drift of an ice-encrusted island in the Arctic Ocean, no matter how large it might be.

His mind thus stimulated, he took the letter to the post box just as the sun was proceeding to set behind a veil of ice clouds and showing such a brightly luminous parhelion that anyone might be forgiven for assuming it were the real sun. Generosity was easy enough if one had only to wait until a cloud passed by to be proved right. If only it were as easy in all cases. For a moment, he thought he couldn't wait for the transatlantic measurement to begin at last.

Unfortunately, as Wegener learnt soon afterwards, the war prevented the undertaking.

Hilde put on more and more weight. Sometimes Wegener called her chubby, which offended Else. She was barely three quarters of a year old when she began pulling herself up by every halfway firm object and standing motionless for minutes at a time. Earnest and fat, she gazed into the distance.

Wegener heard of another planned measurement: Greenwich–Cambridge. Rather ridiculous, in fact—no matter how time-honoured the locations, the drift to be expected was insignificant compared with other pairings. Yet the observatory and university had recently been connected by an ocean cable, which promised to make the measurements sufficiently precise. It was some time before Wegener learnt that the cable had been cut on the outbreak of war. This measurement too could not take place.

Wegener passed the time with minor publications: On the Question of Atmospheric Tides; On Changing Colours in Meteors. He recalled his secret passion for turbulences. He yearned to one day witness a whirlwind for himself and spent many an evening at the foot of the Lahn hills, his gaze fixed upon the trees' leaves hour after hour, like an angler without a rod.

Sometimes he thought he made out a gust of wind less horizontal than vertical. In his mind, he came up with the possibility that a tornado might be invisible if its interior did not condense.

A cloud might be positioned at its upper end, from which a column might be suspended, and the foot would form nothing but a small, fast whirl. As yet undecided how likely such a phenomenon actually was, Wegener decided to give it a name in any case, and thus he dubbed the event of an invisible tornado a 'blind funnel cloud'.

Having estimated the likelihood of such a weather phenomenon occurring in his presence and duly sobered, he decided instead to publish a collection of eyewitness reports.

In Lucretius, he came across a description of a cyclone on the open sea, which he found surprisingly objective. Would he be capable of keeping so calm a head in the face of such a force of nature?

The volume was released the following year. Its title vignette was a drawing from 1827—the waters of Sicily, above them a dozen tornados of all sizes and shapes. The picture had been drawn by a Mr Mazzara from on board his ship, at the moment when the captain had just opened fire on the most threatening of the water columns.

Inspired by Lucretius' sobriety, Wegener had given his book the objective title Tornados and Water Spouts in Europe. He knew, however, that his collection could not possibly be complete. Some newspaper edition, travel account or city record undoubtedly contained descriptions of further weather columns that had evaded him, also memoirs, possibly even sermons. But who was he to view it in its entirety, in times of war to cap it all? Completeness, to speak with his father, was only to be had with God.

The collection was impressive enough as it was.

It also cast all Jews along with their wives and children out of their bedchambers, above the roofs and onto the streets. Likewise they have themselves installed a printing press in their quarter, in which they intended to print the Old Testament in the Hebrew tongue. The weather took also this printing press, blew the copies over all houses into the town's streets, outside the town, even into all far fields, one mixed with another, torn, hung on fences and trees, so that in the morning when day came, in and outside the town and also on the fields, the same printed papers lay so many and so thick, and of which in such masses, as though it had snowed.

When something really did happen it was not a whirlwind, and Wegener was not present in any case. It was a few farmers in Kurhessen who first raised their heads on the afternoon of 3 April 1916, alerted by a thunderbolt, clouds of smoke, by a strange light. They all later stated they had thought at first of artillery. The assault on Verdun had just begun and the canons could be heard all the way to their fields on windless days. Then they looked up—through the cloudless spring sky, a fireball fell at a leisurely pace, leaving a gleaming trail.

The impression of this spectacle on the beholder was enormous. Over the next few days, the newspapers filled up with eyewitness reports, earwitness reports, statements based on hearsay. Even in Sachsen-Meiningen, a hundred kilometres distant, a painter claimed to have heard the sonic effects, with the incident becoming increasingly colourful with distance. The fireball was said to have glowed by turns red, blue and green, which Wegener, having bought a copy of every newspaper on sale at the station, instantly considered indicative of the characteristic colour change from blue-green to red occurring when passing the boundary from the hydrogen to the nitrogen sphere. He read the sheets on his knees, as usual with ruler and pencil so as to underline key aspects immediately; in the swaying train carriage, his tools helped him to keep on the right line. The pages were soon strewn with notes. As the spectacle progressed, the articles reported, the light took on a yellowish hue ('like a brimstone butterfly') or glowed white like the sun or even the colour of acetyl gaslight ('and then playing in all colours of the rainbow'). One observer even claimed a heavenly melody had sounded during the descent.

And he had not been there to see it! Wegener had been called away for a gas course a week before the event. When the news reached him he had dashed to the course leader, explained the phenomenon of falling meteorites in brief words and finally managed to convince him it was his patriotic duty to recover the heavenly body for the Reich. Without understanding in detail what he was talking about, the man had granted two weeks' special leave and Wegener had set out right away. He got down to work the instant he returned to Marburg.

First he sent a notice to all the larger newspapers in the area— Frankfurter Zeitung, Kölnische Zeitung, Der Tag, Magdeburger Zeitung—requesting their readers to send him their observations, which was printed without further ado and free of charge.

The number of letters was enormous. They came from all corners of the distribution area, a detailed protocol of the light phenomenon even reaching him from the Hermann Monument in the Teutoburg Forest. There was some indication, at least, that the Rhine and Main rivers formed a southern and western visibility boundary. Wegener entered every report on his map, with the observer's position and the direction he had been facing. The signs soon coalesced into a clear circle, with only Göttingen apparently under a cloud that day. The pattern grew clearer with every entry, the lines emanating like the rays of a star from an area on the banks of the Schwalm. When the word Treysa was barely legible on the map, Wegener decided to try his luck there.

Else accompanied him, having meanwhile listened to enough of the Schwalm dialect from the market women to serve as his interpreter. They went from village to village, from door to door and soon felt like the Brothers Grimm collecting their fairy tales.

A master baker went on record as saying the fireball had looked like a sponge cake turning in mid-air and he had jumped in the roadside ditch for shock. A little old man whispered in a scratchy voice in Else's ear that there had been a fiery cloud in which the Kaiser's face appeared. He was willing to swear an oath. Wegener had to ask twice before he could believe what his wife translated for him.

After several such experiences, they took to visiting the village teacher first in each place, to find out who might report reliably on the event. The most fruitful exercise was to speak to school classes and ask the pupils to report their observations.

The children could barely hold back, all wanting the professor to give them a turn, and Wegener had to take rapid notes to collect all the wonderful observations, excited by the prospect of the implications that this almost-congruent material promised. At last there were not only contradictions. He was already envisaging what might be derived about the meteor's material from the descriptions of the clouds of smoke.

It took several of these sessions in musty classrooms for Wegener to realize that the uniformity of the descriptions ought to give cause for suspicion. Only gradually did he admit to himself that the pupils agreed on even the most outlandish elements. If the loudest boy in the class said the spectacle had looked like a glowing pear, Wegener could soon be sure that his fellow pupils' comparisons would no longer leave the orchard.

It was that old plague—people in groups. Wegener had always known it and here it was merely confirmed once again. All that was pure became diluted, only the rank and evil added up until nothing remained in the end but raw, common mediocrity. As an individual, man was a highly dubious creature; in the pack, how-ever, he lost all dignity. Wegener shuddered to think back to his time in the army. What else would have brought him to set aside the scholar's prudence, if not the damaging influence of the mob?

From then on, he isolated his sources. He separated spouses and dragged children from their mothers' sides. There was no helping it; there was no other way to get at the truth. People were only of use when they were alone. With every person who could credibly claim to have seen the event with their own eyes, Wegener went separately into the fields, had them lead him to the spot where they'd been working or eating their bread, and then entered the direction and height at which the spectacle had been visible.

It has been a burning lump of coal, they said. A golden arrow, the luminous egg of a goose.

It had emitted a ray of light like a torch, they told him, burning in all colours. It had looked like the yellow flares from the trenches.

A white dove illuminated by the sun.

The least difficult to establish was the time. Sub-postmaster Rühl reported that the Cassel–Marburg passenger train had been just between Neustadt and Allendorf at the time of the first flare of light. He knew that because he had been on board himself. It must therefore have been twenty-five minutes past three. Should the train have had a slight delay, as occurred regularly on this line, admittedly, the meteor would have been correspondingly delayed.

The exactitude of the positional information, however, was low. There were so many obvious delusions and errors of recollection in it that Wegener initially wanted to abstain from making any more precise determination of the meteor's course. Then, however, studying earlier cases, he noted that layman observations included a number of typical repeated errors, which could be systematically calculated.

Wegener had thought he might deepen his knowledge of the movements of heavenly bodies, but in fact he became rather more an expert on all shapes and forms of autosuggestion. How firmly people believed in their mistakes, how unburdened by the slightest doubt.

Cand. theol. Seiwert wrote from Paderborn, at least a hundred kilometres away in other words, that Wegener would do better to search in the vicinity of his house, as the object had landed some 200 metres away from his observation point. Wegener wrote back that that was hardly possible, when all previous observations suggested a landing region far to the south. Seiwert responded in a rather forceful tone that he must apologize but that was not possible. The object had fallen to earth between him and a nearby hill, and he added sketches and eventually declared himself willing to confirm the information under oath.

Wegener needed a few nights lying awake and as many days bent over books until he found an answer. The eye followed the moving light even after it was extinguished, and the afterglow on the retina had fooled the Cand. theol., no doubt a man of good faith, into thinking the motion continued in front of the hillside down to the ground.

The height estimates also proved wrong. Every observer tended to maintain the light had been visible either directly above him or close to the horizon.

Wegener therefore weighted those statements more strongly in which a church tower, a flagpole, a telegraph wire had served for comparison. Before he fell asleep at night, he thought about petitioning the government to cover the country in telegraph wires, thereby ensuring there would always be a reference point nearby.

The rage he gradually developed towards his witnesses. Now that Else was no longer with him because of the child, Wegener had to see for himself how to deal with their hair-raising reports. The meteor had been the size of a child's head. Had they never noticed that a child's head looked larger from close up than from a distance? What he needed was comparisons, relations, best of all angles, azimuths, accelerations. It was such a pity he had not been there himself.

And every enquiry called forth yet more outlandish answers. Where at first a single light had fallen, after his interested enquiry it soon became an entire shower of meteorites. They didn't want to disappoint him, the visiting scholar. So he noted down silently, merely filling the margins with grimacing caricatures of all the childish minds he questioned.

His research was made no easier by the alleged finds. News came from as far away as Wiesbaden that a master bricklayer had discovered a foreign body reeking of sulphur. To begin with, Wegener had them show him the places, but he'd soon had enough of all the pebbles and lumps. How angry people grew when he tried to talk them out of their errors. Wegener remembered Victor Hugo's words about how nothing was as powerful as an idea whose time had come, and he corrected—nothing was more powerful than an idée fixe. What he found was quartzes, bulbs, on one occasion a lump of iron slag, left over from the days when the region's iron ore had been smelted locally.

What surprised him was how rarely sulphur was mentioned. From the literature, he knew that not only every meteor had smelt of fire and brimstone in olden times but also Northern Lights, comets and whirlwinds. After spending an entire afternoon on suppositions of possible reasons, Wegener decided it could only show the dwindling significance of the devil in people's everyday lives.

203

A white strip of smoke had been left behind, as thick as a woollen thread. The smoke had looked like a taut telegraph wire, at the place where the tail had just been. It had been the shape of a spiral staircase. Slightly wavy. Curled, zigzagged.

It had looked like a rupture in the firmament.

Then it had grown gradually paler and finally vanished 'like a fog' (Corporal Karlbaum), 'like a cloud of shrapnel' (Private Wippler), 'like candyfloss' (Master Bülbring, the tailor's son).

Of course, a hissing sound. Descriptions of it came even from distant places. Wegener was not fooled. One heard a hiss because one expected a hiss. The deception was all too easy to expose because the hissing always occurred simultaneously with the light in the descriptions, whereas a genuine hiss would have come chasing after the light, the speed of sound being far slower.

Those reports that spoke of a sudden crack of thunder a good while after the glow, Wegener weighted doubly, however. The lyceum teacher Miss Jehn from Wehrda gained significant credibility through her description of how, only a while after the flash of light ('as long as it takes to pick up a few cubes of sugar'), her coffee cup had begun to clatter.

Consistorial Councillor Weiss in response to the question of whether there'd been a sound: Yes, it had sounded like an 'Oh'. At first he'd thought it was his dear Hedwig, but then it turned out she thought the same of him. They had sat up in bed, where they were taking their midday nap as they did every day. There had been a multiple bang, followed by a gurgling sound, and then silence. Hedwig had taken his hand. Nothing worth further reporting had happened. They had opened the curtains; perhaps the afternoon had been a touch brighter than usual.

In the end Wegener abandoned his field study. He withdrew to Else's workshop for a full week, not even leaving for mealtimes. He calculated, compared, weighted. Even the observations he discarded due to obvious unsuitability, Else had to write up as clear copies, though that was becoming increasingly difficult for her due to her failing eyesight.

He estimated velocities, atmospheric layers, orbits and their slants, relieved that this meteor had fallen into the lap of so competent an expert as himself. Had all his possibly outlandish-seeming tendencies not prepared him ideally for such an incident?

As he left the little room at the end of the week, Wegener knew where he had to look—at 50°57' North and 26°50' East of Ferro.

The spot was right on the boundary of Rommershausen. Wegener guessed at a wooded area next to the village; had the landing been in the open, a farmer would have found something by now. Along with a few assistants, Wegener set out in search of traces of the heavenly body. They paced through the undergrowth in a long row; soon none of them spoke a word, as though they were stalking deer. All the things one could mistake for the mark of a landing! On the first afternoon, every shadow on the forest floor sent them into a frenzy. Over time, however, they grew more suspicious and no longer sounded the alarm for every molehill.

A few days later, the search was abandoned without results, and instead a reward of 300 gold marks was pledged. The local farmers were asked to keep an eye open when tilling their fields that autumn.

It was a whole year before a timber farmer alerted Forester Huppmann to a lightning strike in the woods outside Rommershausen. Huppmann examined the beech tree and established that it showed signs not only of burning but also of scoring. That, he wrote to Marburg, was rather unusual for lightning. Furthermore, he had found a strange opening at the foot of the tree, which he had originally taken for a fox's den, but perhaps the professors might like to see for themselves?

They might indeed. They set off for Treysa immediately. The car encountered a clutch of hens in Cölbe and not all parties survived, as Wegener noticed with a glance over his shoulder.

Huppmann had already had spades brought out. Professor Richarz and Wegener hung their jackets from a branch and the work was begun. The hollow they found had a depth of a quarter of a metre; soil falling subsequently and washed in by rain may have filled an original impact hole.

They made good progress to begin with, the upper layer made up partly of loose forest earth, partly of impure loess clay. After not quite a metre, they came upon clayey sandstone, which Richarz classed as a lower Buntsandstein formation. Digging in it was exhausting, all parties resting on their spades with increasing frequency until they finally decided to leave the work entirely to the forester's two assistants, whom Huppmann had kindly summoned.

The young men made it clear what they thought of the whole matter. Wegener could understand them; in their place, he too would have wondered how anyone was to come across anything at this depth other than more and more layers of sand and earth and rock. Had he not known better.

The men groaned with every shovel of sand they threw over the edge of their pit. All of a sudden, however, the excavation perhaps a good metre and a half deep by now, one of them emitted a sound, nothing but a big, round 'Oh', just loud enough for Wegener to clamber down to them instantly and begin freeing the stone they had hit upon with his bare fingers.

It was gigantic. It was, Wegener thought once they had extracted it, as large and as round as the digger's 'Oh'. Deep black, covered in rough bulges and dents, and yet its surface was as perfectly smooth as black porcelain. There could be no doubt that the surface had at one time melted and then solidified again. Wegener tried to lift the stone, wanting to raise it in the air like a trophy. He was after all the first person ever to touch it. The lump must have a mass of a good hundredweight. Just as he grew dizzy, the forester's men leapt to his aid and the three of them heaved the meteor out of the pit together.

By the time Wegener himself came crawling out and patted down his trousers, Professor Richarz already had his eyepiece in place. 'Pure iron,' he said. 'Indubitably, in every respect.' He looked up. 'A real catch, certainly one of the most significant finds of the modern era.' Not 800 metres from the calculated point of impact. It was the first time a meteor had been found through planned calculations.

Richarz was the first to congratulate Wegener. It was an honour and an embarrassment in equal parts to him that a professor of cosmic physics had to pay respects to a weatherman for an entirely physical achievement. But then, meteor, meteorology, the name did indicate that it was possibly more likely than one might suspect. Wegener gave a tight smile.

Forester Huppmann was handed his reward on the spot. It was barely lighter than the assistants' load.

Once the war ended, they would cut the stone and examine the pieces. For the time being, they didn't have the labour.

The Nature of the Treeline

The minuscule bubbles shimmered away almost joyfully. Every one of them reflected a segment of the world, shown in miniature, distorted reproduction on its smooth surface. Wegener took the spoon out of his cup and leant down further. He recognized a hazy outline of his face, multiplied in the foam of the hot drink. He looked old, which might be due to the liquid's colour. When he moved his head, all the tiny heads circling on the coffee wobbled in synch. What did they take him for? An all-powerful being who struck fear into some and was of no account to the others?

He picked one of the bubbles floating on the edge of the conglomeration and tried to spot the reflection of his eyes in it, but they refused to be seen. When Wegener leant in so deep that he almost touched it with the tip of his nose, the bubble burst. He recoiled in shock. At the moment before the destruction, the shining had vanished for an instant, the coloured streaks stopped moving, the so recently reflective skin had suddenly grown dull, only to shatter with a tiny crackle.

As though nothing had happened, neighbouring bubbles occupied the freed space and went on turning with the liquid. As it circled, the small gathering tore apart, its pieces drifting away from the middle until they were all distributed around the surface. Each of the bubbles adhered alone to the edge of the cup, only isolated examples still drifting without destination across the small brown lake. Wegener stirred again and emptied the cup in a single mouthful.

It tasted appalling. Else was of the opinion that a cup of coffee was an essential part of a proper life, and if there was no proper coffee to be had then false coffee was just as good. She never tired of trying out new recipes, using chicory, beechnuts, acorns. Judging by the taste, she had added dandelion this time.

Wegener heard her playing the piano in the next room, as every afternoon. She played by heart because she could no longer read the notes. Always Richard Wagner, always this same adaptation for pianoforte, as though they went together. Sometimes he wondered what would have to happen to make her stop. Wegener had heard the pieces so often he'd soon be able to play them himself.

A sheet of paper lay on the desk before him. It had been a year since he'd written to his father, in the summer of 1917, and now this was his answer.

'Our daughter,' he had written then, 'is now several years old and still such a small creature. How long it takes man to grow out of his stupidity. I don't imagine we shall have any more children.'

He had not meant to be mean, neither to Else nor to Hilde, it was not meant against his father and least of all against God, or at least it had not been his intention to offend anyone. It was only when no answering letter arrived that Wegener realized how much his rejection of family matters must have upset his father.

And now he was looking at the telegram informing him that his father had died on Saint John's Day. Wegener had not seen him for years.

When they arrived in Zechlinerhütte, his mother was sitting in her wheelchair in the shade of the veranda. The lake shimmered through the trees. The rotund nurse took Wegener aside and explained the situation. 'Madam is brought out in the morning. During the day she simply sits there, and in the evening I roll her inside again.' He pressed a few coins into the woman's hand.

The conversation with the doctor was similarly brief. To begin with, his father had merely felt cold at all times. Not a good sign, but no cause for concern for him as a doctor. Then it had gone quickly. 'Gruel, then soup, later not even that. At the end the pain must have been excruciating.' His father had not said a word, his mouth ever contorted in suffering. It had—begging his pardon— looked like a grin. His eyes widened in fear like a child.

On the way to the cemetery, Alfred pushed his mother's chair at the head of the long procession and was glad to have the metal grips as some kind of hold. It was early July and far too hot for a funeral. Wegener sweated in his suit. How small the grave looked, now that they had all grown tall. How long ago was it that he had last prayed?

He took a furtive look around. The small graveyard was hope- lessly overcrowded. On all the gravel paths and between the graves stood his siblings of all ages, dressed in black and hands folded. Their mouths opened in unison to pray. 'Our Father, who art in Heaven.' Which father was meant? Then they sang the old hymns, 'For all flesh, it is as grass' and 'De profundis', and as if singing in their sleep, each one knew their part. Behind him, he heard Kurt's brittle baritone.

Wegener sang along, not heeding the words. Else clutched his arm and pressed the curve of her belly into his side; against their plans, she was expecting another child after all. The new pastor said the Lord had pleased to take his son to Him by means of a tumour in the oesophagus, and Wegener thought about whether his father would have approved of those words. Then he leant for- ward, took a handful of earth and threw it into the breach.

Silently, he thought, I've won our bet. Without malice but in the certainty of being right. His father had clearly found no con- solation in God at the end of his life. Then he realized he too had yet to prove he might do so in science. How much time did he have left? Was it possible they might both lose in the end?

For the funeral meal there was quince bread and iced water, Kurt and Tony at the table, their mother between them, but no one felt like talking. Else tried to persuade Hilde to try her grandmother's baking but took none for herself.

Afterwards they all went their separate ways. Hilde screamed for the entire return journey, the carriage jolted terribly, and Wegener would have liked to join in the screaming. Once home, he resolved to fall ill. Not even that was a success.

Else now often stayed in bed in the morning underneath her heavy balloon of a featherbed, which was far too hot for Wegener. She could barely make it up the stairs, meaning he had to heave around the full laundry baskets alone. It was inconceivable how much dirty clothing Hilde produced on a daily basis.

Their first child had been born on the outbreak of the war. On 11 November of the year 1918, France and the last remains of the German Empire concluded an armistice in a train wagon in a forest at Compiègne. The war had cost nine million people their lives.

The Wegeners' second daughter was born at midnight. They called her Käte. By the light of the gas lamp, her face was barely recognizable through her screams.

Wegener informed his mother and his parents-in-law of the birth of another granddaughter in two letters, including greetings from a weak but well Else. He was uncertain, he noted in a postscript to Köppen, which of the sixty-seven most pressing subjects he ought to address after completing his meteor essay.

He had meanwhile been appointed a titular professor. Wegener had hesitated a little before he signed the appointment decree in which the minister bestowed him with the title. With his signature, he read, he solemnly declared to remain devoted to His

Majesty the King and the sovereign royal house in unswerving loyalty. Unswerving—what was that supposed to mean?

There was no king any more; on the morning after Käte's birth, the newspapers had reported Wilhelm's abdication.

Käte was an extremely noisy child. The only time she was quiet was when her father sang at her cradle, but could he sing all day long? He was meanwhile camping out in the hall so as at least to have some peace at night. The bed of rough woollen blankets reminded him of his bunk in Pustervig. Before daybreak, he released the infant from her mother's arms and took the bundle into the kitchen so that Else could sleep a little. There he sat, his daughter wrapped in a towel on his lap, and whispered the names of the geological periods to her: Carboniferous, Permian, Triassic, Jurassic, Cretaceous, Palaeogene, Neogene, Quaternary, Modern. Käte looked at him, her eyes huge, like a prehistoric creature.

Wegener linked the syllables into a little song that tended to calm her. He held out his forefinger and she gripped it firmly. And so they passed the hours until dawn.

In the end they both heard by the sounds from the bedroom that the day was beginning. As soon as Else emerged in her dressing gown, eyes swollen with fatigue, Wegener slipped into his shoes and jacket and withdrew to the institute library, hoarse from all his singing.

There was little paper to be had. And the little that there was was used to print nonsense. Wegener suggested to Köppen that they might write a theory of gusts together, but even in the next letter doubted they would find a publishing house for such a manuscript. The gentleman publishers no longer felt the responsibility they had once possessed. 'An intellectual life prevails,' he wrote, 'determined by authors' and publishers' vanity and profit-seeking, which merely complies to the taste of an irresponsible mass readership and its obsession with sensation and hedonism.'

Even Wegener noticed his handwriting was a little uneven on the page. Where did his anger stem from? Köppen did not respond to the letter.

Food too was scarce. Potatoes grew in the front garden and they harvested them before they were ripe so that no one else could dig them up. Wegener observed his wife's hunger with concern. He was glad, on one hand, that she nursed the child as long as possible, because it meant one less mouth at the table. On the other hand, he wasn't sure whether her compulsively increased appetite didn't defeat the purpose.

His parents-in-law kept them supplied with everything the garden in Großborstel provided, and they thanked them with potatoes. That was fine by Wegener; he barely knew what there was left to write in his weekly letters. Now he thanked Köppen in many words for the packages of onions, eggs, beans and flour received in one piece. He noted in all detail what was made out of them, and Köppen responded with suggestions for further nutritious meals: cabbage schnitzel, roasted celeriac, meatloaf. One might have thought the letters staunched their hunger.

What Wegener continued to write with a passion was essays. The scientific journals were published at irregular intervals but because most contributors had been lost in battle, lay wounded in field hospitals or had said a mental farewell to the world, the editors were grateful for Wegener's articles. It was almost irrelevant to him what he wrote about during these years; everything seemed equally pressing.

Proliferation of Sound
Dust Whirls on Iceland
Studies on the Sall Crater on Ösel Island

On the Ice Phase of Water Vapour in the Atmosphere
The Size of the Cloud Elements
Some Main Characteristics of Funnel Clouds
The Moon and the Origin of the World
Hair Ice on Dead Wood

Wegener knew perfectly well that he had to do more. For economic reasons alone. Their third daughter was born in May 1920; they named her Lotte. Her appetite reminded Wegener of Hilde. He wouldn't have minded having a boy. Seeing as he didn't believe in fate, though, there was no one he could blame. So he accepted it and tried to teach his girls the boyish games he had grown up with among all his siblings.

He was not granted a regular professorship; Wegener could imagine what made him suspect to the commission. His drift theory was now only ever cited in ridicule. His esteemed colleagues were like continental floes—their views shifted only through massive forces acting at a geological pace.

Wegener began to turn abroad in his thoughts, sometimes taking the Danish medal out of its box; it was already a little tarnished. He wondered why they did not want him there, in the motherland of his fame.

And then a letter arrived from the Austrian Federal Ministry of Teaching. It offered him a post in Graz; the newly declared republic was concentrating intellectual troops from its neighbour. Wegener sat down at his desk, chose his green ink for so special an occasion and expressed his general willingness to approach the question of a professorship. Except that he had certain concerns; to wit, he was not in a position to accept another extraordinary professorship. Too many aspects of his life had been extraordinary already.

The matter also had to be discussed with Else. The next evening, once all three daughters were asleep at the same time, Wegener steered conversation towards the letter. Else said she had to sit down first of all, not noticing she was already seated. Wegener stood up to make one of the weak teas she liked in the evening, but Else stopped him. After a while she asked where this Graz place was, exactly.

The two of them leant over the old atlas, inherited from Wegener's father. It would no doubt suffice for a rough orientation.

Else feared the distance from her parents and Wegener spoke of the beauty of the mountains, whereupon she looked up, worried. 'Will we have to climb them all the time?' How far was the Mediterranean? Wegener nodded—just around the corner. Else was concerned whether she'd be understood down there, with her north German lilt. People had laughed at her in Marburg to begin with. Wegener was able to reassure his wife; compared to the way people spoke in Graz, her Hanseatic twang was barely noticeable.

'But we've always done fine.'

Wegener pointed out that they were living beyond their means now that there were five of them. And people living beyond their means could change either their life or their means. Which would she prefer?

Else stared at him, shocked. 'You sound like a Spartacist!' And at any rate, she couldn't very well leave her parents behind up in the north. And was it really a better position for him than here? They turned in circles. It was almost midnight when it occurred to Wegener how all parties might be mollified.

He reported for duty at the end of April, initially alone. He had gone on writing letters until the good news finally arrived that he'd be granted an ordinary professorship, tied to an initial salary raised by six increments, calculated on the basis of eighteen years of service at basic pay. Whatever that might mean in detail, Wegener had screwed the lid onto the green ink with satisfaction.

Gertrud, the librarian in the Marburg reading room, had given him a piece of embroidery as a leaving present: For all the land, it is as ice. He fastened the cloth to the wall behind his new desk with two pins.

The family joined him in the autumn, filling the house on Blumengasse where Wegener had spent several months alone in the dark, echoing rooms. It was part of the newly built Bachmann Estate, walking distance from the university; in the event of rain, he could board the tram at the cavalry barracks.

Else felt a little out of place to begin with. Her increasingly poor eyesight made it hard to get her bearings. But the girls conquered their new kingdom with whoops and screams. The walls of their room were papered in an ivy pattern. And they could run straight into the garden, where they played to their hearts' content.

As well as the master bedroom and a small extra room, the first floor had a study for the professor, where papers were already piled up. The small utility room Else had claimed for herself was also up there.

And then there was another room, which was not occupied until November. Mother Köppen embarked carefully from the taxicab and stood for a while in the gutter. She had pulled her red hood low over her face and now peered mistrustfully from beneath it. Vladimir, however, strode around the house leaving every door open behind him. Even Else had to admit her father seemed decades younger.

And the mountains! In their very first week in Graz, Wegener put his daughters on skis in the living room and practised the plough with them. While they squatted low, he slowly recited the stages of their descent—from the top of the Schöckl in countless sweeps down the slope. Another right curve over to the Kalvarienberg. Shooting along a bumpy piste and finally through the swathe at Rastleiten to the banks of the stream, from where they glided at a slow pace ('Faster, Father, faster!') through the beautiful valley all the way down to Sankt Radegund. Quite out of breath, the girls wiped their eyes dry. Their cheeks were flushed by the descent.

Marie Köppen too was enamoured of her new home, at the very latest on harvesting the first crop of gooseberries. The children were soon asking for Topfen and Schlag with their fruit, seduced by the Austrian words for the excellent local dairy products. Even a goldfish had survived the move unharmed; Hilde spent many an afternoon at its bowl and Vladimir occasionally joked that she took after her father when it came to tenacity.

Marie soon joined a literary circle, in which the wives of the university faculty read aloud the most heart-rending novels of the season to one another. Over dinner she recounted the plots in detail and reported on the other ladies' reactions. The robust widow of an economist had a habit of falling asleep during the first sentences, but never forgot beforehand to whisper the now legendary request to her neighbours, 'Wake me when they kiss.'

Aside from these few excursions, Wegener's mother-in-law was always at home. Whenever he entered the living room the old woman would be there, and she'd look up from her embroidery frame, blow her nose and enquire after the weather. 'I have to trim my herbaceous borders!'

Else too liked the way of life in Styria, calling it Mediterranean. She dreamt of a trip to Italy, which was only hailing distance away, after all. She imagined the sun would do her eyes good; their opacity had not abated, unfortunately. Wegener put her off for the time being—first the mountain world was waiting to be discovered, which worried Else somewhat. The snow-capped peaks around them seemed to embody the very opposite of the promised Mediterranean.

For Wegener, however, Graz was a disaster. Not on the surface, not so that he could have proved it on the basis of any particular detail. To be precise, little changed in his life. But perhaps it was precisely that which began to get him down after a matter of weeks. The devastating lack of any change for the better. Wegener felt it was an injustice, an insult. And the extent of the imposition became only harder to overlook as time proceeded, Wegener's cares and woes expanding with every week that passed uneventfully. With every page of the calendar turned in his study—it came from the local pharmacy and month for month linked an illustration of a further Alpine mountaintop with a friendly note that the observer would soon be at the peak of health with the aid of the correct remedy—his realization grew that there was no escape. His entire existence offended him.

Wegener had to admit he had hoped for a decisive change in the progress of his life here in Graz. He had wished the title of ordinary professor would help him to stand more firmly. He had wished for dignity, a little pride, and he had hoped it would come from others. Now he felt that such a stance had to grow within oneself. There, however, nothing was to be found.

What remained instead were his doubts, not only in himself but also in mankind as a whole. At the end of the day the two were the same because he was part of humanity, much to his chagrin. That was the source of his woe, precisely that.

A second hope that Wegener had placed in his new life in Graz also proved deceptive. It had been his aim to share a roof with Köppen, to have access at all times to discussion with him, stimulation. Now, however, it emerged that Köppen too was nothing but a man from close up, merely another man.

Köppen did want discussion and stimulation, but for him that meant conversations until late at night about mutual acquaintances, about current climate zones and their effects on botany, about vegetation. Wegener was no longer interested in vegetation, he had no time for it. And he was even less interested in mutual acquaintances.

And so Wegener sat opposite his father-in-law at the table night after night, between them only a few biscuits and Else's teacup, half emptied before she went to bed, and every time he was assaulted by that feeling of gliding so familiar from Pustervig. Only now it was time he was gliding on, flowing away beneath him silent and unnoticed.

The longer Köppen spoke—about compulsory agricultural service and Esperanto, about land reform, calendar reform and whatever else his current hobbyhorse was, but particularly about anti-alcoholism, to which he had meanwhile succumbed entirely —the more Wegener longed for their old correspondence. For the enforced precision inherent to letter-writing, for all the enlightening interjections from Hamburg—how often they had prevented him from taking the wrong path. But who would write to someone who slept in the next room?

When writing, Köppen had presumably been less cosy than here in person. Wegener had experienced him as more loyal in his letters. It now occurred that Köppen merely raised one bushy white eyebrow in response to one of Wegener's thoughts and looked at him as though they had no need to maintain their little secret about the continents' drifting in this context. It pulled the ground out from beneath Wegener's feet. Was he alone in his belief in the truth?

More than anything else, though, Wegener missed his own letters, the act of focusing his thoughts and experiences for a sympathetic and conscientious reader. He was ashamed that his own writing had apparently been the most important part of the exchange for him.

Instead, now there was their talking, with all it entailed. The deviations, the repetitions when everything was long since clear. The pauses. And in those pauses the sounds of an old man.

Thus, while Köppen sniffed and mumbled into his shaggy white beard and barely recognized him through the small lenses of his spectacles from the other side of the table, Wegener's eyelids soon grew heavy. When he closed them he saw armies of ants running down their insides, uniting to form a single, flickering surface that grew ever brighter, like lights in the sky, like snow. He saw landscapes made of nothingness, between which, to his surprise, floated people with fragile wings like dragonflies, and each of them who saw him put a finger to his lips and pointed at the horizon, where there was nothing at all to be seen, however. Or perhaps there was—in the distance, Wegener made out a curtain of silky black rods bending in his direction. With shock, he watched them rise all of a sudden and recognized them as gigantic eyelashes opening before him, but there was no eye behind them.

In the end Wegener woke with a start, rubbed his face and apologized to Köppen; he ought to be in bed. Exhausted, he went over and lay down next to Else, who sighed softly in her sleep.

As often as he could, Wegener walked out along the Leonhard stream, past the Brothers of Mercy orphanage and up to the Ries hills. Only once he saw the massif of Koralpe, Stubalpe and Gleinalpe rising beyond the slopes did his heart grow lighter. Then he'd stop, his hands clasped behind his back, and look over at the white tips of the mountains. He couldn't get enough of the sight, and even once he'd finally drunk his fill of it and continued on his way, he would stop wherever a new view opened up.

On these walks, he formulated the letters he could no longer write to Köppen, now addressed to himself. But he was not a helpful recipient; perhaps he knew himself too well. He was a bad listener, interrupting himself as soon as he paused for breath. He laughed at himself and sometimes didn't know who was laughing.

When he looked up he recognized the Großer Speikkogel, the sky, the Mur valley. He found hair ice on the wood of a few tree stumps and examined it. After one or two hours he'd had enough and would turn around. Downhill, he walked fast, his hands still behind his back. The small, fragile happiness of these walks never lasted long, his head gradually sinking even as he reached the orphanage. By the time he arrived home he was filled with a kind of homesickness that knew no destination.

In the entrance, he patted down his coat and hung it up. Then he sat down at his desk with a glass of water and had spent yet another whole afternoon not working, not writing, not discovering a thing, not making progress for science. He hated himself for his lack of concentration, for the debilitating tiredness now surrounding him for days and hindering him like a veil. But every attempt to fight the exhaustion, to tear the web, tired him all the more.

At night he lay alongside Else and didn't dare to breathe. They no longer touched one another. They never knew how many daughters lay between them; one after another came over during the night complaining of the heat, the cold, a bad dream. Then their small bodies lay there and dug knees and elbows into his sides as they slept. There was nothing to be done but play dead.

In bed, in the moments before he fell asleep, images of Squirrel now sometimes shot into his head. He was powerless to resist. The two of them squatting behind the pews during the service, her small face close to his. Later the reunion at the dancing class when he had been lost for words. What might have become of her?

Should he have gone to look for her at some point in his life? But at what point?

Wegener tried to imagine how she looked by now. In the bathroom in the morning, he checked in the large framed mirror whether she'd still recognize him, whether he himself recognized the boy he had once been, behind the church pew. There were certainly differences, the thin moustache, the higher forehead, but the essentials seemed strangely unchanged—his colourless eyes, his protruding mouth. He almost thought it was a child staring back at him from the mirror.

Else sought company in the town. She forged a friendship of a kind with the wife of Professor Gangolf Schwinner, another member of the Geological Institute, and soon invited the couple to dinner. She was glad of the prospect of holding regular soirées in their spacious home.

Wegener, however, despised his hunchbacked, permanently perspiring colleague so much, due to his grumpy demeanour, that after the couple had arrived a quarter of an hour early and been led to the formally laid table by a grandly gesturing Else, he had had enough of him by the soup course.

Full of pride, Else told the assembled company that most of the vegetables for the bouillon already came from their own garden. Schwinner, meanwhile, slurped from his spoon. Wegener regretted wasting an entire evening on the fellow. From the main course on—venison—Schwinner talked with his mouth full about his achievements in the field of geological mathematics, not interrupting himself as he wiped his mouth, nose and forehead with his napkin. While he spoke, he stroked away incessantly at a small statue made of dark wood, apparently a gift although he had still not presented it to his hosts. He had clearly brought the carving back from a trip to Africa. The moor's head now shone from Schwinner's moist hand.

Once the visitors had finally left the house, the hosts argued. Wegener considered himself incapable of inviting the couple again. Else reproached him and Köppen too appealed to Wegener's humanity the next morning. One must not let first impressions put one off. He reminded Wegener of their mutual friend, the great Russian meteorologist Voeikoff, whom no hotel in Hamburg would take in due to his neglected appearance. Wegener had no recollection of a man of that name.

And seeing as Schwinner also remained censorious, Wegener was not prepared to go back on his decision. As though his colleague's ridiculous beard and walrus-like eyes were not disqualification enough.

It was no use; Else had to see her new friend on her own. And so the two women met almost every evening for a walk along the slopes of the Ruckerlberg, where they had a view of the sunset.

Else soon abandoned her plan for regular evening invitations to Blumengasse. They did not have a sufficient number of acquaintances to make up a formal occasion, in any case.

Parhelia below the Horizon

Wegener felt he could not escape the misery of his life here in Graz either. He knew by now what his theory lacked in order to reap recognition—what had set things in motion. Even if his description of the drifting continents were correct, he would not be believed until he could name a reason for it.

To begin with, he had resisted this realization, simply because the cause seemed so negligible a matter. He'd always been interested in phenomena, not in the secret forces that might be behind them. Secret forces reminded him of his father.

When it dawned on him that he would not be heard otherwise, he reluctantly sat down to find a cause for the drift. The impetus for the whole thing. His money was on the strength of the tides, and he and Köppen spent long nights calculating the force totalized by the motions of water, moon and the precession of the equinoxes. And even though that force wasn't quite sufficient in the end to set the continents in motion, Wegener stuck by his assumption. He had no better explanation.

He now always carried a small globe in his briefcase, so that he could check his thoughts about continental shape and the location of the poles and climate belts against it at any time. The children wanted to play with it but he refused to let them. Instead, he leant down to the three of them from his armchair and held the miniature globe before him as though he were the divine Atlas. The children looked up at him in wonder and he showed them all that was important about the world, the incline of the equator, the distribution of the landmasses, the arid zones, until they turned to another game.

Sighing, he put the globe away and simply stayed in his seat. After a while his mother-in-law put her head around the door and asked why he was watching instead of joining in the game, and he wondered once again why he hadn't thought of it himself, but then did nothing about it.

When the house grew too constricting he went out, his daughters sometimes coming after him, leaping about him and throwing rosehips. Fortunately, all three of them were equally poor shots, but after Hilde had once caught him on the eyelid he now flinched if they as much as ran to the bushes. To begin with, he tried to laugh under such assaults, then grew suddenly strict, held lectures striking barely less fear into himself than into his listeners, and finally strode off in anger at the children and himself.

Sometimes he wondered whether it was because his daughters had too few siblings that they constantly chose him as their target. Hilde had recently started biting her fingernails, something Wegener could not bear to watch. Whenever he noticed it he'd yank her hand out of her mouth, most severely. In addition, he paid greater attention that she was not in the room when he chewed at his own nails.

All three were now learning to play the recorder, at Else's request. The sound was barely tolerable. And there were instruments all over the house.

Wegener woke amid his daughters. He wished for nothing more than a moment of peace before the day began. It had been a late night; he had spent a long time over his books.

His eyes closed, he heard Else clattering the breakfast plates downstairs. He heard his mother-in-law going about her morning ablutions and could imagine how the bathroom would look afterwards. He heard his own breathing reverberating off the plump down pillow, and beneath it something like whispering. All at once he felt something touch his eye and was just about to swat at the supposed fly when he noticed it was a finger pushing up his eyelid. Close up, he recognized the blurred faces of his daughters. They exchanged whispers as to whether he was awake.

Wegener rolled onto his side but the children would not let him be. He was to tell them one of his stories. Wegener had his doubts as to whether life as a scientist was compatible with founding a family. Grumbling, he sat up and rubbed the sleep from his eyes. Hilde slipped underneath the featherbed, Käte laid her head on his leg, Lotte sat cross-legged in front of him and stared at him with her huge eyes. He sighed.

Had he told them the story of the wind? Wegener cleared his throat; his voice seemed not to be awake yet. They shook their heads.

'Which of you knows what the wind is good for?'

Lotte raised her shoulders and kept them there. Hilde said it brought people fresh air. 'And it keeps kites up in the sky!' Käte remembered that it blew away the clouds. Also, it helped trees to lose their leaves.

Wegener raised his eyebrows. That was all very well. But there was one wind that did none of those things. That wind only ever turned in circles and had no other goal in life. That was how it propelled itself, getting stronger and stronger. In the end it turned so fast that it lifted everything in its path high up into the air.

Lotte looked like she was about to burst into tears.

Once, that wind had blown past a fishpond. It had sucked up all the water and scattered the fish far and wide. The column of water as upright as a steeple. Shining silver, its tip touching the clouds. No stonemason could have carved such beautiful flowers and ornaments as that tower boasted.

Wegener took a breath, then went on telling them how the wind once came to a village. There, it had come across a clutch of chickens. Now, hens couldn't usually fly, as the girls knew. But the wind had lifted those cackling hens up as high as the rooftops. Right after that, it felt like tearing down the village hall. And the neighbouring houses too, and it had disembodied their five inhabitants as well.

Lotte asked what that meant but Hilde shushed her.

Only a child that had been asleep in her cot in one of the houses had remained alive. The villagers asked her what had happened, and she had pointed her finger at the sky. The people had exchanged amazed glances and murmurs; that innocent child must have seen something supernatural.

Lotte looked like a hen thrown up in the air.

On the edge of that wind, there had been a great spray of rain. With that precipitation, all the objects had rained back down again, picked up by the wind on its devastating way: dead crows, larks, starlings, branches, posts and many more things. It had lifted grazing cows off the ground. A boy herding them had been blown twenty-five metres. When the wind dropped him on the road, the boy had knelt down and sung a hymn. Later, he had stammered that it had been boiling hot inside the wind.

Hilde said in a toneless voice that she couldn't even imagine how it had looked.

Wegener nodded. Everyone had wondered about that who hadn't been there. One observer had said, like a column. Another had interrupted him that it hadn't been a stiff object, though, more like a hose. A third person said it had looked like a polypus's sucker.

Hilde asked him why he opened his eyes so wide when he told stories. It scared her, she said. Wegener promised to restrain himself.

More quietly, he went on. He told them about the coiffeur whose bedroom ceiling had been torn off while he slept, and not a scrap of it was to be found. Instead, the beams of other houses had landed on his own roof. As he cleared up the mess, he'd found all sorts of household implements—skewers, flax, hackles, sieves, baskets, a serving spoon and much more. None of it belonged to him so he showed it around in the town. But no one had claimed it.

In the end, the watchman from the town tower had come swaying down to the street. He told them of a feeling like being lifted up in the air by something. He had seen a strange face in the sky. Even days later, he was incapable of saying anything more precise. As soon as he tried, all his limbs started trembling and he went pale with fear.

At this point, the children started crying. Wegener took them all in his arms and hugged them until their sobs abated. In the meantime, he looked out of the window at the sky, which was empty.

On one of Wegener's lone walks, Gangolf Schwinner crossed his path and proved impossible to shake off. Only now, he said, had he found out where their interests intersected.

'You've come up with a really rather interesting theory to deal with the problem of permanence. What the thought lacks, however—if you don't mind me pointing out—is a driving force. I myself have undertaken a number of rather impressive studies on the currents inside the earth, which might be slightly lacking in terms of effects. Doesn't that fit together wonderfully?' He sniffed at length. 'I'm sure I could let you have the article I have written about it. If I'm not mistaken, the work is quite passable.' Schwinner grinned at him through his beard.

As he spoke, Wegener walked half a pace ahead of him, forcing the other man to talk to him from behind and below like a gnome trying to whisper witty remarks in his ear. Now he stopped. Wegener spat on the ground and then asked what currents he was talking about.

'Thermal-based convections,' Schwinner hurried to answer. 'You'll see how naturally our ideas elide. No worse than,' he contorted his face into a laugh, 'the coasts on either side of the Atlantic Ocean.'

Wegener turned to go. Schwinner followed close behind.

'Initially, my studies of these currents were chiefly concerned with mountain-forming processes. In the meantime, though, I have approached the same questions that occupy you. Where your study possibly relies a little too strongly on solidified material, I myself may have immersed myself rather too deeply in molten lava.' Schwinner laughed. 'What links the two of us is tectonics.' He laughed yet again, briefly, and then grew earnest. 'My entire theoretical model is based on tectonic plates, incidentally. Thus we are both looking, if you'll permit me the image, from very different standpoints into the same Promised Land.' Wegener attempted a thin smile.

They had reached the institute for the blind by this point. Wegener looked at Schwinner. He promised his colleague to take a look at the matter, if he cared to let him have the article he'd mentioned. The two men bowed and went their separate ways.

The article arrived by post the next day. It was almost a hundred pages long; Wegener scanned the first few paragraphs and soon understood what his colleagues meant when they referred to the critique-worthy dialectic in Schwinner's work.

He had long since decided not to be drawn into any further discussion on the causes of continental drift. One might just as well question the existence of the universe. No one—with the exception of his father—could explain the cause behind that either.

Secretly, Wegener was making plans for a new expedition. To Greenland, where everything came from, where everything could be measured—the drift, the weather, the ice.

Coming across his notes while cleaning, Else confronted him. What was this trip he was planning?

He spoke long and falteringly about the possibilities such an expedition offered, he spoke about ice thicknesses, position determinations and balloon ascents, he cleared his throat and went on speaking, about firn temperatures and spending the winter.

'The whole winter?' Else stared at him.

Wegener leapt up and ran to her, taking her hands, but the words had been spoken. She looked at him and brushed his fingers away.

'You must promise me this will be your last trip.'

Wegener gasped for air—and then he promised, by all that was sacred to him. She replied that she did not want to know what he meant by that.

On the crossing expedition, they had shown that the old tale of the fixed, perpetual high-pressure area on Greenland's inland ice was a fallacy. That had remained a momentary snapshot, however, and one from summer only. No one knew how it looked there in winter.

Wegener's plan was firmly in place. He would set up a basecamp in which to spend the winter. He would call it Eismitte—

Mid-Ice; he had already marked the spot on the map. Halfway between the coasts, at the thickest point of the ice.

All the things one might do there—sea-level measurements, measurements of the ice thickness using the echo so that subsequent generations could one day establish whether the inland ice was increasing or decreasing. Gravity measurements, measurements of glacier motion. So many glorious measurements! The question of how low the temperature fell there in the winter's night was of the greatest general interest.

No dogs this time. No horses. He was planning the first tour using motorized sleds. And few companions. He would have liked to go alone.

He made a mental list of who might come into question. Wegener would surely manage to gather a few daring souls. One had to pay heed to suitable characteristics. Which meant, essentially, that the men had to be able to shut up for a few weeks at a time.

He wrote letters appealing for support, meaning primarily monetary support. He was of the opinion, he wrote, that Germany should not stand on the sidelines during this noble competition between nations, and the didactic aspects of polar exploration should also be considered. Did crossing unexplored territory not trump a victory on the football field?

He was asked in return what Greenland had to do with the Germans. Was German soil not closer to their hearts? Naturally, Wegener answered, except that this very German soil had been formed by a huge ridge of inland ice exuding from Scandinavia. Any man wishing to understand his homeland must go to the place where that inland ice was still to be found to this day.

They were living in difficult times. Stock markets all over the world were collapsing and submerging like the land bridges in which Wegener no longer believed. He received friendly rejections, he received harsh rejections, he received silence. After two weeks, a letter arrived from the Schuster sports company, agreeing to supply the expedition with pocket compasses at cost price. It was a start.

To get in shape for his trip, Wegener climbed the Dachstein and a few of the lower peaks of the Tauern massif. On the Hintereisferner in the Ötztal Alps, he measured the ice thickness multiple times until his results tallied with the drillings recently undertaken there.

After her initial furore against the expedition, Else displayed discretion and spent hours typing requirement schedules, baggage lists, itineraries as dictated by Wegener. She now found typewriting easier than writing by hand because she could close her eyes as she did while playing the piano. She and Hilde lay down on the floor in the living room and Wegener used the measuring tape from Else's sewing box to determine the length and width of the planned two-man tents. He sent the measurements to the Schuster sports company, which had additionally offered to make special models, this too at cost price, in recognition of his planned heroism. Wegener sent Schuster his hooded jacket, the gift from his saviours on the crossing. Might it be possible for them to manufacture such an item for each participant of the expedition in good quality?

Schuster was enthusiastic. This time, he would even refrain from charging for the material, asking in return for the licence to use the pattern for his collection. All it needed was a name. Wegener declared himself willing to grant such a licence. In his postscript, he added that the garment was called an annuraaq. It was Greenlandic for 'against the wind'. He was sure they would think of something.

Käte was now attending the fourth grade of a progressive girls' lyceum. One day, the unpopular German mistress was absent, launching the girls into instant high spirits. All the things they could do with the gift of a free afternoon! By the time the headmaster had sent a young colleague to cover the lesson, the girls had long since sneaked out of the school building. In a wavering row, they snaked out onto the frozen Mur River.

The moment they were on the ice, Käte let go of her friends' hands and ran so fast that the wind blew threw her hair. How the world blurred on either side, becoming nothing but a shadow play of white and snow and frost. Then the moment when she abandoned herself to the ice and simply glided onwards. The glinting of the crystals in the light, the low gurgle of the Mur deep beneath her and the icy air; she didn't care what might happen to her at the end of her trajectory. At that moment, Käte thought she was flying.

When she did stumble then, falling to her knees, rising with a laugh and patting herself free from snow, the small figure of the headmaster stood all at once on the bank. A cloud of anger steamed from his mouth. He made the girls step up to him individually and remove their hats so that he could pull their ears one after another. Käte was the last in line. He already had her earlobe gripped between his fingers when he leant down to her once more, his fat face close to hers, and said quietly, 'And you, Wegener, you too?' And then he pulled so long and hard that Käte thought her head would come off, imagined it rolling through the snow and down the frozen river towards the weir, and just before it sank there in the maelstrom of open water, the headmaster let go.

Gangolf Schwinner rang at their doorbell on one more occasion, this time unannounced and after nightfall. Wegener opened the door in his nightshirt, quietly so as not to wake the others, and Schwinner lunged at him and grabbed at his arm. He had been thinking.

Wegener was to forget his article. What he had written distracted from the essential issue. It was all a matter of remaining a decent person. And it was a matter of the truth, of course, the truth first and foremost, first and last. 'Have you heard of Margules?'

Wegener had not.

'Max Margules, decent fellow. I've no doubt you'd have taken just as much a liking to him as I would have. Had I been granted the gift of meeting him.'

Schwinner appeared to have been drinking.

'From Galicia by birth. A little older than the two of us, if you'll beg my pardon. Studied physics, PhD in philosophy. A good combination, what?'

Wegener gave an imperceptible nod.

'The first to link the force of a storm with its heat content. Not at all uninteresting, as an approach.'

Wegener conceded he was right. It might indeed be worthy of further consideration. If a person were to find the time.

'In short,' Schwinner was already continuing, 'this Margules fellow came to the idea of combining weather predictions with the principle of mass conservation. Don't ask me why.'

Wegener did nothing of the sort.

'He put all these assumptions into one huge equation. As is right and proper. And realized to his horror that almost everything could be cut out of it again. In the end it led to flawed, even absurd results.'

Wegener silently congratulated his unknown colleague.

'Max Margules therefore . . .' At this point, Schwinner, whose eyes had been closed during the last few sentences, paused and looked up. Wegener could make out the whites of his eyes, as glossy as raw egg. 'Max Margules therefore concluded that predicting the future weather is generally impossible. A principle that earned him no friends. But that's not the last of it. He also deduced from his observations that even the attempt at such a prediction is immoral.'

Wegener wondered whether the time had come to close the door. He had goose pimples under his nightshirt.

'In his later years,' Schwinner went on, 'Margules concluded from the impossibility of weather prediction that God too was an impossibility.'

Hoping to end the conversation, Wegener asked what this Margules was doing nowadays. Perhaps they could meet up at a conference. In daylight.

'He's dead!' Schwinner exclaimed. 'Died, starved, out of stupidity. He didn't know how to take care of himself.'

Wegener promised to include the gentleman in his bedtime prayers, and closed the door.

On the last weekend before he set out, with everything safely packed, he took Else and the children along on an excursion. Via Maria in der Zirbe, they hiked to the Zirbitzkogel. Lotte had been in a miserable mood since the morning and Else tried to perk her up with stories.

Wegener carried the backpack and his walking stick, walking a few steps ahead of the others. He only noticed he was singing when Else joined in after a while. 'If there's a song to be sung, I shall be the one.' His father had often hummed it to himself on walks by Lake Zechlin. 'Cross mountain and vale you'll hear my tale,' and over again from the beginning. Else sang at an interval, which annoyed Wegener. Why would she never let him do anything alone? Lotte stopped crying, at least. And even Wegener had to admit it sounded pleasant, their duet. Nevertheless, it remained a mystery to him why one should sing a tune like that as a canon.

They reached Lake Lavant in the afternoon. While Wegener pitched the tent in a clearing, the ladies picked mushrooms in the underbrush. It was late in the year, one last good day. By the time the guy ropes were in place, the four were back with their harvest, sweaty and their hair mussed.

It was an impressive haul—parasols, honey mushrooms, dotted-stem boletes. Hilde had brought along a toadstool as a trick on her father. Else told her off and Hilde had to return it to the woods.

They toasted the mushrooms over an open fire. Most of them burnt, the rest tasted passable. Hilde said they tasted of earth, Käte said of smoke, Lotte said of worms. Wegener added a silent 'of ersatz coffee'.

Else and he had agreed to stay awake for a while to discuss his trip in peace. But even once the children were finally ready to sleep beneath their covers, there was still a twig cracking somewhere, a cone falling somewhere, a distant wail to be heard, probably a wild cat.

After a full hour of incessant singing, storytelling and reprimanding, Else and he sank exhausted onto their raffia mats. They could only hope, Wegener thought as he drifted off, that the children would fall asleep at some point too.

When he opened his eyes, Wegener saw the shadow of an animal directly in front of him. The shape crept across the canvas.

An ant, quite slowly, was labouring up the slope. And just as the shadow on the fabric enlarged its image, so the taut canvas amplified the crackle of its steps—a tiny, threatening monster. Wegener rubbed his eyes and saw that ants were crawling all over the tent; they must have pitched camp on an anthill.

He looked around. The children had kicked off their pale sheets and now lay scattered across the ground of the tent. Lotte's eyelids were slightly opened, showing their whites. She was snuggled close to Else's belly. Hilde seemed to be cold, her arms wrapped around her drawn-up legs. Käte held both hands pressed to her head, her hair falling over her eyes. In the morning light, the ants' shadows crawled across their bodies. Was this the image he would take along of them? All four had their mouths open.

Wegener slipped out of the tent and went to collect firewood. When he returned with his load, the entire campsite was bathed in morning sun. The girls were sitting clothed outside the tent, combing each others' hair. While he made a fire, Else helped them with their plaits. She gave her daughters fishbone braids every Sunday. How proudly Else looked upon her finished work. She was a great devotee of all things Nordic, like Wegener. Else could spend hours on the subject of the beauty of youth or the strength in her children's eyes. At times, Wegener suspected Else understood Nordic to mean something entirely different than he did.

After breakfast he set out to catch the post bus in Mühlen; Else and the children wanted to spend the day out in nature and would return to Graz later. Wegener had to make the night train to Berlin, where he was meeting Dr Georgi, the meteorologist who was to head the central firn station. They would set out for Copenhagen the next morning and the expedition participants would make the last preparations there during the weeks before their departure.

He had an inkling of how often the image of this farewell would return to him. And so he had asked to say goodbye out here rather than at a station or on a quay in the midst of reporters, like the last time.

As he stood before them with his backpack shouldered, Hilde curtsied and conjured up a bunch of daisies from behind her back. He took the bouquet and sniffed at it but there was nothing to smell. Then it was Käte's turn and she pressed his hands so long and hard that he feared Hilde's flowers would be damaged. She gazed at him with such desperation that he had to look away. Fortunately, Lotte was already tugging at his coat and then clambered swiftly into his arms. Her small palms pressed both his eyes closed, and as he stood there like that, laden and blind, she planted one of her almost imperceptible kisses on each eyelid.

Then his farewell from Else. For a moment they stood facing one another, neither knowing what to say. In the end he swallowed and said, 'You'll be able to go to the south at last. To the Mediterranean.'

She smiled. 'Yes, while you bury yourself inland.'

'Look after the children. And your parents. And yourself.'

'You'll have enough to do looking after yourself. Promise me you will?'

Wegener nodded.

How long it had been since he last looked at Else. She screwed up her eyes a little against the light; she had sacrificed more and more of her eyesight for all her sewing. He should never have left her alone during the war. Fortunately, Hilde was now sensible enough to lend her a hand where necessary. Still, though, Wegener recognized in her the woman whose hand he had once gripped on a dyke. The face that had stared aghast at him over the edge of a balloon basket. His joy, his ballast. He closed his eyes and leant down to give her a kiss. Another thing he hadn't done for an eternity.

But Else had put her hands in front of her face because her tears were flowing. His mouth connected only with her knuckles. Then Else opened a gap in her hands so that they could kiss, and from below them Lotte asked why they were laughing.

The path down to the valley cut steeply across country. Wegener had promised to leave markers, so he broke off dry branches here and there and stuck them in the wet earth. He collected loose stones and piled them into small, wobbly towers, hoping to leave something behind that might help Else and the children along their way. At the foot of the mountain, he paused and inserted the remains of Hilde's bouquet into a fork on the last of his planted branches. Then he looked around to see whether his traces were clear enough, but from down below there was nothing to be seen of them.

Studies on Air Blasts

The sea flowed upwards. He was aware that he was being taken in by an illusion, yet there was no other way to describe it. When he stood by the ship's rail and looked around, it really did look as though the sea rose towards the horizon. Only slightly, but sufficiently to render it hard for a ship to make it up. A barely perceptible warp in the blue-black, almost-smooth sea, similarly weak as the curvature to be expected of the earth's surface, except that they were now, if he were to believe his eyes, not on the outside of a sphere but in its interior.

Wegener shook his head. The impression remained. He wondered whether the knowledge that something was impossible helped to refute an illusion, or whether it was absolutely unimpressed by such an objection. The feeling of sailing up a slope would not be shaken off, in any case.

Yet they weren't even moving. The Gustav Holm had stood by the edge of the ice at Kekertat for two weeks now, motionless. April, and they were still waiting for the ice to open up at last. They should have long since unloaded. With every morning that the passage remained blocked, their plan was delayed by a new day.

They had spent longer than planned sorting and stowing the cargo at Copenhagen. Almost as long as it had taken Else to type up the baggage lists in the autumn, categories, hazard groups, weight. In total, it was a hundred tons of cargo they had brought across the water. Now it had to be taken onshore, and then up onto the inland ice.

Captain Vestmar had gone berserk during loading, with all the baggage. Even just the prefabricated walls for the winter house, and then the dog food, crate after crate of measurement equipment, barrels of consistent fat. Above all, though, hay, hay and more hay; it had come to two full wagonloads in the end.

They would not do without animals after all, now. They had made a long stop in Iceland to load horses, which Wegener anticipated would help transport the baggage over the edge of the glacier. Vigfus had also joined them; to Wegener's delight, he was determined to be part of the expedition again. A few stables had been installed on the Gustav Holm under his instructions. Wegener wanted to find sled dogs in Greenland; one could not rely entirely on modern technology, especially when it was untested.

If they ever managed to dock.

Not until they had fastened everything else in place had the motorized sleds arrived in Copenhagen. Vestmar had dashed straight to Wegener on the lower deck. On the quay, he said, were three gigantic crates, each the size of a freight car. Only over his dead body were those monstrosities coming on board. It took all of Wegener's persuasive powers to refrain the captain from throwing himself overboard.

During the Copenhagen night that followed, he had once again been assaulted by the memory of his Pustervig exile. He lay awake for hours, amazed at the radiant black before his eyes that would not be driven out by blinking. The snow had glowed in the darkness that way whenever Wegener had ventured outside back then.

In the morning, he had asked the glaciological assistant Dr Loewe to request a little pleasure for the long winter's night in the local music shop. That very evening, nine gramophones stood on the quay, coated in frost. Plus records—'Adieu, mein kleiner

Gardeoffizier', 'Ich bin die fesche Lola' and several copies of a song warning of the dangers of blondes. What did people know of the needs of a polar night? Wegener had briefly considered leaving some of the donations behind but then decided they would make welcome gifts for the Eskimos.

And now—after a stormy crossing of several weeks, after the stop in Iceland where they had only managed to drag the horses on board through a combined effort, after the winter trip to the west coast of Greenland—now they lay, as thirsty for action as they were exhausted, within eyeshot of Kamarujuk, their destination, and unable to unload.

The land a few hundred metres away, a mix of snow and the grey of the scree slopes. The colourless fjord. The jagged hands of the mountains petering out to the coast, as though stretching their stony fingers out for them.

Above it all the line of the inland ice. Before that the water, dark. One could spend hours staring at the landscape without making out the slightest motion.

It was now May. Sitting on deck, shielded from the wind by the canisters, it was veritably warm in the sunshine. As soon as one stood up and stepped around the corner into the shade, however, the air punched ice-cold at one's face, a frigid draught coming from the inland and destroying all hope of an end to the frost.

The ice edge still divided the sea into a liquid and a solid part. A passage from one to the other was not provided for. Their attempt to break the ice failed.

The plan was this—dock, unload, then get the baggage onto the inland ice with the aid of the horses via the tongue of the glacier, which offered the only vaguely straight ascent. It would take weeks. Up there, set up the winter house at the western station. Only Georgi was to go ahead to Eismitte to begin with the measurements, in the company of Dr Sorge if circumstances required. Take everything out into the ice on several tours, using dogs or motorized sleds, whichever proved effective. Best of all both.

Wegener caught himself humming a tune but could not remember the words for some time: 'In the long hard winter weather, that's when a wolf, a wolf, a wolf eats its brother.' His mother used to sing it to him, and later he sang it to his daughters.

He looked around. The petrol canisters were piled ship-high on the entire middle deck, swaying gently in the swell. The explosives were stored at the front of the ship, with the hay. Any open flame was strictly forbidden on board. At Iceland, the entire crew had lined up along the quay the minute they got on land and spent at least half an hour smoking in silence. Now too, a few of them could barely resist. Manfred Kraus had come to him that morning, the propeller-sled driver, and asked whether he'd let him move to the lifeboat temporarily so as to smoke there. Since their journey had been interrupted, though, the lifeboat had been storing the detonators.

At night the full moon stole low along the horizon with a reddish shimmer. Ducked down in the shadow of a single cloud, like a thief.

There were three fatal things about waiting. Firstly, every day postponed their plans further into the winter. Secondly, it wasn't merely time they'd lack later but also all the hay the horses were now eating during the wait. They had fodder for a hundred days and every horse got another ration tossed into its box every morning, which it chomped lazily over the next few hours. And thirdly, it became clearer with every passing day that each of them was paying a moral tribute out here. Vigour, courage and trust were perishable goods too.

Early every morning, that brief moment with still-closed eyes when he was nowhere, in no place, as though he were floating far above everything and would only be allocated a place to start the day when he awoke. It was the same morning after morning—the swaying in the swell, the click of the waves beyond the boat's side, the cramped bunk where he heard Georgi breathing in his sleep beside him, the little desk with their books, the porthole to which he crept to look out. And every morning the very same view—the untiringly falling snow, the never-parting clouds. Sometimes ice floes drifted past them to the south. The wind still calm, the barograph Georgi had put into operation still drawing a line as straight and unruffled as the horizon.

For breakfast there was a black bowl of gull soup.

By day they sat in the cramped mess and passed the time with games. They did not even have dice with them. Wegener remembered that playing cards had been on one of the baggage lists, at Else's suggestion. He must have crossed them off, probably for reasons of space, more probably because he'd thought them unnecessary.

Having preferred to stay in his berth to begin with, after a few days Wegener began to join the others. Alone, he only became more and more entangled in anger over the pointlessly wasted time. And there were only so many times he could grease his boots.-

Dr Sorge, who would be responsible for measuring ice thickness, showed them an Eskimo game where they had to grab small objects from the table as quickly as possible. They practiced with sugar cubes but Wegener knew from Mylius-Erichsen that the Eskimos used knucklebones. He was not particularly skilled at it. Secretly, he dreaded the game.

Then they'd talk again for hours, and Georgi said it would be interesting to record their conversations, especially before they went to sleep at night. They came to the question of where the motivation for particular achievements stemmed from and what had brought them all there. A desire for adventure? An excess of energy? After a while Wegener told them how he had come to lack fine motor skills, the shot through his thumb, whereupon all those old enough interrupted each other to list their war experiences, first the highlights and then, after a brief silence, the moments of shame. They spoke about nihilism, cynicism, they spoke about optimism and its limits. On several occasions, they touched upon the problem of marriage and the question of whether marriage was the reason why they were sitting there. These things occupied them more than they cared to admit.

Messrs Loewe and Sorge soon emerged as opponents in these conversations. Loewe seemed sceptical but terribly well informed, no doubt slightly melancholy, mistrusting himself even more than the others. Sorge, by contrast, was a youthful optimist, a daredevil, likewise unusually knowledgeable and versatile but with stronger emotional drives. Despite all their contradictions, one could understand both their standpoints.

While Vigfus and Georgi attempted to distil alcohol out of the liquid obtained by soaking prunes, Loewe entertained the group with speeches. They were drafts for the ceremonial addresses that would be held for them on their return, once the institutes of the world were open to all of them. In his opinion, nothing less than worldwide fame and glory awaited them. Wegener failed to establish whether he was serious.

Sorge, at least, was disturbed by his polemical tone and an embittered dispute soon arose. In the end Loewe lay down his weapons and withdrew to the prospect of all of them ending up porters at the meteorological institute, as their limbs would no doubt have frozen off by their return.

It was Karl Weiken, a geodesist with experience in the field of gravity measurement, who suggested a new game. He dipped his forefinger in the stove's ash box and wrote a name on Georgi's forehead: Gandhi.

The men stared at him in surprise. The most surprised was Georgi, who was trying to squint at his own forehead.

'The aim of the game,' Weiken said, 'is to guess who you are. You're allowed to ask questions as long as they can be answered with Matthew 5:37.'

Gudmund Gislanson, an Icelandic medicine student who had joined them as a horse wrangler, dared to ask what that entailed, apologizing for his limited German skills.

Wegener was able to assist. 'Beatitudes. "But let your communication be, Yea, yea; Nay, nay: for whatsoever is more than these cometh of evil."'

Weiken nodded. Then he wrote Al Capone on Loewe's forehead. The geophysicist Dr Wölcken was now Haile Selassie, Gislanson himself became Socrates. In the end Weiken came towards Wegener with his ashy finger and began to run it across his forehead. Wegener closed his eyes and tried to think of something else. A, J, an E, an S. Was Weiken teasing him? When the finger traced the bend of a U on his head, Wegener whisperingly asked Weiken to write less clearly.

The finger stalled, then wiped swiftly across Wegener's skin and began anew, now using so many swerves, loops and underlinings that it was genuinely impossible to decipher the word.

After that Wegener opened his eyes, dipped his own finger in ash and baptised Weiken with the name of Schrödinger.

The guessing was a long process but really did prove to be a pleasurable pastime. Loewe had guessed his way through all the stars of the American movie industry before it occurred to him he might be a big name in the underworld rather than entertainment. Wölcken got entangled in the idea that he must be one of the three wise men. Poor Gislanson grew most unsettled when his sigh that he did not know prompted a chorus of nods. For a long time, Georgi assumed he was Buddha until the tip of thinking of a rather different stature put him on the right track.

In the end Wegener was the only one left. Or, rather, whoever he was supposed to be. While the others chewed on their seal meat he grew increasingly desolate, despite having quickly found out he was the son of a Berlin pastor. Wasn't that him?

When he found out he had recently died, Wegener gave up.

Georgi told him the solution, 'Horst Wessel!' Wegener stared at him, uncomprehending. 'He just died, Hitler's martyr.' Wegener had to apologize. Had it been due to the preparation for the journey that he had not heard about it? He asked who Hitler was. No one dared to laugh at him.

Then he stood at the ship's rail with Georgi; from time to time, Kraus' dim silhouette lit up down on the ice in the glow of a cigarette. He had overcome his reluctance and now let himself down to the surface to smoke in the evenings.

Georgi said if they waited much longer this way they'd drift once around Greenland with the ice floes.

'Or around the whole world,' Wegener added.

'Where would it take us, I wonder?' Georgi looked up at him.

Wegener broke off an icicle from the rail and licked at it. 'We'd drift over to the Canadian shelf,' he said, 'at the level of New Brunswick, then down the American East Coast and then melt in the Caribbean at the latest.'

'Melt? Us?'

247

Wegener apologized; he meant the ice floes. 'We'd probably simply go on shore.'

They fell silent for a while, then Georgi murmured a goodbye and left.

Unlike his fellow travellers, Wegener hardly missed smoking. When he stood out here in the dusk and emitted a new cloud with every breath, more impressive than any smoke ring, there was nothing he missed. If only the ice down there would get out of the way at last. They'd have to make up with industry for what fortune had failed to bring.

Kraus' tiny cigarette ember still lit up the eternal twilight from time to time. Wegener wouldn't have minded joining him down there for a pipe, but he'd have had to find his smoking equipment first.

A knock on the ship's side directly in front of him gave Wegener a start. It was Kraus returning on board, the rope ladder hitting the metal. When his pointed hood appeared over the edge, Wegener remembered what he had been thinking about.

What was it they said? If the prophet wouldn't come to the mountain, the mountain would have to come to the prophet. But then if they couldn't make it to the land, wouldn't the land have to come out to them? It was doing nothing else, though. The ice extended the land across the water. All they had to do was set foot on it. Wegener leant forward and reached a hand out to Kraus. He had to summon all his strength to pull him over the rail.

Half an hour later, the crew was gathered in the mess, some of them in their nightshirts, and Wegener explained his plan. They would take the equipment to the coast across the ice, all 100 tons of it. Not an easy task but better than waiting until midsummer. And in the final analysis, it was no different to the inland ice.

The next morning, the motor sleds were the first to go. The unmoored ship listed strongly as the first of the huge crates inched down the outer wall. Wegener stood on the ice and conducted while Captain Vestmar ran up and down the ship's rail like a captive animal just before feeding time.

At last all three monstrosities stood on the edge of the ice shelf; Manfred Kraus levered the side walls open and set about installing the runners. The next task was the horses, they too lifted off board by crane. They dangled as still and attentive in their belts as kittens in their mother's mouth, not even twitching a hoof.

By the next morning they hadn't even taken two loads over to the shore. The ice was already thinner than anticipated, and it melted as they watched over the next few days. Now of all times, a foehn came up, the curve of Georgi's thermograph crossing the zero-degrees line for the first time, like a ship bridging the equator on a nautical map. On the third day, they could stab their sticks through the ice in places. The dogs fell in at the edges on the afternoon of the fourth day.

So they left all the other cargo on board and set about blasting a channel into the ice. Wegener calculated the points and they buried powder for eighteen simultaneous blasts of a kilo and a half each. It took them two hours to lay all the fuses. Then Wegener raised his hand and everyone sank to their knees and pressed their gloved hands to their ears.

How the noise was cast back from the walls of the inland ice. Rolling, the echo surged over them as though wanting to take them along with it.

Although the first attempt brought them only minuscule progress, there was unanimous enthusiasm at the method. No matter how much time, dynamite and detonators it cost, at least something was happening. The men ran laughing across the ice; the explosion had attracted a number of Greenlanders, their dogs leaping around among the detonation wires and barking while the ship reversed anew and pressed against the ice's now ragged edge with all its might.

Once they had worked from six in the evening to three in the morning, the ice sprung a tear. Not directly where they were, though, but a little way further south. A gigantic floe, its surface surely half a kilometre wide and several kilometres long. All their work in vain; they might as well have gone on smoking, thinking, sleeping. But that was no matter now. What counted was the free passage. The cargo was heaved back on board, including the baffled horses. The open stretch was reached with a few detonations and everything still on the ice was taken on board, dynamite, crew, Greenlanders, dogs.

They arrived in Kamarujuk on the morning of 17 June, six weeks behind schedule.

The Size of the Cloud Elements

They worked day and night; it was always light anyway. Someone had to visit the coastal settlements with the local catechist to find sled dogs. Buy up the grass harvests and spread them out to dry. Catch halibut as dog food. Then repair packsaddles. Choose dog drivers. Set up a drying frame for shark flesh. Make a path over the glacier with ice axes. Manage less than twenty metres in three days. Despair. Then a memory by night, of the fireplace at Zechlinerhütte, the dustpan full of soot, the frozen lake, the holes melted into it. So charcoal was scattered on the glacier and the sun's warmth hollowed out steps. What relief. The men's faces, joy and soot on them. Build bridges. Regulate streams. Set up depots. Build a bridle path in the western moraine of the glacier. If a single man managed half a section at the steepest point in four hours, how many men would be needed for the whole length?

The single man was Wegener himself. When he returned he found Vigfus, who still hadn't finished all the packsaddles. They'd have to go on without a third of the horses. Gislanson was no great use either. Finding Greenlanders to help prepare the paths, in that case. Then shouting at Vigfus again, who still maintained they couldn't make full use of the horses at the outset or they'd go stiff. In the meantime, swift measurements of the key parameters. Above the pathway, they broke out a rock and dropped it, and it made the earth boom.

Harnessing horses, dogs and people before the first motor sled, the ropes crossing the entire slope. How dashingly the sled was shaped, and how poorly that matched the effort with which it struggled uphill. Metre for metre they moved it forwards, the people spurred on by shouts, the animals by kicks and cracks of the whip.

Moving depots onwards. Estimating daily distances. Finding Greenlanders prepared to accompany them up to the inland ice. Singing as they worked; the Greenlanders now knew many German songs. With one of them, Rasmus, Wegener sang 'Singe nicht, Nachtigall' in two parts. Untangling the sled lines. Cooking shark soup. Cooking bread soup.

There had been invitations to begin with, to the catechist's house, to the head of the local colony, to their helpers' family homes. They were expected to be constant witnesses to the locals' hospitality. Wegener had to bend over in the low doorways, and in the early days he always brought a gramophone along. When their stocks depleted, Wegener took along some of the carbon paper he used to write his letters, as a gift. The sheets caused an even greater sensation than the musical appliances. As soon as Wegener took a seat at the table he'd begin to nod off, and even when he talked to keep himself awake, his thoughts would incessantly slip away from him.

If the daily load was 4,000 kilograms and they had twenty-one horses with eighteen saddles and could thus use three of the horses for the sleds, they'd have the remaining load in the Else depot in seventeen days. Perhaps more like twenty. Three drivers for the horses, two sled drivers, someone had to go on building paths and repairing initial damages to the steeper stretches. If they went twice a day, the seventy-five tons of the interim camp would be in the next depot after twenty-two days. They needed more Greenlanders. Perhaps they'd make it in nineteen. He'd talk to Vigfus, see if he couldn't make three trips a day instead of two. It depended on how many hours one counted as a day.

They had to make progress, there was barely any hay left. The first horses would soon have to be slaughtered. They had only been planned for this initial transport up onto the inland ice in the first place. Yet some of them had not been used at all, due to the lack of saddles. He'd have to persuade Vigfus to have only two people leading the horses from now on. They now had thirty-one Greenlanders working for them. A hundred krona a day, per head. Plus the catechist. And still the sleds hadn't been used; that test was yet to come.

The plan would not hold up to a single further mistake. They had to get a move on at all times, otherwise winter would come over them.

They returned to the ship to sleep, that was the simplest. There could barely be any thought of sleep in the first place. In the mornings, when they came back from work, Wegener stood on deck for a moment. Despite his exhaustion, he had never felt so determined.

When the snowfall was interrupted for a few instants he looked up into the grey spread of clouds that revealed nothing. A few flakes were still up there, refusing to fall down to them. Small and white, they circled at dizzying heights and didn't give a fig about gravity and earthly laws. Perhaps that was the right way to go about things.

Just as Wegener was about to lose faith in gravitation, the snowflakes beat their wings and proved to be albatrosses. It was a whole flock moving on, heading for another, more hospitable corner of the world.

After breakfasting on board, Wegener stood up and asked the team to stay where they were for a while; he had something to say. 'What we're doing here is tiring for everyone, and there'll be no less work over the weeks to come. Expeditions in the polar region are mainly a transport problem. As students, many of us no doubt dreamt of a life in research. And where has that brought us now? What we have to do here is closer to building the pyramids than calculating their surface area. And all for a few numbers and series, with which we'll return next year, God willing?'

Wegener looked around. How old the faces had grown since he'd taken them on board. Perhaps it was because no one here had time to shave; all of them sported beards.

'I'm going to tell you a method that has often helped me. It's universally valid and extremely useful. To survive in an emergency, we have to work on imagining our deeds are indispensable, our research questions are the most interesting in the world. Only such a valuation of our own work, exaggerated when regarded in cold blood, enables us to achieve what is demanded of us here. Looking at the history of polar accidents, we come across a mysterious rule. To be precise, there is no compelling cause for any of the past disasters. For no obvious reason, the expedition gets stuck and suddenly becomes unable to continue. The real reason is always the loss of the illusion. Like an Arctic down draught, doubt descends upon the mind, as cold as Scott's disappointment. Strength disappears exactly when the insight prevails that one is nothing but a miserable incompetent in the end.'

The men cleared the table in silence. From the coast came the incessant howling of the dogs.

Wegener cancelled their free Sunday afternoons, despite knowing the lost time could not be made up. He travelled along the whole coast to find more dogs and persuade every village head to have even the smallest patches of sparse grass torn up. Separately, they were tiny amounts, but they soon had 600 kilograms in total, which would produce 200 kilograms of hay. Plus 240 kilograms of half-dried grass that had already been delivered to the foot of the moraine path.

There were sacks of hay and dogs underfoot everywhere there. It was a mystery how every dog was to find its way back to its owner after finishing its task. But he couldn't let that worry him for the time being. For now, Wegener was grateful that the dogs lay there, a huge, breathing carpet in the snow.

This was how it might work. If only they didn't lose their tenacity. Their endurance. Courage.

They named the depots after their wives. It gave them additional motivation.

In early August, Wegener found the first louse in his shirt. Unpleasant but not surprising. They were living in such close confines with the Greenlanders that they could hardly avoid contagion. He put the creature on his open palm and examined it. Its angry horns didn't scare him. Six minuscule legs crawled in mid-air, the body billowing below them like a pregnant bride's wedding dress. Impossible to tell whether it had drunk his blood yet or not.

It was not the louse that shocked him, but the hand on which it lay. Deeply furrowed, yellowed, rough—what life had done such harm to his skin? He traced the lines with his eyes. Hadn't Squirrel once tried, years ago, to read his future from this palm? How long his nails had grown; there was little time for manicures here. Wegener picked up the louse between forefinger and thumb and cracked it with the edge of a fingernail.

In the mornings, after a day's work, he wrote letters to Else. One heard, he wrote on one occasion, that the Eskimos had so very many words for snow. She was not to believe a word of it; he had looked into the matter. In actual fact they only had two, he wrote. One for falling and one for fallen snow, which seemed wise to him. And pretty, besides. There were of course compounds as well, no different to at home, new snow, powder snow, snow storm and so on. In some dialects there was apparently another term for the snow that wafts close above the ground. That was owing to the local conditions, he explained. And finally, with a great deal of goodwill, one could also count the expression muruaneq, which referred to everything in which one sinks. As a rule, it did denote snow. That, though, was it. Four words in total, no more and no less than in German: Schnee, Firn, Graupel, Harsch. There was no need, he told her, to come to this end of the world for that reason.

Before he lay down to sleep he added a postscript to the letter: For today, you are my muruaneq.

What a slog they were putting themselves through. Two-fifths of the load was now up on the ice. Wegener's fears persisted, however. They were drifting ever more clearly into a wretched predicament. The short summer would soon come to an end and the distance to the site where the western station's winter house was to be built was still long.

There, once all the parts had finally made their way, they would assemble the motorized sleds and begin the transport to Eismitte on the flat inland ice. But the amounts of food, fuel, instruments and material needed there before the winter came— it was inconceivable how it would ever work.

Or was it merely the louse to blame for his dark thoughts? Wegener spent full hours washing, assembled the Flit pump and sprayed himself from head to toe with repellent. He boiled all his clothes and washed them in petroleum—another two days. At midnight, the sun was now sinking so far below the horizon again that it grew veritably dusky.

When he came home in the morning from work, having once again made so little progress, Wegener thought of Clausewitz.

What would the old man have advised him? They needed new reserves to cast into battle. But where to find them? The whole affair seemed under immense threat.

Since the louse, all difficulties increased in a way that grew more terrifying with every day. Since the louse.

When Wegener dreamt, he dreamt of journeys to the south, the Mediterranean, more peaceful coasts. If only the duty of heroism might come to an end one day.

They bagged an ermine with white fur and a black tip to its tail. At the foot of the glacier, a beautiful Arctic fox escaped them at the last moment, almost looking disappointed not to have been caught as it peered back at them from the scree.

At the top end of the glacier, where the motor sleds now stood waiting for Kraus to put them into operation at last, a polar bear made an appearance. The small ears, the huge paw it raised at them, in welcome or defence. The hump behind its shoulders. Wegener was out with Loewe and Georgi that day with only baggage, mainly petroleum but no rifle. Perhaps the bear had cast an eye on their horse. Loewe had just returned from a two-week transport to the Karoline depot, which he had set up with a few Greenlanders at 200 kilometres' distance from the coast, halfway to Eismitte. With the exception of his two comrades and the horse, the bear was the first creature he had seen since then. And while the sight instilled Wegener with more than respect, Loewe seemed to regard the encounter as absolutely unremarkable. Had he lost his senses in the firn? Loewe stood in front of the horse to protect it, even taking a few steps towards the polar bear.

The bear began to snarl.

Loewe snarled back.

The bear raised its paw anew and that too, Loewe emulated. Where had his fear gone? Left behind in the ice? Did he not know what he was doing? Behind him, the horse began to whinny. The bear walked towards them and stood upright. Loewe too raised his arms. They stood facing each other, clearly intoxicated on their own strength and yet unwilling to make use of it. The horse behind them was now foaming at the mouth, dancing nervously on the spot to the clanking of the petroleum canisters.

At last, Wegener called Loewe's name and he began to walk very slowly backwards, never taking his eyes off his opponent. Only once the bear dropped onto all fours, lowered its head and beat a retreat, allowing Loewe to look back at him in search of applause, did Wegener vent his anger. What had he been thinking, he shouted, to risk the mission so recklessly. They weren't in the circus. His voice cracked with anger, at Loewe and at himself for not intervening earlier.

Wegener moved into the large Hilde tent high up on the edge of the inland ice, along with Loewe and Dr Wölcken. The view was sublime—the sun wandered low above the water for hours, as though fearing it might extinguish in it. The colours changed only very gradually. Out before the bay, an iceberg had come loose; against the evening light it looked like a gigantic archway, radiantly green and cold and violet. Floating ice all the way to the horizon, loose, broken, interlocking.

A week before, Georgi had set out alone for Eismitte so that the measurements could finally be started.

They now named the campsites after relatives too. The longing was hard to bear, at times. At least the lice had grown fewer.

The singing of an engine. They all shot to the tent's entrance, Loewe still in his sleeping bag, his hair stuck to his forehead and one hand stretched out, obviously unable to find his glasses in the rush. Wölcken reached for the spade and began to shovel the entrance clear. The drift was considerable, with new snow slipping in and in to them, but Wölcken did his best. As soon as there was space, Wegener pushed past him to crawl out, and then the three of them stood in the snow outside the tent, barefoot and in underclothes, and kept watch.

The low sound was still suspended in mid-air like heavenly music. Then they spotted a black dot in the distance, creeping slowly closer. They didn't move from the spot, merely standing there and watching the approaching miracle—every motion of the fragile body, every side-slip, every leap as it was thrown upwards by the uneven ground.

And then the sled drove up to them in a wide curve, braked, slid a little and then stopped, and while the propeller went on circling idly, the cab roof opened and out clambered Kraus.

As the others leapt into their boots and tumbled to the sled, Wegener simply stood there and thought about what it all meant. A new chapter of polar exploration was beginning before their very eyes. How sleek the motorized sled looked, how modern. A being come to them directly from the future. For their journey too, it opened a door, at least a crack, and Wegener eyed the new promise incredulously, like he had through the tent's entrance that morning. Perhaps they might manage to slip through it after all.

Kraus brought good news. As they lugged petrol canisters to the depot, he reported, out of breath, that Uvkusigsat had seven tons of grass, meaning at least 2,000 kilograms of hay. Then there was Umanak with another sixty sacks, plus Satut, Ikerasak, Kaersut and Akuliarusersuak. Wegener was triumphant. What a difference it made for morale whether one harvested by the sweat of one's own brow or merely placed an order and had the work done by the local women and children. They now had more than enough fodder for the horses. And if everything did work out?

They spent the rest of the day in the Snow Sparrow, as the first of the sleds was soon christened, driving to and fro along the edge of the inland ice. They perched in the cramped cab and looked out at the bay. Wegener was allowed to steer, under Kraus' critical gaze. Not fast but steadily, they drove across the rippled ice. On the return trip, Kraus was back at the wheel and Wegener lit a pipe next to him. Wasn't it a marvellous luxury? If only Scott were there to see it, or Shackleton. How vain their sacrifices seemed from this passenger seat. But no, one must not even think such a thing. Who was to say how miserable their own trip would seem to the very next generation?

In the afternoon they drove together to the upper end of the glacier to fetch the second motorized sled, which they named Polar Bear. Starting in fresh snow proved difficult but as soon as they were in motion there was no stopping them.

It was now victory all the way. Wölcken and Dr Sorge set out with a large dogsled party to Eismitte. On the coast, Vigfus finally managed to get the most out of the horses, reporting rising daily loads. In the crevassed icefall, the horses were simply superior to every other means of transport.

The following day, Wegener and Kraus started on their first propeller sled tour with payload, to move part of the Karoline depot ahead. It was almost impossible to pick up speed on the sticky new snow. In the end, however, they found a fairly comfortable method. A board beneath each runner, and while one person shook at the sled from the outside the driver had to go full throttle, then with a little luck things would get started—whereby the helper had to make sure he got out of the propeller's way in good time. In the end that meant running after the moving sled and taking a leap to get on board.

Yet if there was a weather god, he was not in the best of moods that day. The snowfall so dense that they could barely see a few steps ahead. After a very short time they lost sight of the black pennants Georgi had placed, and simply went on driving across the ice with not the slightest idea of where they were heading. The noise of the propeller, Kraus' jolting body beside him in the driving seat, ahead of them the falling snowflakes, leaping away in all directions like a swarm of shooting stars. To begin with, they had sometimes exchanged shouts but they could not hear each other anyway.

All around them the radiant grey, motionless and without the slightest contour, sometimes seeming to float as though they were no longer of this world. None of the flags were visible, no depot. Finally, they turned around and followed the last remains of their own tracks back to their tent above the coast. The day had been good for nothing in the end but an utter waste of petrol. They could have loaded half a ton and taken it up to kilometre 200. Instead, they had collected nothing but a heap of experience, which now weighed as heavy on Wegener in his sleeping bag as a fully loaded Snow Sparrow. It was the last day of August.

The next weeks brought more new snow, sticky and erasing all traces. How easy everything would have been if they'd only been able to start the transports ten or twenty days earlier.

They loaded up, set out, drove a tiny distance at immense effort, then got stuck, unloaded and returned, discouraged. They barely made any progress against the wind and driving snow. As soon as a slight inclination arose, they came to a complete standstill with their load. There were now interim depots all along the route, consisting of all the goods that absolutely had to get to the Eismitte station—above all the house and large amounts of petroleum.

Huge snowdrifts piled in the wake of the crates, everything gradually sinking.

It was no use. The first half of September passed with no improvement in the weather; the summer with its smooth paths for the sleds and windless days was over. Only very gradually, as slowly as the new snow covered the old, making it denser and firmer, turning it to firn and then at last to ice, did Wegener come to realize that time was ripping up his plans and scattering them to the four winds.

Or at least, the hope placed in the motorized sleds proved an illusion. It was too late in the year for the devices. They needed another large-scale dogsled trip to get all the material to Eismitte that was essential in the approaching Arctic winter. Why on earth had Georgi, who had organized the first transports, not taken everything necessary to the central firn station to begin with? It had been a mistake to give him free rein.

Wegener would have to take part in the trip himself.

On the day before they set out, Wegener was the first to slip out of the tent. The sun was rising between crimson clouds, the dark margin of a stratus cloud marked by strips of rain drawn across all the rest of the horizon. Wegener wanted to take a few pictures to send in a Christmas parcel for Else. The last post ship would soon be passing down at the harbour. What better gift could he give her but a view of their life out here?

He photographed again what he had seen in the past months, the mountains of ice, the fells of stone; it wasn't much. He had first seen it all from the water as they approached, while waiting, and then on the coast on returning from a dinner at the catechist's house in the evening's dusk. He had seen it from the moraine when they turned around during a break in their work, and later from the glacier, driving the horses—the sea, smooth as a mirror, with the white flecks upon it. The charcoal line in the ice that wound like a garland around icicles smoothed by a storm. Scattered in the snow, the furry bundles of dogs, every gust casting waves across their pelts. The horses standing alone, turned away from the wind.

On his attempt to climb back into the tent, Wegener caught his foot in a rope, slipped and fell. At first he couldn't explain the stabbing in his side, and then he realized he had fallen on a corner of the camera. The pain grew no less when Wegener saw the damage to the casing, but he paid it no further attention. It turned out the rear wall of the camera had been bent open; in comparison, the bruise to his hip was insignificant.

Wegener immediately began to develop the plates. He spent hours warming the baths, the thermometer at hand at all times, to reach the correct temperature. Then the first grey appeared on the plates, growing darker and at last utterly black. Wegener took prints nonetheless by exposing them for several minutes before the petroleum lamp. But the photos remained entirely colourless, a pure white, only covered here and there by a nebulous shadow and once by a frost pattern formed while drying. Before he put the pictures into Else's Christmas letter he wrote on the back of each one what they depicted.

The dogs in the morning, buried under fresh snow
A snow-covered horse in the light
The moraine path before using charcoal
The tent at the Else depot
A polar bear in retreat
View of the sky

Elementary Theory of Atmospheric Reflections

Wegener set out on 22 September, accompanied by twelve Greenlanders. Also by Dr Loewe—not his first choice but all the other expedition participants were otherwise engaged.

They rode out with cries of 'íu, íu' and cracks of the whip. At noon, the cloud cover opened up for the first time in days. The blue of the firmament—Wegener thought he might be looking into another world, feeling strangely exhilarated. Only above the coastal fells did the föhn clouds squat, motionless.

He, though, was at last on the move again. The loose snow drifted low above the ground, leaving a snaking pattern. A marvellous ride, galloping through the white waves, a strong cold north-easterly into their faces, plus blowing snow and once again the most wonderful lights, colours and views across the coastal mountains.

'Today—for dessert—inland ice—with whipped cream!' Wegener yelled over at Loewe, but it was no doubt incomprehensible.

They met the returning dogsleds at kilometre three. Wölcken appeared exhausted and his Greenlanders no less so. He had a letter from Eismitte with him, which sounded rather desolate. Georgi and Sorge announced their intention to take the hand sled to the coast of their own accord if no further transport arrived by 20 October. A hazardous plan. For the event that another sled trip was to be undertaken, they placed a number of orders: seventeen large petrol cans, a drill, a sufficient amount of explosives. Georgi had the audacity to complain of the lack of meteorological equipment. He needed balloons for the winter, especially small models, plus kites, kite wire, registration strips, and also two metres of rubber hosing.

Rubber hosing! The man had a cheek. Georgi threatened an unspecified catastrophe if the material did not arrive. At the end of the letter, he asked to put his agitation down to the extreme situation. He seemed still to consider it a mere meteorological emergency.

They were now well beyond meteorology.

Wegener watched his Greenlanders in heated conversation with Wölcken's Greenlanders, their concerned faces. The men placed their hands on each others' shoulders.

Feeding the dogs every evening. When approached with the meat, the dogs threw themselves against their belts with such energy that the material threatened to tear. The bucket had to be emptied high above one's head while the dogs leapt up.

How their rear ends stabbed into the air as soon as the meat tumbled to the ground, erect tails pressed close together. In the end they bit at the bloodied snow, licked the splashes from one anothers' fur and only slowly realized the feeding was over.

How quiet the Greenlanders were in comparison. Their fear of the inland ice. Wegener would very much have liked to understand what they said to one another. Their conversations broke off whenever he came close. Silently, they turned to the dogs, scratched the ice from their fur or castigated them; it made no apparent difference.

At kilometre 62, the Greenlanders refused to go any further. They couldn't breathe, they said, the dogs would die and then they'd have to walk back in the end and eat their boots to fend off starvation. Hours of palavering brought no outcome.

Eight of them returned to the coast; it took some effort to keep the other four with them. Wegener raised their pay to six krona per day. There was now an icy frost, driving snow and headwinds.

They decided to abandon the winter house. They could always dig down into the firn at Eismitte, where it was no colder than behind the thin walls. All that mattered now was the petroleum.

The whole affair was heading for a major disaster, it was no use denying it.

In addition, the soft new snow hindered their progress considerably. Every day threw the previous day's plan into disarray. Wegener had promised the Greenlanders an expedition watch each if they stayed up to the halfway point. Three of them would no longer play along, even fifty kilometres before that. Wegener sent them back with a letter to Weiken, in which he asked him to give them the watches nonetheless. He would continue with Loewe and Rasmus, the last remaining Greenlander.

Their objectives—firstly to reach Eismitte. Only there could they establish whether Georgi and Sorge had in fact been foolish enough to attempt a return on foot. How could the team at the western station even think of working sensibly, while fearing for the two men's welfare?

Secondly, maintaining the winter station at any price. Loewe and he were determined to spend the winter in the firn, should Georgi and Sorge want to go back. The five of them together would hardly be able to stay at the station, however, without sufficient food and fuel.

Georgi and Sorge could use the dogs and there was no lack of depots, at least on the outer leg. In good weather, the return to the coast ought to be possible.

On the first Sunday of October, they marked the harvest festival by opening two tins of macaroni, with a little broth to wash it down. That night they all tossed and turned in their beds with happiness and overfed stomachs.

Then the line of black flags that had previously shown them the way came to an end. Wölcken had warned them the markings got rarer out here; apparently, most of the pennants were stowed away in a poorly marked crate. Sloppy preparation would cost them their necks.

Fortunately, Georgi had been so kind as to build a snowman every five kilometres on his first trip out. The structures themselves were barely recognizable from a distance, but their shadows stood out clearly in the general whiteness. And thus the caravan paraded past a guard of mute soldiers, caught in utterly rigid salutes.

Huge wheels of cloud now rolled across the sky.

The ground they crossed was the last vestige of the Ice Age in the northern hemisphere. While waiting on the Gustav Holm, Georgi had calculated that the oceans would rise six and a half metres if the entire inland ice were to melt. In a world like that, Wegener would have played not by the canal as a child but on a beach.

They reached the 200-kilometre depot. Halfway. At least they had no sign of frostbite yet.

What they needed was every polar explorer's most elegant aid: good fortune.

The thermometer fell relentlessly—thirty degrees. Thirty-five degrees. Forty degrees. Their daily distances fell too; in some cases they made no progress at all. The effort required at 2,000 metres above sea level was an additional burden.

Atmospheric condition: good view, yet with no contrast in the sky and the snow. Every snowdrift and every crevasse an unpredictable hurdle.

At kilometre 280, a dead dog by the side of the path. A monument to the cold.

Then came 20 October, the date for which Georgi and Sorge had announced their departure with the hand sleds. They now expected to meet the two of them every day on their march. Every dark fleck in the distance was examined for hours as they approached it. The days grew swiftly shorter; there were more and more such dark flecks. And in the end it was merely one of Georgi's snowmen after all. They trooped past the cold figures in silence; it felt like running the gauntlet.

They had to spend entire days in the tent. The lice had meanwhile grown so rampant that Wegener wanted to tear off his clothes and run out into the firn. Loewe complained of pains in his foot but refused to let anyone look at it. On several occasions, a snowfinch fluttered around their tent, 340 kilometres from the coast.

They sustained themselves from the supplies they were supposed to be taking to Eismitte. Loewe came up with a recipe using dried apricots, which he soaked in sugar-water, producing a tasty decoction. The procedure could be repeated several times before the depleted remains were stewed into compote. Out of gratitude, Wegener gave the recipe the name Good Beasts. It could also be made with frozen apples.

More and more, they simply stayed in their beds in the morning. There was no need to look outside; the winds gave them a vivid impression of the weather. So as to pass the days in the tent in more interesting a fashion, they made a stew of soaked ship's biscuits. Sardines in oil were served on the side.

The dogs' howling every evening. One of them began, another joined in, and at some point they all lamented, in wave after wave.

Out once more to stand beside the tent. The full moon in the eastern sky polished silver, the snow beneath it almost black, as though it had swallowed up all the moonlight and would never give it back. Above the western horizon a dull, orange glimmer, which curved in a pale dusk towards the zenith, above it an abandoned pack of stratus clouds. The sky itself lustreless blue, decorated with a few exhausted stars. From time to time, the sharp crack of firn breaking under the weight of the snowpack interrupted the silence. It sounded like the rumbling stomach of a gigantic icy whale. Nature in its own company, paying them not the slightest attention.

Loewe's pain grew more intense; sometimes he screamed at night, waking himself up, and then he gagged himself with something to stop him from disturbing the others. His wheezes and Wegener's relief at the end of the noise.

How slowly they progressed, as though their path stretched out towards the end. The differences between days spent moving and rest days barely registered now. The few steps they managed on some days served essentially to maintain their morale. The deep snow as sharp as sand, the dogs sinking in almost entirely. It seemed to Wegener as though they might just as well have left the tents where they were. They'd have walked back to sleep and would at least have saved themselves the work of pitching.

They saw the snowfinch several more times in the drifting snow. As they walked behind the sleds side by side in the headwind so as not to overtax the dogs, they conversed about the likelihood that it was a real bird, interrupted only by Loewe counting his footsteps; he mistrusted the pedometer. They could spend hours discussing whether the finch was imaginary or reality.

When he wrote in his journal, pencil clutched in his gloved hand before he went to sleep, Wegener tried to describe the bird as though it were an illusion.

It grew colder with every further day, and with every day it grew darker. They abandoned another canister daily, knowing they would make no progress otherwise. Had they really once set out to provide the Eismitte station with petroleum for the winter?

Soon they had nothing more than themselves.

Visible from some distance—a tower of snow, the structures of the weather hut, the bare black silhouettes of the radiometer, a few skis stuck into the firn, the anchoring ropes, between them scattered petroleum cans. As they came closer, they saw that a wall of snow blocks surrounded the inside area of the station in a semicircle, almost overpowered by snowdrifts. The theodolite, the tripod for the firm scales—what use were they now? All of it absolutely motionless, apart from a thin red pennant fluttering from the anemometer mast like the useless rigging of a boat wrecked on the open sea.

The dogs, the crunching snow. Was there no one there to hear them? Then a call, 'They're here,' and Georgi dashed outside in long underwear. Hugs; perhaps for the first time in his life, Wegener understood why people hugged one another. Joy at the reunion and possibly even stronger relief at not having to go on any further. The fear Georgi must have endured over the past weeks was still visible on his face, the feeling of being given up, abandoned. Did he not see they had no supplies with them? When would he understand that they had not brought help?

Sorge now appeared, embraced Wegener, stared at him for some time and then cautiously broke a few lumps of frost out of his beard and eyelashes. Rasmus was greeted with equal enthusiasm.

Loewe was the last to arrive, on foot because his dogs had refused to pull his sled. It would have been his turn for embraces now, but that failed because he instantly sank to the ground and seemed unwilling to stand up under any circumstances. Georgi pushed a canister towards Wegener and patted unceasingly at the metal, as an invitation to take a seat. The amazement at no longer having to struggle.

And yet—there were five of them and they wouldn't all be able to stay, they didn't have enough for the winter. Loewe's exhausted face in the small opening of his hood. Sorge with his voluminous beard, arm in arm with Rasmus, the dogs leaping about their legs while still attached to the empty sleds; no one had released them.

At last, Georgi asked them in, which in this case meant asking them down. He went ahead to the entrance, a simple hole in the snow. Over his shoulder, he explained the situation—as the autumnal storms picked up, the tent had become uninhabitable, so they had ended up withdrawing beneath the firn's surface. Sorge had dug into the ice like a man possessed since his arrival, to get temperature readings from various depths. He was planning an essay, 'The Warmth of the Perpetual Ice'. Sorge gave an embarrassed smile. He held an arm out to Loewe, who was clearly having trouble staying on his feet.

The staircase was steep and deep in snow. Icy-smooth steps led downwards. Ahead of Wegener, Georgi felt his way through the dark, then Sorge with Loewe and at the rear Rasmus, who had fed the dogs. It might be five or six metres' depth, the narrow aisle and driven snow everywhere. Did it really get warmer in the ice? Wegener enquired as to the external temperatures of the past week; on their way, they had not even managed the most basic of tasks in the end. He registered with satisfaction that the previous days had set new records. Minus fifty-four degrees—so it hadn't been merely their exhaustion that made them feel cold.

Measurements were scored into the walls of the shaft, height markings but also pictures, an animal, possibly a wolf. Alongside them hands, melted into the ice. How slowly time must have passed.

Then a step down. And while the actual aisle led almost vertically downwards, caverns branched off on either side, the right-hand one presented by Georgi as the living space. The bathroom was opposite, he said. Wegener understood now where all the blocks of snow came from, fashioned into the storm wall up above.

The parlour lay behind a curtain of two reindeer skins, in darkness. Before Wegener entered he broke a handful of snow out of the wall, lumped it together into a decently round ball and threw it down to the depths. There was not a sound. But perhaps the firn on the ground was merely so soft that it muffled the landing.

Sorge lit the stove in their honour. Wegener saw that the cave was overgrown with white ferns, thousands of tiny leaves trailing down the walls. It took him a moment to realize it couldn't be plant life. What covered the ceiling was expelled breath congealed into frost.

The walls of the cavern looked like white marble, the soot having added the typical streaks and ribbons. Once the fire was alight, Sorge turned almost apologetically to them and said they actually rarely heated the place now. Since deciding to stay there, they had spent all their time in sleeping bags to save petroleum.

How swiftly the room warmed up. Yet it remained dark despite the fire and the air soon grew stuffy. Wegener did not have the impression that the change of light and temperature did him much good, after all his weeks in the fresh air. Rasmus grew veritably apathetic and had to sit down. Someone provided them with squares of chocolate, which stayed in their mouths without melting for a surprising length of time. When it did dissolve, it flooded their mouths with its sweetness and stickiness, making Wegener have to walk back to the exit to disgorge it.

Once he was back and felt strong enough to speak, Wegener thanked Georgi and Sorge in a brief speech for holding the station, and explained the situation. Their three sleds were the pitiful last remains of their undertaking. Apart from Rasmus, all the Greenlanders had let them down, he said; he could still barely withstand the disappointment. Instead of the planned two weeks, they had taken forty days to get to Eismitte.

'Like Jesus,' Sorge quipped. Wegener made no response.

Georgi uttered the question Wegener had feared. Why had they come at all? There was no hint of accusation in his voice.

Wegener tried to make his answer sound just as composed. 'By the time we realized we would be no help, our supplies were not sufficient to consider turning back. We hoped only to find food here.'

The small petroleum stove hissed. 'And,' Wegener continued, 'I wanted to spare the two of you from abandoning the station of your own accord.'

No one answered. Perhaps it had come out rather too blunt. What he had meant was, from leaving on your own initiative. Tacking that on would have sounded like an apology, however. So Wegener merely added, facing Georgi, 'It was your decision in the summer, at least, to take along instruments on the first journey rather than provisions and fuel.'

A drip of melted ice loosened from the ceiling and fell onto the table between them.

'This seems to be a futile conversation,' Georgi said then. 'We ought to see how to make the best out of the circumstances we're in now. Don't you want to get an impression of the station first?'

They did.

'Just a quick tour of the house,' Georgi promised. Like a country gent, he shuffled around the living area in woollen socks and cardigan, presenting the sleeping bunks fashioned out of snow as though his family estate were on show. Impressed, Rasmus and Wegener listened to his explanations. Loewe, however, was too weak for the tour. Sorge made him a provisional bed and he lowered himself onto it with a great sigh.

They were shown the chapel—a niche above the lamp and Primus stove where the rising heat had melted a cupola into the ceiling of firn.

'No pictures of saints?' Wegener asked with a hint of ridicule, and Georgi shook his head in silence. Sorge, having followed the conversation from the margins, shook his head likewise but more in amazement.

Next to the chapel, the ceiling opened up to a ventilation pipe going all the way outside. 'Perhaps,' Georgi said, 'you saw the cloud of thin steam crossing the ice as a kilometre-long trail of fog.' None of them had noticed it. Georgi reported how an Arctic fox had sat outside the opening one morning, due to the warmth or the nutritious scent. 'We couldn't get rid of it for days. When things did get too monotonous for it in the end, it ate up the anchor rope of the anemometer mast and trotted off.'

In one corner of the cavern, a gramophone, a camera and a radio were stowed away. Wegener stopped and was about to say something but Georgi beckoned him over to the exit. Wegener followed without a word. At the foot of the staircase, Georgi was preparing his descent by knotting a long rope firmly to a mounting.

There was presumably no need to show them the privy across the hall, he noted.

Then he let himself slowly down into their icy crypt, as he called the excavation. As he disappeared into the darkness he called up to them that their house had originally been only two metres below the surface. Through the incessant falling snow, however, they had got gradually deeper and anticipated residing twice as far from the outside world on their departure than now. 'It's Sorge's greatest ambition,' his voice called from below, 'to get deeper and deeper down here. He spends every free moment digging, or actually cutting. It's considerably easier to excavate the firn in blocks.'

Then the sound of an impact, followed by a muffled shout that he had now landed and Wegener was free to follow.

Wegener let himself down with due caution. The first section led down steep steps, whereas the last four metres were a vertical drop. Georgi conducted him, from below, having meanwhile lit a lamp.

Wegener landed on his hands and knees, patted himself down and then looked around at where he'd landed. What an undertaking. Holes were bored into the firn at a metre apart, the walls impacted here almost to pure ice. The mercury thermometer was installed in the lowest opening. Georgi presented the instrument with some awe; it was the most sensitive device they had brought to Eismitte. Wegener understood him completely, even sharing his pride, although he doubted whether the two of them were correct in their assessment, from a higher perspective. When Wegener considered how spaciously padded the thermometer's transport crate had been—how much petroleum could they have transported in its place?

Georgi held the station's entire electrical equipment in one hand: a flashlight for reading the thermometer. Because the dry battery had stopped functioning at these temperatures, Sorge had come up with the ruse of swaddling it thickly in socks to feign a milder climate.

They stood side by side, embarrassed like in a cramped elevator. The leader of the Eismitte station and the leader of the expedition as a whole. How was it to go on for them? Georgi took the flashlight between his teeth to enter the current temperature in his notebook. Wegener cleared his throat.

'Loewe is too weak to go back, I'd say.' Georgi nodded. The flashlight nodded along with him.

'We can't possibly all stay here.'

Georgi removed the light from his mouth and said they'd have to do an inventory of provisions and fuel, and then they'd see.

He gave a swift overview of the results of their measurements in the firn, which Wegener followed half-heartedly. His mind wandered constantly to the question of what he would do if he were down here alone and the rope came loose from its anchor.

The outcome of the calculation was that the supplies were sufficient for three persons at most, who could live on them for six months in an emergency; until the end of April. At that point, however, it would only just be possible to start the first sled trip of the new year.

Loewe was meanwhile feverish; returning soon was out of the question for him. He lay cowered on his bed, his knees drawn up to his chest; the others sat around the table.

Wegener asked after further scientific findings. Georgi reported on the difficulties of keeping the carbide dry for filling the pilot balloons.

'And the ice thickness measurements?'

Georgi and Sorge exchanged glances. They had stored the crates of explosives some distance away for safety's sake, perhaps a hundred paces from the station. After several days of snow, the marking had been gone, they said, and the crates untraceable. They had spent several days prodding the entire surrounding area with rods. Sadly, to no avail. They were optimistic about finding the explosives, however.

Wegener withdrew to his thoughts. How was one to come to a decision when it was impossible to gain an overview, a patch of firm ground from which to decide? All certainties were floating away from him.

One could at least assume that both were equally pernicious, the passage to the coast and spending the winter in the ice. He didn't notice the others stealing out of the room. One had to apply systematic criteria to the problem until it could be appeased. Work through all possible combinations. How many possibilities were there if one decided the station had to remain occupied? At that point in the year, one couldn't send anyone to the coast alone. And after Wegener's experiences in Pustervig, it was out of the question to leave someone out here alone all winter. After some thought, he even questioned it for himself. And Loewe was not capable of being moved in any circumstances. They still had twenty dogs.

He went through all the options in his mind. Rasmus could not be called upon to spend the winter in the ice, even though he didn't show his fear outwardly. But he had cried out at night in terror. And Wegener himself was needed more urgently on the coast, where so many decisions awaited him, than here.

All at once someone cleared his throat behind him. When Wegener looked around, there were Georgi, Sorge and Rasmus, each holding a petroleum lamp. The little flames flickered wildly. Was he having hallucinations? It was only when they began to sing 'For He's a Jolly Good Fellow' that Wegener understood midnight had arrived.

The 1st of November, his fiftieth birthday. Before he could say anything, Sorge was patting him on the back. Georgi gripped him by the shoulders and looked him in the eye for a long time. Loewe smiled over from his bed, then it was Rasmus's turn and he held out his small, plump hand, and they did not let go of one another for a good while.

To mark the occasion, Sorge thawed an apple for each of them in hot water. They sang all the songs Rasmus had learnt in the moraine, children's songs, meteorologists' songs; the atmosphere grew very informal. They talked about their families, they argued about where it was more dangerous—here or in highly strung Europe with its automobiles.

Georgi talked himself into a rage; an electric tram came shooting around every corner at home. With all the haste and mechanization, one was constantly at mortal threat, or at least he was more concerned about his wife and son than for himself. Wegener was too tired to contradict him.

When they asked Sorge whether he had children, it emerged that he had married directly before their departure and had joined the expedition straight from his honeymoon.

For a while, they stared into the dancing petroleum flames, each man thinking of home. Then Loewe's groans grew louder and they decided to declare the festivities over and turn to the practical sides of life.

For the first time since leaving the west coast, Loewe removed his socks. His right foot proved to be frostbitten, all the toes already in a state of rot.

They stood silently around the foot. Although the cold had the considerable advantage of reducing smells, it still reeked to high heaven. Georgi thought he saw early signs of blood poisoning.

There was no other option but to operate. Wegener was to perform the removal. Before that, however, he requested half an hour's rest to regain his strength. The others stayed by Loewe's side while Wegener lay down on Georgi's bed.

He did not find the sleep he had hoped for, however. Over and over, he felt at his feet to memorize where and how far he had to cut so as to separate the toes smoothly from the joints. Just as he had drifted off after all, Georgi came and woke him.

They tried to make Loewe's foot slightly less sensitive by applying crushed ice. They had no painkilling medications, no syringe, and the crate of alcohol was deposited at kilometre 62. Sorge held Loewe's foot in his lap, held the lamp and handed over instruments and bandages.

Wegener used a pair of shears to cut. What self-control Loewe possessed. He had had so many travel plans. It took a full hour.

Later, they sat together. Loewe was running a fever in his bed but was capable of answering them when they managed to wake him. He said he saw animals, lots of animals. What beautiful animals they were. When they asked him to describe them he fell asleep again.

They made all manner of lists that night. Classifications, considerations, inventories of the various depots from memory. Plans for the first trip in the spring, assuming various weather conditions. As time passed, they grew rather exuberant. Sorge fed Wegener and Georgi bread with butter. No one wanted to remember that it would be time to set out again in four hours. As winter approached, every day counted. Wegener had still not yet decided who had to leave.

He watched Sorge playing with the shears. Lost in thought, he began to cut his nails, finger by finger. Then he made the scissors dance on the table, the pair of blades ending up pointing at Wegener and Rasmus. It was impossible to overlook but none of the others paid any attention.

He would return, with Rasmus. Against all adversities. Wegener announced his decision, emphasizing that Georgi and Sorge were undoubtedly the best suited to complete the work they had begun. He stressed the word 'begun'.

The two of them consented and agreed to ration their supplies even further, so as to hold out until June as a last resort.

While - Wegener and Rasmus repacked the crates and Georgi assembled provisions for their return journey, Sorge was so kind as to deal with Wegener's underwear. His shirt alone must have harboured some 5,000 or 10,000 eggs. Over and over, Sorge heated the metal surface of a ski with the soldering lamp and used it to iron the fabric so firmly on the inside and outside that he was just shy of making holes in it. Wegener urged him to hurry; he was cold as he packed. Sorge handed him his clothes with a grim smile, commenting that he hoped he had either destroyed the beasts or at least damaged them severely.

In the end they decided to lie down for a moment after all. Georgi and Sorge surrendered their beds to the guests; they would rest on the floor of the cave, they said. Wegener was too exhausted to contradict, only hoping he wouldn't leave too many lice behind for them. Then he lay there trembling with fatigue and the cold, which kept him from sleeping for a long time.

He cleaned his fingernails with the nail of his thumb. How long they had grown. After that he dealt with the other hand in the same manner and then began all over again. Their method of gaining knowledge was no different, a constant pushing to and fro of certainties that held each other up but provided no real support. And as soon as a firm place had been found for once, someone was sure to make it falter in the next moment.

Had it been different one or two generations before, in the days of the great heroes? Was doubt only a part of their present day? Would it ever pass? The impossibility of comparing one's own era with a previous one, simply because one could not yet see it from outside. How hard it was to assess developments. No one experienced time passing without aging in the process. The never-ending talk of youth, fashions, progress said less about the actual external development than about the passing of each individual's internal time.

Wegener's last thought before he did fall asleep—the first half of his life was now over.

The External Audibility Limit

It was early morning when Georgi woke them. An unreal, magical light came down through the ceiling.

Wegener put on his passably dried clothing—the cloth trousers, the ironed vest, dogskin trousers, his thick, stuffed fur boots, the skiing shirt, the blue sleeveless cardigan.

After a breakfast of shark in bread soup, Wegener tended to Loewe's wounds one last time. Small pieces of bone had festered out over night. As they had no more bandages, he plucked the splinters out of the gauze with tweezers and reused the material.

The woollen cardigan, over it the dogskin anorak, his woollen windbreaker, the head protector, plus the wrist warmers, his hat and the fur gloves.

Georgi looked at him. Did he feel sufficiently rested for the long journey? Wegener dismissed the question with a gesture. The sooner they got out there, the more time they'd have before it got dark for good. And apart from that, he felt stronger than ever, he felt on top of the world.

Georgi smiled. 'You are, in a way.'

The steep stairs once again. How the weariness came welling up as Wegener stepped outside, out into the winds, snow, light and cold, into emptiness, frost and hostility to all life. All that greeted him with a desolate, unchanging exorbitance, which he was powerless to combat.

A moving farewell on both sides, the hugs perhaps a moment longer than the previous day's. Georgi seemed to have taken no offence at their dispute over the station's equipment. And Wegener's anger had evaporated. What was he to be angry about? No matter how much one hoped, while preparing at one's desk at home, to calculate everything in advance—no traveller in this territory was entitled to remain unharmed by mistakes, by mishaps, by the uncertainty in which they all lived.

Wegener sensed that their parting was harder for Georgi and Sorge than for themselves. They could at least take some action, they could save themselves. Georgi looked as though he'd need to withdraw to the privy after they left to regain his composure.

Before they set off, they slaughtered the three poorest dogs. One was fed to the remaining animals and two stayed there, as a reserve supply of meat for the winter.

Strapping on the skis. Grabbing the poles. Heading out. Eyes narrowed to slits, putting one foot in front of the other. Wegener walked behind the dogsled, stumbled over furrows ploughed by the wind. Within minutes, he had lost sight of Rasmus, although he was probably directly alongside him.

Was he merely imagining it had been his father's fiftieth birthday when they'd made that unfortunate bet? How could he have thought during the night that he was in the middle of his life? What did the psalms have to say on the subject? The days of our years are threescore years and ten; and if by reason of strength they be fourscore years, yet is their strength labour and sorrow; for it is soon cut off, and we fly away. Wegener clenched the fingers of his left hand in a fist inside their glove. Five. Then he did the same on the right. Ten. Was it that, that strange decimal system, that made him think of the half? How was one to determine the middle of a life without knowing the end? He had solved equations with considerably more unknowns, but now he made no progress with only one missing factor.

The difficulty out here was, one rushed into the falling snowflakes with open eyes, simply because they did not differ from the background. Had he been asked twenty-five years ago where he would spend his fiftieth, he would never have thought of this remote place. And yet—had he been asked where he'd most like to spend his birthday, his ideal would have been identical with this view.

Moving on, towards the dusk that was now all around him. Driving out these thoughts, thoughts of darkness. In fact any thoughts of time, which was a disease. An infectious disease; everyone succumbed to it sooner or later.

It made no difference now whether he kept his eyes open or closed. Always, the same empty, lightless white.

His eyelashes froze to the fur on his hood. Every time he adjusted the jacket a few of them were pulled out, which was not only painful but also left his eyes without protection from the snowflakes. He had long since stopped counting the snowmen. Numbers had proved unreliable. How was he to know he hadn't overlooked one of the white shapes? He didn't spot a single one for a full day. Had they sunk beneath the snow? Were they hiding from him, or had he taken a wrong turn? Rasmus was not visible either; perhaps he was in it with them. As long as he wasn't buried in the snow with them. Sometimes Wegener thought he made out a white head next to him, protruding from the firn and watching him as he walked on, but it was probably nothing but shadows on the ice.

There was a great deal to discover now, in general. He hated to admit it but the entire contourless world was becoming populated,

in a rather shocking manner. Snowfinches were a daily phenomenon and the Arctic fox was apparently back too. On one
occasion, Wegener thought he spotted a snow leopard in the distance, though he couldn't be sure. But then, where would a snow
leopard feel more at home than here? If ever Wegener were to turn
into a snow leopard, he could wish for no habitat more suitable.
For the moment, that was rather different.

New animals now awaited him every day: snow hares, snow
bears, all manner of beasts. Would he be transformed into a snow
human in the end? Into one of the snowmen by the side of the
path?

What if he were to die here? Of exhaustion, of fatigue? He too
would sink gradually into the firn. His fingernails would go on
growing for several days, at the speed at which continents shift.
He would drift gradually westwards with the inland ice, just as
Greenland's continental shelf drifted westwards, in harmony with
the results of his work. In the end he would thaw his way off
inside an iceberg and drift out to sea.

He would be outside of the world. How often had he dreamt
of that?

As soon as the light disappeared in the evening, the temperatures
plummeted. Then he'd wait for Rasmus, or Rasmus would wait for
him. Sooner or later they found one another every time, in some
inexplicable way.

So as not to assault their supplies excessively, they thinned
down their food. The stomach was primarily concerned with getting a full litre, so they filled it with firn before cooking. When
they were too tired even for that, they nibbled at ship's biscuits
until they felt sufficiently nauseous to sleep. At night, Wegener
lost the breathing hole of his sleeping bag and woke from night-
mares. Then there was no other cure but to open the carefully tied

tent entrance and rub his face with snow until all memory of the dreams was driven out.

Rasmus' lead dog fell ill and Wegener killed it. He took off his dogskin anorak to do so—but so carelessly that it was instantly chewed at by the other dogs.

Wegener's fingertips now displayed deep cracks, which were painful. They also caught on things. The frost that formed on the sleds was now unbearably severe, affecting even the tethers and the barometer case. Not that anyone read the barometer any longer.

All at once one night, he knew he had a gap in his life, like every other man. A way out not taken, which he regretted. Where, he asked himself, where do you dream yourself to when you dream yourself away? The question went unanswered.

Then he believed he was the ur-continent. He simply lay there and was an entirety. All alone, he was everything in one place. He was the whole world.

He lost sight of Rasmus for days on end, or at least it seemed that way to him, simply because there was now no way to determine when one day ended and the next began.

Wegener no longer believed in days.

What he did believe in was aeons. Whirlwinds. Snow. He believed in the instability of his thoughts, in instability in general. All the things that had proved instable in the end, faith, knowledge, the continents. The most instable of all, however, was man.

And finitude; Wegener believed in that too. In the finitude of humanity and the finite nature of weather, to state two general examples.

He no longer believed, however, that this snowfall would ever come to an end. Would the ants outlive them all? Insects had proved incredibly adaptable. Continents had come and gone but the ants remained. What made them so robust? Their exoskeleton? Hardly; it was far too easily crushed. Their indefatigability, their number? Oh, to be an ant, one among many. What did ants believe in?

All at once it occurred to him that he did know how it went on. He could calculate it; he had invented it himself. He had only ever looked backwards, into the past. He had studied the movements of the lands for the brief moment of his present. How everything had come about. Yet one could just as well continue those motions, narrate them onwards, out into a future that was suddenly less unpredictable than his closest surroundings.

He spent the following kilometres calculating that future. How good it did him to hold onto a task. He had always done so whenever something came too close to him, just as he had come too close to himself over the past days. To begin with, he was annoyed at having to make all the calculations in his head. He couldn't even use his fingers as an aid; they were out of reach in his gloves.

How sad that he couldn't write it all down. How sad that it remained trapped in his mind. Wasn't there already rather a lot trapped there?

By the late afternoon he had calculated that, at constant velocity and direction, the North Pole would reach the southern tip of Greenland in twenty-three million years. He waited for a feeling of calm that did not arise. Late that evening, he finally found out that in forty million years, Europe would break apart along the Rhine. For a moment he was worried for Else and the children. Then that too was over.

He wished they would remember him as the man he might have been. It was of no matter to him what coming generations would make of his life. Everything over again from the beginning, over and over. One had to let the pasts drift by like the land. In the end they'd collide again.

A secret friend to humankind. He'd had no other wish than to leave them their possibilities. A lover of the Arctic, perhaps its greatest. Although the nature of the Arctic now seemed to be overcoming him. His skis sank ever deeper into the new snow.

He wished he could write a letter to Else but he feared his hands were no longer capable. He would have written this—an apology for using her as ballast on their balloon trip. The question of whether she remembered him saying when they first met that it would never be the way it had once been. The ur-continent was lost. They had been expelled, there was no way back. That view had been mistaken; he had to correct it. Only today had it occurred to him that the Earth was of course spherical. Great gratification at this realization, as she could no doubt imagine. Not until today, due to the fact that he had a rather generous amount of time to think out here, had he established what ensued from that basic fact. In 250 million years' time, all the land would come back together, on the rear side of the world, all the continents would come together and would be reunited at last. And with the land, he hoped, all of them. Else, the children, the Köppens. His parents, including his father. All his siblings, natural and adopted, with their own children and children's children, for whom he hoped there would be sufficient space on the huge new continent. They would all be there; he could hardly wait to see Mylius-Erichsen again, and Nansen, even Suess and the various Kaisers, this time with their bread rolls. And his friend from the back of the church would be there. What had he called her again, Squid? Something like that. He looked forward to her in particular.

How empty and unpopulated it was. Heaven knew what he was looking for here. Though he valued the many types of white found on this so-spaciously-laid-out field of snow, he could have used a human soul by his side now, perhaps for the first time in his life.

He tried to fill the emptiness of the landscape with images from his memory but all he saw remained hidden behind a cloud of icing sugar—Jungfern Bridge, beneath it the canal with a dead butterfly floating on it. A bride disappearing in the distance. An empty snow globe, a swinging pendulum, a pipe gone cold.

He tried to summon it all up, their games by the water, the crowd of his siblings. How boisterous they were. He thought of Willi, who had fallen through the ice, and all at once he was scared to break through the ice himself. But he knew it was strong enough, far stronger than he was. He heard his mother's voice but could not find her image, only ever her voice, scolding him in a foreign language. He saw his father but could not quite make him out because his face was hidden in his hands, in prayer or desperation. It took a moment for Wegener to recognize he was holding his own hands in front of his face, as protection from the snow. He knelt on the ground, his head lowered, and was glad of the warmth suddenly within him. Perhaps he was lying on his side with his legs drawn up and it merely felt like he was kneeling. How glad he was. The joy that no dog came to bite at his sleeves. The joy of experiencing all this consciously and one day being able to sum it up in an article. The joy that his father was no longer watching him. Unfortunately, it was still unclear which of them was triumphant in the end.

The wind came from all sides simultaneously, seemingly untroubled by him. The unrest subsided, the crawling of his thoughts. Wegener felt the leisurely drifting of the magnetic poles. When he closed his eyes he saw ancient, extinct animals, and he held out his hand to them. He walked across land bridges, he walked across the sea. He heard the glassy ring of the air layers and recognized every one of them. He thought of the frozen meadows of his youth, of the snow-laden plum tree in the garden in front of the house in Zechlinerhütte, he thought of himself sitting up there as a boy and imagining it all, the polar night and what it would be like to perish in it. He thought of the frost on the last leaf as yet unfallen, of the icy air. Of climbing down from the tree in the end, his hands chapped by the wind and the bark. Why here?

All at once, Rasmus was with him and led him back to their tent. What a marvel such a tent was. And what a marvel this Rasmus was. An angel, a devil of a fellow. Unfortunately, the tent did not manage to banish the cold spreading within him. It seemed to come from inside him, from his bones.

How cramped it was in the tent, how little air it held. And so many ants now approaching from all directions.

White ants, radiant white, snow ants perhaps, the itching everywhere, the first of them already inside his trouser legs, on his hands, on the sleeves of his jacket. How they reared up for battle; what had he done to them? The feelers, the tiny teeth. How robust they were. Their unique ability to predict earthquakes, always finding time to relocate their nests. They were the ones who would outlive mankind.

All at once he saw all their armour split open at the back, something emerging, as crumpled as old parchment, and dividing. Wings—they could fly, of course. And the next instant the first of them were in the air, fluttering for a moment around the tent like snowflakes, like a flock of snowflakes in the wind, then they flew up and away and took him along with them, out of the tent and away to a new colony.